445 9825

Discerning Critical Hope in Educational Practices

How can discerning critical hope enable us to develop innovative forms of teaching, learning and social practices that begin to address issues of marginalization, privilege and access across different contexts?

At this millennial point in history, questions of cynicism, despair and hope arise at every turn, especially within areas of research into social justice and the struggle for transformation in education. While a sense of fatalism and despair is easily recognizable, establishing compelling bases for hope is more difficult. This book addresses the absence of sustained analyses of hope that simultaneously recognize the hard edges of why we despair.

This volume posits the notion of critical hope not only as conceptual and theoretical, but also as an action-oriented response to despair. Our notion of critical hope is used in two ways: it is used firstly as a unitary concept which cannot be disaggregated into either hopefulness or criticality, and secondly, as an analytical concept, where critical hope is engaged and diversely theorized in ways that recognize aspects of individual and collective directions of critical hope. The book is divided into four parts:

- Critical hope in education
- Critical hope and a critique of neoliberalism
- Critical Race Theory/Postcolonial perspectives on critical hope
- Philosophical overviews of critical hope.

Education can be a purveyor of critical hope, but it also requires critical hope so that it, as a sector itself, can be transformative. With contributions from international experts in the field, the book will be of value to all academics and practitioners working in the field of education.

Vivienne Bozalek is Professor of Social Work and Director of Teaching and Learning at the University of the Western Cape, South Africa.

Brenda Leibowitz is Director of Teaching and Learning at Stellenbosch University, South Africa.

Ronelle Carolissen is Associate Professor of Community Psychology in the Department of Educational Psychology at Stellenbosch University, South Africa.

Megan Boler is Professor in History and Philosophy of Education at the University of Toronto, Canada.

Foundations and Futures of Education

Peter Aggleton *The University of New South Wales, Australia*
Sally Power *Cardiff University, UK*
Michael Reiss *Institute of Education, University of London, UK*

Foundations and Futures of Education focuses on key emerging issues in education as well as continuing debates within the field. The series is inter-disciplinary, and includes historical, philosophical, sociological, psychological and comparative perspectives on three major themes: the purposes and nature of education; increasing interdisciplinarity within the subject; and the theory-practice divide.

Discerning Critical Hope in Educational Practices
Edited by Vivienne Bozalek, Brenda Leibowitz, Ronelle Carolissen and Megan Boler

Education and Masculinities: Social, cultural and global transformations
Chris Haywood and Mairtin Mac an Ghaill

Bullying: Experiences and discourses of sexuality and gender
Ian Rivers and Neil Duncan

Language, Learning, Context: Talking the talk
Wolff-Michael Roth

Postfeminist Education? Girls and the sexual politics of schooling
Jessica Ringrose

The Right to Higher Education: Beyond widening participation
Penny Jane Burke

The Struggle for the History of Education
Gary McCulloch

Radical Education and the Common School: A democratic alternative
Michael Fielding and Peter Moss

The Irregular School: Exclusion, schooling and inclusive education
Roger Slee

School Trouble: Identity, power and politics in education
Deborah Youdell

Schools and Schooling in the Digital Age: A critical analysis
Neil Selwyn

Being a University
Ron Barnett

Education – An 'Impossible Profession'?
Tamara Bibby

Re-Designing Learning Contexts: Technology-rich, learner-centred ecologies
Rosemary Luckin

Education and the Family: Passing success across the generations
Leon Feinstein, Kathryn Duckworth and Ricardo Sabates

Learners, Learning and Educational Activity
Judith Ireson

Gender, Schooling and Global Social Justice
Elaine Unterhalter

Education, Philosophy and the Ethical Environment
Graham Haydon

Schooling, Society and Curriculum
Edited by Alex Moore

Discerning Critical Hope in Educational Practices

Edited by Vivienne Bozalek, Brenda Leibowitz, Ronelle Carolissen and Megan Boler

LONDON AND NEW YORK

First published 2014
by Routledge
2 Park Square, Milton Park, Abingdon, Oxon OX14 4RN

and by Routledge
711 Third Avenue, New York, NY 10017

Routledge is an imprint of the Taylor & Francis Group, an informa business

© 2014 V. Bozalek, B. Leibowitz, R. Carolissen and M. Boler

The right of the editors to be identified as the authors of the editorial material, and of the authors for their individual chapters, has been asserted in accordance with sections 77 and 78 of the Copyright, Designs and Patents Act 1988.

All rights reserved. No part of this book may be reprinted or reproduced or
utilised in any form or by any electronic, mechanical, or other means, now known or hereafter invented, including photocopying and recording, or in any information storage or retrieval system, without permission in writing from the publishers.

Trademark notice: Product or corporate names may be trademarks or registered trademarks, and are used only for identification and explanation without intent to infringe.

British Library Cataloguing in Publication Data
A catalogue record for this book is available from the British Library

Library of Congress Cataloging in Publication Data
A catalog record for this book has been requested

ISBN: 978-0-415-82632-7 (hbk)
ISBN: 978-0-203-43111-5 (ebk)

Typeset in Galliard
by Cenveo Publisher Services

Printed and bound in Great Britain by
TJ International Ltd, Padstow, Cornwall

Contents

List of contributors vii
Preface xi
Foreword xii
MICHAEL W. APPLE

Introduction 1
VIVIENNE BOZALEK, RONELLE CAROLISSEN, BRENDA
LEIBOWITZ AND MEGAN BOLER

PART I
Critical hope in education 9

1 Affective, political and ethical sensibilities in pedagogies of
critical hope: Exploring the notion of 'critical emotional praxis' 11
MICHALINOS ZEMBYLAS

2 Teaching for hope: The ethics of shattering worldviews 26
MEGAN BOLER

3 A pedagogy of critical hope in South African higher education 40
VIVIENNE BOZALEK, RONELLE CAROLISSEN AND BRENDA LEIBOWITZ

PART II
Critical hope and a critique of neoliberalism 55

4 "That's scary. But it's not hopeless": Critical pedagogy and
redemptive narratives of hope 57
GUSTAVO FISCHMAN AND ERIC HAAS

5   Plasticity, critical hope and the regeneration of human
    rights education   69
    ANDRÉ KEET

6   Critical hope: Deconstructing of the politics of HOPE at
    a South African university   82
    HENK VAN RINSUM

PART III
Critical Race Theory/Postcolonial perspectives
on critical hope   99

7   Critical hope and struggles for justice: An antidote to
    despair for antiracism educators   101
    RONALD DAVID GLASS

8   Agents of critical hope: Black British narratives   113
    PAUL WARMINGTON

9   Decolonizing education: Discovering critical hope in
    marginal spaces   126
    MERLYNE CRUZ

PART IV
Philosophical overviews of critical hope   141

10 Hope: An emancipatory resource across the ages   143
    JOHN HORTON

    *Afterword: Critical hopes – gratitude and
    the magic of encounter*   157
    MARY ZOURNAZI

    Index   164

Contributors

Michael W. Apple is John Bascom Professor of Curriculum and Instruction and Educational Policy Studies at the University of Wisconsin, Madison and Professor of Educational Policy Studies at the Institute of Education, University of London, and World Scholar and Distinguished Professor of Educational Policy Studies at East China Normal University in Shanghai. Among his most recent books are *The Routledge International Handbook of Critical Education*, *The Routledge International Handbook of the Sociology of Education*, and *Global Crises, Social Justice, and Education*. He is an internationally renowned academic in the field of critical pedagogy.

Megan Boler received her PhD at the History of Consciousness Program at the University of California, and is Professor in the Department of Theory and Policy Studies, at the Ontario Institute of Studies in Education/University of Toronto; and Associate Faculty of Knowledge Media Design Institute. Her books include *Feeling Power: Emotions and Education* (Routledge, 1999); *Democratic Dialogue in Education: Troubling Speech, Disturbing Silences* (Peter Lang, 2004); and *Digital Media and Democracy: Tactics in Hard Times* (MIT Press, 2008). She teaches graduate studies in philosophy of education, and her essays have been published in journals including *Educational Theory*, *Women's Studies Quarterly*, and *New Media and Society*.

Vivienne Bozalek is a Professor of Social Work and the Director of Teaching and Learning at the University of the Western Cape (UWC), South Africa. Prior to this she was Chairperson of the Department of Social Work, University of Western Cape. She holds a PhD from Utrecht University. Her areas of research, publications and expertise include the use of post-structural, social justice and the political ethics of care perspectives, critical family studies, innovative pedagogical approaches in higher education, and feminist and participatory research methodologies. She has co-edited a book entitled *Community, Self and Identity* with Brenda Leibowitz, Ronelle Carolissen and other colleagues.

Ronelle Carolissen is an Associate Professor and Chair of the Department of Educational Psychology at the University of Stellenbosch. She holds a doctorate from the University of Stellenbosch. Her research expertise and publications explore social justice and critical community psychology perspectives in the context of transformation and innovation in higher education. She is the co-editor of the book *Community, Self and Identity*.

Merlyne Cruz is a Research Fellow at the Equity and Childhood Program in the Youth Research Centre, Melbourne Graduate School of Education at The University of Melbourne. Merlyne is currently involved in several action research projects that investigate the practices and processes of creating pedagogical change in educational settings. Merlyne's research interests are in anti-colonial thought, indigenous knowledges, critical spirituality and diasporic identities. Merlyne holds a PhD from The University of Melbourne.

Gustavo Fischman is Professor in the Mary Lou Fulton Teachers College at Arizona State University. He obtained his PhD in social sciences and comparative education at the University of California, Los Angeles in 1997. His areas of specialization are comparative education, higher education policy studies, and gender studies in education. His books include *Imagining Teachers: Rethinking Teacher Education and Gender* and *Education, Crisis and Hope: Tension and Change in Latin-America* and numerous articles on comparative education, teacher education, and gender issues in education. He is the lead editor of *Educational Policy Analysis Archives* and co-editor of *Education Review/Reseñas Educativas*.

Ronald David Glass received a PhD in Philosophy of Education from Stanford University. He is an Associate Professor of Philosophy of Education at the University of California Santa Cruz, and Director of the Center for Collaborative Research for an Equitable California (CCREC; http://ccrec.ucsc.edu), a University of California multi-campus research program initiative. He has co-published a book with Pia Lindquist Wong examining the links between school reform and transformation of teacher preparation: *Prioritizing Urban Children, Teachers, and Schools through Professional Development Schools*. Dr. Glass has published essays in leading journals (such as *Educational Researcher*, *Reading Research Quarterly*, *Teacher Education Quarterly*, and *Democracy and Education*), and has contributed chapters to a number of edited books.

Eric Haas is a Senior Research Associate at WestEd, where he conducts research on education issues, with a focus on English language learners and the link between education research and policy development. His research on the influence of cognitive frames and education research on the development of specific education policies has been published in academic journals, including the *American Educational Research Journal*, the *Peabody Journal of Education*, and the *Bilingual Research Journal*, as well as in books and the popular press. He obtained his PhD in Educational Leadership and Policy Studies from Arizona State University in 2004 and his law degree from Catholic University in 1990.

John Horton holds Master's degrees in English and Education, and is currently completing his doctoral studies in educational theory at the University of Toronto. He is an educational practitioner and has worked as a teacher, principal and school system administrator in suburban Toronto. He has authored textbooks and acted as a consultant and curriculum developer. He also trained teachers in the Caribbean and co-ordinated cross-Canada educational projects for the federal government, United Nations Association of Canada (UNAC) and non-profit organizations.

André Keet holds a PhD degree from the University of Pretoria and is currently the Director of the Institute for Reconciliation and Social Justice at the University of the Free State. He has headed the human rights and inclusivity task teams appointed by the Minister of Education from 2000–2003. André also served as the Deputy Chief Executive Officer (DCEO) of the South African Human Rights Commission and briefly functioned as a Commissioner on the Commission for Gender Equality. He presently serves on the ministerial oversight committee on the transformation of higher education in South Africa. He publishes in the field of human rights, social justice and education.

Brenda Leibowitz holds a PhD from the University of Sheffield and is an Associate Professor of Education and Director of the Centre for Teaching and Learning at Stellenbosch University. Her research interests include professional academic development, identity and higher education, action-based research and social justice in education. She is currently a co-editor of the *International Journal for Academic Development* and has edited a book entitled *Higher Education for the Public Good: Views from the South* and co-edited the book *Community, Self and Identity*, both in 2012 and authored a book *The Significance of Academic Literacy in Higher Education: Students' Prior Learning and their Acquisition of Academic Literacy in a Multilingual South African University* in 2010.

Henk van Rinsum holds a PhD from Utrecht University and currently works as a researcher at the Utrecht School of Governance and as Secretary of the Board of the Faculty of Social and Behavioural Sciences. His research focuses on the history of governance of universities, both in Europe and South Africa. He has a particular interest in the history and transformation of the University of Stellenbosch. His PhD study, published in 2001, entitled *Slaves of Definition: In quest of the Unbeliever and the Ignoramus*, dealt with the Western dominance in the discourse development on African traditional religion. In 2006 he published a book on the history of the relationship between Utrecht University and South Africa, stressing the major influence of this Dutch university in the establishment of the University of Stellenbosch.

Paul Warmington is a Senior Lecturer in the School of Education, University of Birmingham and Deputy Director of its Centre for Research in Race and Education. He gained his doctorate at the University of Birmingham in 2000. His research focuses on race and education, black British educational movements, widening participation in higher education. His books include *Improving Inter-professional Collaborations: Multi-agency Working for Children's Wellbeing* (with Edwards *et al.*) and *Atlantic Crossings: International Dialogues on Critical Race Theory* (with Hylton *et al.*). Paul is a member of the editorial boards of *Race, Ethnicity and Education and Educational Review*. He is currently completing a history of black British intellectuals and education.

Michalinos Zembylas is Associate Professor of Education at the Open University of Cyprus. His research interests are in the areas of educational philosophy and curriculum theory, and his work focuses on exploring the role of emotion and affect in curriculum and pedagogy. He is particularly interested in how affective politics intersect with issues of social justice pedagogies, intercultural and peace education, and citizenship education. His most recent book (with Zvi Bekerman) is entitled *Teaching contested narratives: Identity, memory and reconciliation in peace education and beyond* (Cambridge University Press, 2012).

Mary Zournazi is an Australian writer and philosopher. She teaches in the sociology program at the University of New South Wales, Sydney. She is the author of several books including *Hope – New Philosophies for Change*, and *Keywords to War – Reviving Language in an Age of Terror*, and most recently *Inventing Peace* co-authored with German film maker Wim Wenders.

Preface

The idea for this book was conceived during a panel presentation on Critical Hope at the 2011 American Education Research Association (AERA) conference. Megan Boler, as one of the panelists, suggested that we convert the presentations into an edited collection on critical hope. A group of interested people then met in June 2012 in Cape Town at the beautiful rural conference centre of Mont Fleur to deliberate about how to take this project forward and to put a book proposal together. Vivienne Bozalek, Ronelle Carolissen, André Keet, Brenda Leibowitz and Michalinos Zembylas were some of the authors and editors there. To this meeting we also invited a group of critical friends including academics and authors such as Joan Tronto, Leslie Swartz, Tammy Shefer, Dorothee Holscher and Sue Clegg who shared ideas about what such an edited collection could incorporate. We decided at this meeting to approach Routledge as a potential publisher and approached Anna Clarkson and Clare Ashworth about this. We were delighted that the proposal was accepted by Routledge in the *Foundations and Futures of Education* Routledge Series edited by Michael Reiss and Peter Aggleton. Clare Ashworth, Anna Clarkson, Michael and Peter have been a pleasure to work with. We are very grateful to Michael and Peter for their insightful and speedy editing of the chapters. Before we submitted the final manuscript to the series editors, each chapter was blind reviewed by two independent reviewers. We would thus also like to express our appreciation to all who agreed to review chapters for us – Judy Aulette, Nasima Badsha, Chrissie Boughey, Sherran Clarence, Richard Ballard, Valerie Clifford, David Gillborn, Jacqui Goldin, Patti Henderson, Cecilia Jacobs, Theresa Lillis, Sioux McKenna, Carolyn McKinney, Wendy McMillan, Maureen Robinson, Christopher Sonn, Leslie Swartz, Melanie Walker, Shirley Walters, Denise Wood and Wendy Woodward. We would also like to express our gratitude to the South Africa-Netherlands Research Partnership Development (SANPAD) for making research funding available for the proposal workshop.

Foreword

Michael W. Apple

Hope in a time of crisis

For many deeply committed educators, our impulses toward critical theoretical and political work in education are fueled by a passion for social justice, economic equality, human rights, sustainable environments, an education that is worthy of its name – in short a commitment to connecting education to the process of building a more critically democratic society. Yet, this is increasingly difficult to maintain in the situation in which so many of us find ourselves. Ideologically and politically much has changed. The early years of the twenty-first century have brought us unfettered capitalism which fuels market tyrannies and massive inequalities on a truly global scale (Davis 2006). "Democracy" is resurgent at the same time, but it all too often becomes a thin veil for the interests of the globally and locally powerful and for disenfranchisement, mendacity, and national and international violence (Burawoy 2005: 260).

The rhetoric of freedom and equality may have intensified, but there is unassailable evidence that there is ever deepening exploitation, domination, and inequality and that earlier gains in education, economic security, civil rights, and more are either being washed away or are under severe threat. The religion of the market (and it does function like a religion, since as I have demonstrated elsewhere it does not seem to be amenable to empirical critiques) coupled with very different visions of what the state can and should do can be summarized in one word – neoliberalism, although we know that no single term can actually totally encompass the forms of dominance and subordination that have such long histories in so many regions of the world (see Apple 2006; 2013a).

At the same time, in the social field of power called the academy – with its own hierarchies and disciplinary (and disciplining) techniques, the pursuit of academic credentials, bureaucratic and institutional rankings, security of tenure, indeed the entire panoply of normalizing pressures surrounding institutions and careers – all of this too often seeks to ensure that we all think and act "correctly." Yet, the original impulses are never entirely vanquished (Burawoy 2005). The spirit that animates critical work can never be totally subjected to rationalizing logics and processes. Try as the powerful might, it will not be extinguished. As the chapters in this book signify, it certainly remains alive in a good deal of the work in critical pedagogy.

This is especially important given what is currently happening in education. Increasingly, under the growing power of neoliberal, neoconservative, and new managerial ideological forms, education is being commodified. Its institutions are being turned into "producers" that are to be subjected to the logic of markets. And the people who work in educational institutions at all levels – and the students with whom they work – are to be valued only by their contributions to an increasingly unequal economy, with test scores as a proxy for national and international competitiveness. Not only is this amoral (if not immoral) set of assumptions destructive for an education worthy of its name; but it devalues and is deeply disrespectful of the critical work that education must perform and just as deeply disrespectful of the labor of love, care, and solidarity that underpins so much of educational activities inside and outside of formal institutions of education (Lynch *et al.* 2009). Indeed, these "affective" norms can act to directly counter the demands for audit cultures and for the constant production of evidence that one is a source of profit making and that one is acting in entrepreneurial ways that are so dominant in our current neoliberal age (Apple 2006). The immense pressure in the USA and other countries to judge teaching only through performance "assessment" is but one indication, but a powerful one, of these tendencies.

In times such as these, language makes a difference. How someone or some situation is described, especially by powerful forces who wish to remain in power, is crucial. The language employed carries with it a whole raft of assumptions of course; but it also creates boundaries for what is seen as legitimate action and what is seen as not useful, not efficient, not workable, and quite often too radical. Take the current dominant forms of education that have been guided by neoliberal assumptions and policies to which I have been pointing. Neoliberalism opens a space for certain identities and closes down others. It gives people *one* option of who they are. They are *consumers*. They are to be motivated by one thing – individual gain based on one's choice of "products." Collective responsibility and an immediate concern for social justice, care, love, and solidarity – these things will take care of themselves.

This is a desocializing sensibility. Do not think of oneself as a member of a group of oppressed people who have a long history of struggling for social justice or as deeply and fundamentally connected to other people. Think of oneself instead wholly as a "chooser" of goods and services. Consumer choice will ultimately provide for all – even if you and your community have little say in what these choices are or you actively attempt to refuse to allow these neoliberal programs to include the institutions that have had partial victories associated with them. The message is "Trust us." "We" are the reformers; we will give you what you do not yet know you want. We will transform schools at all levels so that (for now, selective) students will get schooling that will be better. The growing movement to commodify and privatize education (and teacher education as well) and to make it into an arena for the generation of profit that is so visible in so many countries is but the tip of the iceberg here (see Ball 2012; Burch 2009).

Of course, the "we" here are the powerful, the true believers, and at times simply the profiteers (see Burch 2009; Ball 2007, 2012). The "non-we" are those who are told to trust the competitive market and the choices it makes available. And no matter what the rhetoric, like so many people defined as the "Other" in our societies, the students and teachers who must live in a world where inequalities are so very visible are definitely part of the non-we (Buras 2011). This entire situation speaks of something that has a long history. It is one more instance of dominant groups speaking the language of transformation at the same time as power shifts even more radically into their hands. Let us be honest. This is simply the center masquerading as the margins.

In situations such as this, it is all too easy to lose hope, to feel as if the continued attempts to create a critically democratic and responsive education that is linked organically to larger movements of redistribution, recognition, and representation (see e.g. Fraser 1997, 2010) are doomed to failure. Yet let us remember that despair and cynicism only help those in dominance. In *Can Education Change Society?* (Apple 2013a), I examine the long history of attempts to answer the question of whether, and in what ways, education can play a major role in such social transformations and point to a number of current examples as well in which education participates in crucial social and cultural movements that are of considerable significance around multiple relations of differential power. There is hope.

In this regard it is important to remind ourselves that schools and other educational arenas have been and continue to be sites of victories not only defeats. After all, why would the neoliberals, neoconservatives, and new managerialists who are so powerful now be so angry at schools if these institutions were already doing only what the Right wanted? Thus, let us also remember, for example, that nothing that we are facing today is any more difficult than the struggle to end legal and state enforced apartheid in the USA, South Africa, and elsewhere. As Raymond Williams so aptly stated, we are involved in "The Long Revolution" (Williams 1961). Struggles over the politics of culture, over what counts as "official" or "legitimate" knowledge, over collective memory, over voice, recognition, representation, and identity, and over how all of this is to be dealt with in our teaching – all of these are crucial areas that are deeply involved in this process.

This is exactly where the book you are reading enters. One of the aims of *Discerning Critical Hope in Educational Practices* is to provide a more ethically and politically nuanced set of perspectives, and new linguistic, social, and practical resources that would enable us to push the boundaries of education in more critically democratic directions.

The volume is a welcome combination of critique and praxis. Thus, in many of the chapters theory is recursively connected to pedagogic action. It is also international in scope, something that can act against our damaging assumption that one country or region can stand in for everywhere else. Furthermore, and in my mind just as importantly, the chapters not only rightly criticize dominant forms of education, but also (supportively) critique some of the major forms of critical education themselves. This is significant. As I have argued elsewhere, too much of the writing on "critical pedagogy" is largely rhetorical. It seems to treat criticism as nearly a form of treason. Yet the development of critical educational theories, policies, and practices is and must be seen as a *collective* act, one that requires serious discussion, deliberation, and transformation if it is to remain organically connected to the multiple and diverse struggles against the relations of dominance and subordination that so clearly characterize the societies in which we live (Apple 2006, 2013b).

The fact that, unlike many edited books, the individual chapters in *Discerning Critical Hope in Educational Practices* often build upon each other makes it clear that this collective sensibility is recognized by the editors and authors of this book. The words "diverse" and "collective" are significant here. The volume recognizes that there are multiple relations of exploitation, domination, and subordination – and multiple political projects that interrupt these relations in education and the larger society. Each of these projects is valuable. The task is two-fold: to find ways of forming what I have called elsewhere *decentered unities*, ways in which a politics of redistribution and recognition can work in a manner that does not interrupt or contradict each other; *and* to seek ways of forming alliances on educational and social issues and mobilizations that have mutual benefits (Apple 2013a).

I was heartened, as you will be I am sure, to see the honest treatments of multiple relations and multiple politics in the book. Honesty is crucial here. When Williams used the phrase "the long revolution" to describe what we face, he also implied that progress will at times not be easily made, that it will take hard work and will face obstacles. A number of the chapters in this book describe and discuss these conceptual, political, institutional, pedagogic, and practical obstacles, the dilemmas, and the partial gains associated with doing what is best seen as counter-hegemonic actions in education theory and practice. It is hard work. But whoever said it would be easy to interrupt dominance?

The act of becoming (and this too is a *project*, for one is *never* finished, *always* becoming) a critical scholar/activist is a complex one. Because of this, let me further situate *Discerning Critical Hope in Educational Practices* in the role of critical research, and the critical researcher, in education. My points here are tentative and certainly not exhaustive. They are meant to begin a dialogue over just what it is that "we" should do.

The tasks of the critical scholar/activist in education

In general, there are nine tasks in which critical analysis (and the critical analyst) in education must engage (Apple 2013a, 2010).

1. It must "bear witness to negativity."[1] That is, one of its primary functions is to illuminate the ways in which educational policy and practice are connected to the relations of exploitation and domination – and to struggles against such relations – in the larger society.[2]
2. In engaging in such critical analyses, it also must point to contradictions and to *spaces of possible action*. Thus, its aim is to critically examine current

realities with a conceptual/political framework that emphasizes the spaces in which more progressive and counter-hegemonic actions can, or do, go on. This is an absolutely crucial step, since otherwise our research can simply lead to cynicism or despair.
3   At times, this also requires a broadening of what counts as "research." Here I mean acting as critical "secretaries" to those groups of people and social movements who are now engaged in challenging existing relations of unequal power or in what elsewhere has been called "non-reformist reforms," a term that has a long history in critical sociology and critical educational studies (Apple 2012). This is exactly the task that was taken on in the thick descriptions of critically democratic school practices in *Democratic Schools* (Apple and Beane 2007), and in the critically supportive descriptions of the transformative reforms such as the Citizen School and participatory budgeting in Porto Alegre, Brazil (see Gandin and Apple 2012; Apple 2013a; Wright 2010). The same is true for CREA, an interdisciplinary research center at the University of Barcelona that is a model of how to build a research agenda and then create policies and programs that empower those who are economically and culturally marginalized in our societies (Flecha 2011; Gatt *et al.* 2011; Alexiu and Sorde 2011; Aubert 2011; Christou and Puivert 2011; Flecha 2009) and for The Centre for Equality Studies at University College, Dublin. It too has been at the center of research and action that stresses not only poverty and inequality, but movements towards equality (Baker *et al.* 2004; Lynch *et al.* 2009). The fact that the richly detailed descriptions of critical pedagogical and cultural work with diverse students in diverse settings play a key role in *Discerning Critical Hope in Educational Practices* provides even more evidence of its value.
4   When Gramsci (1971) argued that one of the tasks of a truly counter-hegemonic education was not to throw out "elite knowledge" but to reconstruct its form and content so that it served genuinely progressive social needs, he provided a key to another role "organic" and "public" intellectuals might play. Thus, we should not be engaged in a process of what might be called "intellectual suicide." That is, there are serious intellectual (and pedagogic) skills in dealing with the histories and debates surrounding the epistemological, political, and educational issues involved in justifying what counts as important knowledge and what counts as an effective and socially just education. These are not simple and inconsequential issues and the practical and intellectual/political skills of dealing with them have been well developed. However, they can atrophy if they are not used. They are clearly in use in this book. But we can also give back these skills by employing them to assist communities in thinking about this, learning from them, and engaging in the mutually pedagogic dialogues that enable decisions to be made in terms of both the short-term and long-term interests of dispossessed peoples (see Apple *et al.* 2009; Burawoy 2005; Freire 1970; Borg and Mayo 2007).
5   In the process, critical work has the task of keeping traditions of radical and progressive work alive. In the face of organized attacks on the "collective

memories" of difference and critical social movements, attacks that make it increasingly difficult to retain academic and social legitimacy for multiple critical approaches that have proven so valuable in countering dominant narratives and relations, it is absolutely crucial that these traditions be kept alive, renewed, and when necessary criticized for their conceptual, empirical, historical, and political silences or limitations. This involves being cautious of reductionism and essentialism and asks us to pay attention to what Fraser has called both the politics of redistribution and the politics of recognition (Fraser 1997; see also Apple 2013a, 2013b; Anyon 2009). This includes not only keeping theoretical, empirical, historical, and political traditions alive but, very importantly, extending and (supportively) criticizing them. And it also involves keeping alive the dreams, utopian visions, and "non-reformist reforms" that are so much a part of these radical traditions (Apple *et al.* 2009, 2010; Apple 2012; Jacoby 2005; Teitelbaum 1993). This is a key element in the traditions and resources mobilized in this book.

6 Keeping such traditions alive and also supportively criticizing them when they are not adequate to deal with current realities cannot be done unless we ask: "For whom are we keeping them alive?" and "How and in what form are they to be made available?" All of the things I have mentioned above in this taxonomy of tasks require the relearning or development and use of varied or new skills of working at many levels with multiple groups. Thus, journalistic and media skills, academic and popular skills, and the ability to speak to very different audiences are increasingly crucial (Apple 2006; Boler 2008). This requires us to learn how to speak different registers and to say important things in ways that do not require that the audience or reader do all of the work.

7 Critical educators must also *act* in concert with the progressive social movements their work supports or in movements against the rightist assumptions and policies they critically analyze. This is another reason that scholarship in critical education implies becoming an "organic" or "public" intellectual. One must participate in and give one's expertise to movements surrounding movements to transform both a politics of redistribution and a politics of recognition. It also implies learning from these social movements (Anyon 2005). This means that the role of the "unattached intelligentsia" (Mannheim 1936), someone who "lives on the balcony" (Bakhtin 1968), is not an appropriate model. As Bourdieu (2003: 11) reminds us, for example, our intellectual efforts are crucial, but they "cannot stand aside, neutral and indifferent, from the struggles in which the future of the world is at stake." The authors included here are clearly not neutral but "engaged."

8 Building on the points made in the previous paragraph, the critical scholars/ activists have another role to play. They need to act as deeply committed mentors, as people who demonstrate through their lives what it means to be *both* an excellent researcher and a committed member of a society that is scarred by persistent inequalities. They need to show how one can blend these two roles together in ways that may be tense, but still embody the

dual commitments to exceptional and socially committed research and participating in movements whose aim is interrupting dominance. It should be obvious that this must be fully integrated into one's teaching as well. This may not always be "successful" and as a number of chapters here show it may involve a "pedagogy of discomfort;" but to interrupt dominant understandings, we must also interrupt aspects of common sense.

9   Finally, participation also means using the privilege one has as a scholar/activist. That is, each of us needs to make use of our privilege to open the spaces at universities and elsewhere for those who are not there, for those who do not now have a voice in that space and in the "professional" sites to which, being in a privileged position, you have access. This can be seen, for example, in the history of the "activist-in-residence" programme at the University of Wisconsin Havens Center for Social Structure and Social Change, where committed activists in various areas (the environment, indigenous rights, housing, labor, racial disparities, education, and so on) were brought in to teach and to connect our academic work with organized action against dominant relations. Or it can be seen in a number of Women's Studies programs and Indigenous, Aboriginal, and First Nation Studies programs that historically have involved activists in these communities as active participants in the governance and educational programs of these areas at universities.

Conclusion

These nine tasks I have discussed above are demanding and no one person can engage equally well in all of them simultaneously. What we can do is honestly continue our attempt to come to grips with the complex intellectual, personal, and political tensions and activities that respond to the demands of this role. And this requires a searching critical examination of one's own structural location, one's own overt and tacit political commitments, and one's own embodied actions (Youdell 2011), once this recognition in all its complexities and contradictions is taken as seriously as it deserves.

Discerning Critical Hope in Educational Practices takes many of these tasks seriously. If it assists you in this critical examination and gives you a clearer appreciation of what Raymond Williams (1989) called "resources of hope," then it will have fulfilled its editors' and authors' hope as well.

Notes

1   I am aware that the idea of "bearing witness" has religious connotations, ones that are powerful in the West, but may be seen as a form of religious imperialism in other religious traditions. I still prefer to use it because of its powerful resonances with ethical discourses. But I welcome suggestions from, say, Muslim critical educators and researchers for alternative concepts that can call forth similar responses. I want to thank Amy Stambach for this point.

2 Here, exploitation and domination are technical not rhetorical terms. The first refers to economic relations, the structures of inequality, the control of labor, and the distribution of resources in a society. The latter refers to the processes of representation and respect and to the ways in which people have identities imposed on them. These are analytic categories, of course, and are ideal types. Most oppressive conditions are partly a combination of the two. These map on to what Fraser (1997) calls the politics of redistribution and the politics of recognition.

References

Alexiu, T.M. and Sorde, T. (2011) 'How to turn difficulties into opportunities: Drawing from diversity to promote social cohesion', *International Studies in Sociology of Education*, 21: 49–62.
Anyon, J. (2005) *Radical Possibilities: Public Policy, Urban Education, and a New Social Movement*. New York: Routledge.
Anyon, J. (2009) *Theory and Educational Research: Toward Critical Social Explanation*. New York: Routledge.
Apple, M.W. (2006) *Educating the "Right" Way: Markets, Standards, God, and Inequality*, 2nd edn. New York: Routledge.
Apple, M.W. (ed.) (2010) *Global Crises, Social Justice, and Education*. New York: Routledge.
Apple, M.W. (2012) *Education and Power*, revised Routledge Classic edn. New York: Routledge.
Apple, M.W. (2013a) *Can Education Change Society?* New York: Routledge.
Apple, M.W. (2013b) *Knowledge, Power, and Education*. New York: Routledge.
Apple, M.W. and Beane, J.A. (eds) (2007) *Democratic Schools: Lessons in Powerful Education*, 2nd edn. Portsmouth, NH: Heinemann.
Apple, M.W., Au, W. and Gandin, L.A. (eds) (2009) *The Routledge International Handbook of Critical Education*. New York: Routledge.
Apple, M.W., Ball, S. and Gandin, L.A. (eds) (2010) *The Routledge International Handbook of the Sociology of Education*. New York: Routledge.
Aubert, A. (2011) 'Moving beyond social exclusion through dialogue', *International Studies in Sociology of Education*, 21: 63–75.
Baker, J., Lynch, K., Cantillon, S. and Walsh, S. (2004) *Equality: From Theory to Action*. New York: Palgrave Macmillan.
Bakhtin, M.M. (1968) *Rabelais and His World*, trans. H. Iswolsky. Cambridge, MA: MIT Press.
Ball, S. (2007) *Education Plc*. New York: Routledge.
Ball, S. (2012) *Global Education Inc*. New York: Routledge.
Boler, M. (ed.) (2008) *Digital Media and Democracy: Tactics in Hard Times*. Cambridge, MA: MIT Press.
Borg, C. and Mayo, P. (eds) (2007) *Public Intellectuals, Radical Democracy and Social Movements*. New York: Peter Lang.
Bourdieu, P. (2003) *Firing Back: Against the Tyranny of the Market 2*. New York: The New Press.
Buras, K.L. (2011) 'Race, charter schools, and conscious capitalism: On the spatial politics of whiteness as property (and the unconscionable assault on black New Orleans)', *Harvard Educational Review*, 81: 296–330.

Burawoy, M. (2005) 'For public sociology', *British Journal of Sociology of Education*, 56(2): 259–94.

Burch, P. (2009) *Hidden Markets: The New Education Privatization*. New York: Routledge.

Christou, M. and Puigvert, L. (2011) 'The role of "other women" in current educational transformations', *International Studies in Sociology of Education*, 21: 77–90.

Davis, M. (2006) *Planet of Slums*. New York: Verso.

Flecha, R. (2009) 'The educative city and critical education', in Apple, M.W., Au, W. and Gandin, L.A. (eds) (2009) *The Routledge International Handbook of Critical Education*. New York: Routledge.

Flecha, R. (2011) 'The dialogic sociology of education', *International Studies in Sociology of Education*, 21: 7–20.

Fraser, N. (1997) *Justice Interruptus: Critical Reflections on the "Postsocialist" Condition*. New York: Routledge.

Fraser, N. (2010) *Scales of Justice: Reimagining Political Space in a Globalizing World*. New York: Columbia University Press.

Freire, P. (1970) *Pedagogy of the Oppressed*. New York: Herder and Herder.

Gandin, L.A. and Apple, M.W. (2012) 'Can critical democracy last? Porto Alegre and the struggle over "thick" democracy in education', *Journal of Education Policy*, 27: 621–39.

Gatt, S., Ojala, M. and Soler, M. (2011) 'Promoting social inclusion counting with everyone: Learning communities and INCLUDE-ED', *International Studies in Sociology of Education*, 21: 33–47.

Gramsci, A. (1971) *Selections from the Prison Notebooks*, trans. Q. Hoare and G.N. Smith. New York: International Publishers.

Jacoby, R. (2005) *Picture Imperfect: Utopian Thought for an Anti-utopian Age*. New York: Columbia University Press.

Lynch, K., Baker, J. and Lyons, M. (2009) *Affective Equality: Love, Care and Injustice*. New York: Palgrave Macmillan.

Mannheim, K. (1936) *Ideology and Utopia*. New York: Harvest Books.

Teitelbaum, K. (1993) *Schooling for Good Rebels*. Philadelphia, PA: Temple University Press.

Williams, R. (1961) *The Long Revolution*. London: Chatto and Windus.

Williams, R. (1989) *Resources of Hope*. New York: Verso.

Wright, E.O. (2010) *Envisioning Real Utopias*. New York: Verso.

Youdell, D. (2011) *School Trouble: Identity, Power and Politics in Education*. London: Routledge.

Introduction

*Vivienne Bozalek, Ronelle Carolissen,
Brenda Leibowitz and Megan Boler*

At this millennial point in history, questions of cynicism, despair and hope arise at every turn, especially in the struggle for transformation in education and the work for social justice. While a sense of fatalism and despair are readily apparent, establishing compelling bases for hope is more elusive. Given the ongoing and cataclysmic developments on the international stage in the late twentieth and early twenty-first centuries, new social arrangements, and new culture of communication modalities and practices, it is timely to reconsider our resources for hope, including central texts on hope, and how they can be interrogated to address the challenges posed by our times. This book is intended to contribute sustained analyses of hope that take into account the reasons for despair in our current educational contexts by contributing to reconsiderations of hope in the form of 'critical hope'. This collection also focuses on the crucial role that education can play in fostering critical hope where education is understood as ranging from formal settings such as the school or university, to informal settings, including the public pedagogical roles or educational spaces of non-governmental organizations and non-profit organizations.

The book posits the notion of *critical hope* not only as a crucial conceptual and theoretical direction, but also as an action-oriented response to contemporary despair. Critical hope may thus be understood as central to many forms of resisting injustice and to collective organizing against injustice. As a concept, critical hope invokes the histories, theories and praxis associated with critical theory such as the Frankfurt School and neo-Maxist critiques to the humanism of Freire.

Our notion of critical hope is used in two ways. First it is used as a unitary and unified concept which cannot be disaggregated into either *hopefulness* or *criticality*. Second it is used as an analytical concept, where critical hope is engaged and diversely theorized in ways that recognize the *affective, political, intellectual and spiritual* aspects and features of critical hope, namely:

- aspirations towards social flourishing and alleviating social injustices which induce human suffering
- acknowledgement of the role of values and ethics in education
- creativity and imagination
- critical empathy

- re-evaluation of the present through historical scrutiny
- discomfort in relation to 'shattering world views'[1]
- exploring the relationships of ambiguity, uncertainty, hope and despair
- affirmation of the importance of praxis
- a concern with power relations and their impact on privilege and marginality
- an emphasis on process itself as significant, i.e. *how* we strive for flourishing
- a forging of alliances across differences in social sectors and groups
- an affirmation of the importance of dialogue and humility within aims of democratic and participatory citizenship
- a focus on relationality and affect as central to thinking and learning
- the importance of connectedness and solidarity – and thus social networking – for twenty-first century education
- flexibility and openness.

Critical hope departs from 'naïve hope' and unquestioned perceptions of reality. Critical hope is embedded in flexibility and openness rather than being rooted in rigidly held assumptions (Duncan-Andrade 2009; Halpin 2003; Rorty 1999). The flexibility and openness in turn reflect not a naïve sense of wishing but rather always a recursive form of critical reflexivity. Critical hope is an ongoing process, expanding capacity for perception and insight, rooted in materialist recognition of both the present and the past as formative but not fixed, influential but not over-determining.

There is an important component of imagination in the idea of critical hope. It is not just critical in the sense of adding critique. It encompasses participatory inquiry and dialogue – in the broadest sense of a 'lived' critical pedagogy and curiosity about what is possible – helps foster conditions for critical hope and for manifestations of change and social flourishing based in realistic appraisals of current conditions' (Shade 2003: 212; Boler 2004; Shor 1992). Thus imagination in critical hope suggests alternatives in possibilities of praxis and action (Freire 2004; Giroux 2003; Zournazi 2002).

Education can be a purveyor of critical hope, but it also requires critical hope so that educational practices can be transformative. Critical hope is an ongoing *process* which requires constant re-evaluation and revision for renewal and sustained critique. Like radical democracy, by its very nature it is an ever-unfinished project (Laclau and Mouffe 1985). It is both a practice and a disposition (a comportment, a *dispositif*) which can be enacted in every generation and may potentially be engendered in each individual. Critical hope can be considered an intervention in 'reality'. What we come to accept as given and as unmoveable, unchangeable 'realities' are opened to question and critique.

As one finds critical hope translated into transformative educational aims, one turns to the ever-burgeoning field of critical pedagogy and, increasingly, critical pedagogical approaches that acknowledge the affective dimensions as equally important to the cognitive.

In an apt description of this role of a pedagogy of critical hope, Zembylas, in Chapter 1, describes that:

pedagogies of critical hope require that the pedagogical intervention needed to initiate individual and collective transformations can be nothing less than a radical subversion of the existing regime of truth. This process must, therefore, work simultaneously at several levels that identify and critique one's affective, ethical and political commitments and attachments.

Critical hope also emphasizes care for the other and the self, not from an individualistic perspective, but in a manner always embedded in relationality understood within their sociopolitical dimensions. As Zembylas writes:

> Critical hope, then, entails an ethical and political responsibility for constant vigilance in the process of change and becoming. Creating pedagogical spaces for embracing critical hope in educational settings may therefore be seen as an act of ethical and political responsibility that has the potential to recover a lost sense of connectedness, relationality and solidarity with others.
> (Chapter 1)

The complex and nuanced inquiry into the nature of the term 'critical hope' in historical and philosophical contexts, as well as the challenges faced in particular educational settings, are central to this book. The concept of critical hope has previously been shared in the public domain through publications by two authors in this collection, Megan Boler and Michalinos Zembylas. The concept of 'pedagogy of discomfort' illustrates graphically what critical hope may mean, and how it may be realized in classroom contexts (Boler 1999; Boler and Zembylas 2003).

Discerning Critical Hope in Educational Practices extends and builds on critical hope as theory and praxis, providing theoretical and empirical contributions revealing from myriad perspectives *how* critical hope is manifest in different settings. By suggesting how critical hope manifests itself, we can propose why there should be different and more complex theoretical tools that advance critical hope in contemporary contexts, as well as different and more complex understandings of educational aims and pedagogical practices across all modalities of education and learning.

In particular, this book focuses on the following questions:

- What tools, social arrangements, and positionalities are necessary to promote critical hope in various educational and social contexts?
- What forms of scholarship and critique can help us develop a notion of critical hope?
- How can discerning critical hope enable us to develop innovative forms of teaching and learning and social practices that address issues of marginalization, privilege, and access within different contexts?

The literature on critical hope is by no means vast. Collections include work by Raymond Williams (1989), Mary Zournazi (2002) and Cornel West (2008). The fields of educational studies, cultural studies, gender and women's studies, critical psychology, and philosophy have historically addressed questions of the political and cultural significance of hope. Zournazi's volume of collected interviews (2002) represents an important development in critical, ethical and imaginative thinking about hope. In educational studies, the writings of Paulo Freire (2004), Henry Giroux (2003), David Halpin (2003), Tony Monchinski (2010) and bell hooks (2003) come to mind. Most of these writings on hope in education are from North and South America, with few exceptions, such as the special issue on hope in the *South African Journal of Higher Education (SAJHE)* in 2011, to which the first three editors contributed and which offered a case study of different perspectives on hope at one South African Higher Education Institution (Carolissen *et al.* 2011).

The chapters in this volume, coming from different geographical and cultural contexts, allow for an exploration of further questions in relation to critical hope. The contributions in this collection are both conceptual and empirical, thus reducing the conceptual/empirical binary. The authors represent diverse sites of practice and struggle for social justice within education. The collection includes contributions from different geo-spatial contexts including Canada, Cyprus, the Philippines, South Africa, the UK, and the USA. These specific contexts represent sites marked by historical and contemporary conditions of conflict, post-conflict, neo-liberal, post-colonial and racial divisions. These geographies also pose specific educational challenges for critical hope and hopeful pedagogies. The diverse voices in this collection contribute a multi-faceted interrogation of the notion of critical hope, thus situating our exploration of critical hope within the necessary and challenging context of diverse international perspectives and differences.

Outline of the book

In Chapter 1 Michalinos Zembylas discusses how it is possible to think about and enact an agonistic politics of critical hope in education and sketches some of its fundamental dimensions. He theorizes the relationship among the pedagogical, the affective, the political and the ethical sensibilities in educational practices that attempt to instill critical hope and transformation. He elaborates on how pedagogies of critical hope constitute a particular politics of affect in education, reflecting the values and visions of teachers and students. These pedagogies enable the construction of an affective praxis that is anchored in critical action to interrogate the role of emotions in perpetuating hegemony. Pedagogies of critical hope can thus be regarded as decolonizing pedagogies in the sense of challenging dominant knowledge and practice and inspiring hope for change. He details how critical resistance can be achieved through an example which illustrates the constitution of strategic affective alliances between teacher and students.

In Chapter 2 Megan Boler writes about the necessity for an emotional willingness to have one's worldviews shattered through encounters with difference, uncertainty and ambiguity. She distinguishes between *naïve hope* which she sees as espousing the humanist rhetoric of individualism, with its accompanying beliefs in equal opportunity and sameness, and *critical hope*, which she sees as an acknowledgement of inequalities and privileges and an emotional willingness to interrogate one's own world views and position regarding these inequities. Critical hope for Boler also encompasses a historical review of oneself in the world, and of the shifting power relations in this context. She examines how a 'pedagogy of discomfort' can be used to develop a critical inquiry regarding emotional investments which shape both educators' and students' attachments to hegemonic habits of belief. She uses a description of a difficult classroom encounter to show how critical hope can be used as one way of rebuilding what is lost through a pedagogy of discomfort, by following the affect rather than what is expressed in words, and by responding compassionately with loving kindness to this loss.

In Chapter 3 Vivienne Bozalek, Ronelle Carolissen and Brenda Leibowitz build on the previous two chapters to explore possible avenues through which critical hope may be achieved in educational practice. The authors describe aspects of the South African higher education context in some depth, as background to why a focus on 'critical hope' might be necessary. The chapter discusses what a 'pedagogy of discomfort' entails and pedagogical approaches that might be adopted in order to encourage students to engage in the kinds of activities that might lead to the shattering of worldviews and elements of hopefulness. The authors reflect on how this project could contribute to critical hope and how it may also perpetuate hopelessness or despair.

In Chapter 4 Gustavo Fischman and Eric Haas situate critical hope within the influential body of literature on progressive pedagogy, including Freirian, critical, feminist and anti-racist approaches. They contend that the use of these approaches may lead to despair due to an inherent tendency in progressive pedagogy to use a 'narrative of redemption' when arguing for educational change. Using the reflections generated in a class for teachers based on the teaching of Paulo Freire, and one student in particular, they illustrate the dangers of this tendency. Rather than an expectation that educators become progressive 'superheroes', pedagogic support should be provided for them to become 'committed intellectuals'.

In Chapter 5 André Keet discusses human rights education, which, he argues had immense transformatory potential, but has become a purveyor of naïve hope due to its oversimplification and its being submerged within a plethora of instruments, standards and declarations. A critical version of human rights education can be restored with reference to the concept of 'plasticity'. With reference to the work of deconstructions including Derrida and Maibou, he argues for a deconstruction of human rights education in its current form, allowing the kernel of the paradigm to emerge. This will lead to a more productive reading and use of human rights education, and thus its ability to contribute to the emergence of human rights themselves.

In Chapter 6 Henk van Rinsum provides an example of a modern university's attempt to realize its mission with regard to corporate social responsibility via a 'Hope Project'. The context of an institutional history bearing traces of the apartheid past is presented. Using critical theory, which he maintains has Freirian foundations, and Degenaar's concept of the second reflection, van Rinsum questions the degree to which this Hope Project has been able to deal critically with its own institutional culture. He maintains that for an emancipatory critical hope to flourish, hope, struggle and criticality are vital.

Ronald David Glass begins Chapter 7 by exploring Paulo Freire's insight that 'hope is an ontological need'. He sees critical hope as being grounded in actual situations and their complexity, and in the necessary steps towards recurrent struggles for justice inspired by a vision of a better world, despite the situational limits. Thus critical hope can be seen as an act of striving which in itself is an antidote to despair. He uses the example of the hopes of whites working towards anti-racism, who require maps or routes of how to accomplish anti-racism. This chapter provides the means to reconsider the notions of hope and despair that identify opposite psychological and political poles. These typical notions presume that hope requires some specific achievable aim (otherwise it is simply faith), and that despair is evoked when all choices seem unable to generate a new ground for understanding and action. The chapter shows how the hope that infuses liberatory education and struggle keeps despair at bay not because of some specific aim or the possibility of achieving it, but rather because of the human capacity to open new spaces through the very process of struggle itself.

In Chapter 8 Paul Warmington argues that over the past 50 years, black UK identities have emerged around educational hope and educational despair. He shows how, historically, education has been one of the key sites in which the mass consciousness of being black and UK originated. Despite this, histories of black British thought and activism have often remained hidden. In examining some of the landmark black UK educational work from the 1960s to the present, this chapter repositions black UK educators and communities as agents of educational and social transformation. Importantly, it suggests that while their intellectual and political takes on education have been diverse, they have been predicated upon critical hope, wherein a critical understanding of the school system's maintenance of race–class inequalities and a belief in education as potentially transformative, a site of liberation and solidarity, have existed in tandem and in tension. In black UK educational struggles, critical hope has been an emancipatory resource.

In Chapter 9, Merlyne Cruz shares her own decolonizing journey, drawing attention to the discourses that have shaped her colonized/decolonizing lives. Honoring a tradition of critical Filipina feminist thought, she uses a nativist/indigenist epistemology to examine the nature of brown women's knowing and the epistemic patterns that underpin it. Many of the themes she covers in her chapter – suffering and criticality, spirituality and activist praxis – are central to indigenist pedagogies. She challenges the practice of dismissing and marginalizing such elements and argues for these to be a potent force for individual and social change.

Chapter 10 by John Horton offers a reflection on the word 'hope' as it is featured in cultural artefacts and philosophical texts across the ages, beginning with the story of Prometheus unbound. It covers the contribution of Francis

Bacon and the early enlightenment, the contributions by Immanuel Kant and Georg Hegel, before moving on to the more revolutionary perspective of Karl Marx and Friedrich Engels. The history continues with a utopian as well as critical perspective on hope by Ernst Bloch, and the significant contribution by Paulo Freire on a pedagogy of hope. A crucial point made by Horton in this survey is that hope may be based on emotion and reason, but it is always engaged in struggle. This notion of hope resonates throughout the book.

Taken together, the contributions that comprise this volume add to an understanding of critical hope which has been succinctly expressed by Torre *et al.* (2001) as 'where what could be is sought; where what has been, is critiqued; and where what is, is troubled' (p. 150). This edited collection also establishes the basis for a critically reflexive practice in which affect, imagination, relationality and resistance are inserted into the concept of hope. We hope that this volume contributes to debates that take forward the notion of critical hope in educational praxis.

References

Boler, M. (2003) 'Teaching for hope: The ethics of shattering world views'. In: D. Liston and J. Garrison, (eds.) *Teaching, Loving, Learning: Reclaiming Passion in Educational Practice*. New York: Routledge. (pp. 117–31).

Boler, M. and Zembylas, M (2003) 'Discomforting truths: The emotional terrain of understanding difference'. In: P. Trifonas (ed.) *Pedagogies of Difference: Rethinking Education for Social Change*. New York: Routledge Falmer. (pp. 110–36).

Carolissen, R., Bozalek, V., Nicholls, L., Leibowitz, B., Rohleder, P. and Swartz, L. (2011) 'bell hooks and the enactment of emotion in teaching and learning across boundaries: A pedagogy of hope?', *South African Journal of Higher Education*, 25(10): 157–167.

Duncan-Andrade, J.M.R. (2009) 'Note to educators: Hope required when growing roses in concrete', *Harvard Educational Review*, 79(2): 181–94.

Freire, P. (2004) *Pedagogy of Hope. Reliving 'Pedagogy of the Oppressed'*. London: Continuum.

Giroux, H. (2003) 'Utopian thinking under the sign of neoliberalism: towards a critical pedagogy of educated hope', *Democracy and Nature*, 9(1): 91–105.

Halpin, D. (2003) *Hope and Education: The Role of the Utopian Imagination*. London: Routledge Falmer.

hooks, b. (2003) *Teaching Community: A Pedagogy of Hope*. New York: Routledge.

Laclau, E. and Mouffe, C. (1985) *Hegemony and Socialist Strategy: Towards a Radical Democratic Politics*. Verso: London.

Monchinski, T. (2010) *Education in Hope: Critical Pedagogies and the Ethic of Care*. New York: Peter Lang Publishers.

Regan, P. (2011) *Unsettling the Settler Within: Indian Residential Schools, Truth Telling, and Reconciliation in Canada*. University of British Columbia: UBC Press.

Rorty, R. (1999) *Philosophy and Social Hope*. London: Penguin.

Shade, P. (2006) 'Educating hopes', *Studies in Philosophy and Education*, 25: 191–225.

Shor, I. (1992) *Empowering Education: Critical Teaching for Social Change*. Chicago: University of Chicago Press.

Stanford, S. (2011) 'Constructing moral responses to risk: A framework for hopeful social work practice', *British Journal of Social Work* 41: 1514–1531.

Torre, M.E., Fine, M., Boudin, K., Bowen, I., Clark, J., Hylton, D. and Upegui, D. (2001) 'A space for co-constructing counter stories under surveillance', *International Journal of Critical Psychology*, 4: 149–66.

West, C. (2008) *Hope on a Tightrope: Words and Wisdom*. New York: Hay House.

Williams, R. (1989) *Resources of Hope: Culture, Democracy, Socialism*. London: Verso.

Zembylas, M. (2007) *Five Pedagogies, a Thousand Possibilities: Struggling for Hope and Transformation in Education*. Rotterdam: Sense Publishers.

Zournazi, M. (2002) *Hope: New Philosophies for Change*. Sydney: Pluto Press.

Part I
Critical hope in education

1 Affective, political and ethical sensibilities in pedagogies of critical hope

Exploring the notion of 'critical emotional praxis'

Michalinos Zembylas

Introduction

In a previous book (Zembylas 2007), I discussed the pedagogical potential of 'critical hope' and some of the transformative possibilities that *pedagogies of critical hope* entail. In that book I argued that critical hope could inspire the formation of pedagogical spaces in which educators and students identify, narrate, explain, advocate or resist certain aspects of their emotional, historical and material lives; however, I did not pursue the political and ethical implications in much detail, especially in relation to the development of 'pedagogies of critical hope' as spaces for the constitution of strategic affective alliances. In this chapter, I wish to come back to my original discussion, utilizing an enhanced theoretical perspective and focusing specifically on how pedagogies of critical hope are valuable resources that respond to feelings of despair, pessimism and fatalism about social injustices in the world. I will argue that we need pedagogies which recognize the political, ethical and affective sensibilities of hope and that educators and students need to mobilize those sensibilities towards new social imaginaries that are grounded in social praxis and solidarity.

Although the role of hope in education has been receiving increasing attention by educational researchers in recent years (Boler 2004; Duncan-Andrade 2009; Edgoose 2009, 2010; Halpin 2003; Hytten 2009; Webb 2010), its theorization within a comprehensive framework that is simultaneously political, ethical and affective has not always been undertaken. This chapter, then, wishes to suggest that there is a nascent ethics and politics of hope, which involves engaging with emotions when grounding our pedagogies. This should not be interpreted as blind optimism, sentimentalism or utopia; rather, it is an argument for an agonistic politics of critical hope in education that involves critique, reflection, vision, strategy and action regardless of seemingly intractable difficulties (Halpin 2003). When critical or transformative hope is infused within a collective emotional orientation (Webb 2008), it can be argued that pedagogies are (re)constituted in new and meaningful ways that may foster change.

It is important to note that this chapter theorizes 'criticality' and 'hope' not as two separate notions which, for the most part so far, have remained relatively separate and come together to formulate 'critical hope' in an additive manner; on the contrary, 'critical hope' is theorized as a unified and integrative pedagogical tool and a profound political and ethical practice. To exemplify a particular manifestation of pedagogies of critical hope in practice, this chapter explores the notion of *critical emotional praxis* (Zembylas 2008, 2012) through a vignette. Critical emotional praxis is a pedagogical tool that helps educators and students to identify patterns in their emotional, historical and material lives, to realize how these patterns are made and what their consequences are for maintaining the status quo, and to motivate action for change. The notion of critical emotional praxis, then, is explored here as a particular process of developing and sustaining critical hope in schools, while paying attention to the affective, political and ethical sensibilities in pedagogies of critical hope.

A brief genealogy of critical hope

The chapter begins with a brief genealogy of critical hope and how various interpretations of this concept have evolved over the years. The point of departure is Freire's entire philosophy of education, which is founded on his *ontology* of hope (Webb 2010). As he writes in *Pedagogy of Hope*, Freire does not "understand human existence and the struggle needed to improve it, apart from hope and dream" (1994: 8). His thoughts on pedagogy of hope are "written in rage and love, without which there is no hope," and they are meant "as a defense of tolerance—not to be confused with connivance—and radicalness" (p. 10). For Freire, hope is an "ontological need" and "an existential concrete imperative" (p. 2) that keeps us alive thus "it is impossible to exist without it" (p. 72). This is why hope entails such strong emotions as love and rage; love as an ethical, critical and social stance that is open to otherness and nurtures difference, and rage as a commitment to be vigilant and to struggle against injustice and discrimination. Freire is careful, however, not to espouse a naïve rhetoric, thus he writes:

> I do not mean that, because I am hopeful, I attribute to this hope of mine the power to transform reality all by itself, so that I set out for the fray without taking account of concrete, material data, declaring, "My hope is enough!" No, my hope is necessary, but it is not enough. Alone, it does not win. But without it, my struggle will be weak and wobbly. *We need critical hope the way a fish needs unpolluted water.* The idea that hope alone will transform the world, and action undertaken in that kind of naiveté, is an excellent route to hopelessness, pessimism, and fatalism. But the attempt to do without hope, in the struggle to improve the world, as if that struggle could be reduced to calculated acts alone, or a purely scientific approach, is a frivolous illusion (Freire 1994: 8, added emphasis).

For Freire, fatalism is expressed not only by those who invest everything in a naïve hope about the transformation of the world, but also by those who reject any possibility of action and deny struggling because they are paralyzed by the notion that nothing will ever make a difference. Instead, critical hope is grounded in careful critical analysis and understanding of how emotional attachments, historical circumstances and material conditions have led us to the present, and signifies a willingness to be open to the implications of this analysis. This recognition does not theorize the present as the inevitable outcome of some progress, but problematizes how we have become who we believe we are. Thus, hope exists in the face of cynicism not because progress is an inevitable process or because God is with us or because we believe it is our destiny to fulfill a particular mission (Weiler 2003), but because struggle and possibility are precisely what constitute our lives.

It is important, therefore, to distinguish naïve hope – which is similar to optimism or a blind faith that things will get better – from critical hope, which is grounded in reflexivity and action for transformation. Drawing on this distinction in Freire's work, Boler (2004) writes that naïve hope essentially serves the status quo because it espouses a humanist rhetoric of individualism – e.g. hard work inevitably leads to success or everyone is the same underneath the skin. On the contrary, argues Boler, critical hope "recognizes that we live within systems of inequality, in which privilege [...] comes at the expenses of freedom of others" (p. 128) and adds:

> Critical hope requires seeing one's self within historical context, reevaluating the relationship of one's privilege to others in the world. It entails as well seeing how these relations of power shift and change over time and in one's lifetime. This pedagogical relation is a negotiation of the hegemonically constructed habits, internalized as attachments to particular beliefs and corresponding emotional reactions to change (Boler 2004: 130).

Critical hope, therefore, is a *relational* construct that is *both* emotional *and* critical. To say that someone is critically hopeful means that the person is involved in a critical analysis of power relations and how they constitute one's emotional ways of being in the world, while attempting to construct, imaginatively and materially, a different lifeworld. This effort, asserts Boler, demands an "emotional willingness to engage in the difficult work of possibly allowing one's worldviews to be shattered" (2004: 128). Therefore, critical hope – contrary to naïve hope – entails a willingness to exist within "ambiguity and uncertainty" (p. 129).

Naïve hope is also viewed by Duncan-Andrade (2009) as false hope that poses roadblocks to the road for social change and school reform. Duncan-Andrade describes three such forms of false hope that are problematic and need to be identified and tackled, if critical hope has any change to find its well deserved place in schools: *hokey hope*, *mythical hope*, and *hope deferred*. Hokey hope is the hope that ignores systemic and structural inequities and is grounded in "an individualistic up-by-your-bootstraps hyperbole that suggests if urban youth just work hard, pay attention, and play by the rules, then they will go to college and live out the 'American dream'" (Duncan-Andrade 2009: 182). Mythical hope is the hope grounded in "a false narrative of equal opportunity emptied of its historical and political contingencies" (p. 183); mythical hope celebrates the poor and marginalized individual who somehow manages to overcome oppression. Finally, hope deferred is constructed on a progressive vision but it quickly becomes into an empty rhetoric of despair about the 'system;' that is, although there is a critique of social inequity, this critique cannot be manifest "in any kind of transformative pedagogical project" (p. 184).

To summarize the insights from this brief genealogy of critical hope, I highlight two issues that are valuable in the theorization of pedagogies of critical hope in this chapter. First, critical hope is a unified concept and praxis that approaches that which is 'missing' through the affective, political and ethical engagement of participating individuals and communities. Thus, critical hope is what makes seeing one's self with a critical eye, and creates feelings of connectedness, solidarity and relationality with others. This connectedness is precisely what makes us bear witness to oppression, social injustice and past wrongdoings (Oliver 2001).

Second, critical hope entails an ongoing process of critiquing present negatives in the light of the desire for their future negation; that is, it emphasizes future-oriented critical thought, emotion and action. In addition, critical hope moves beyond critique and emphasizes the necessity of transforming society through goal-directed social praxis, individually and collectively (Webb 2008). In other words, although critical hope as an agonistic process entails the potential of affective connections that enable transgressions, such connections are not inevitably emancipatory. This recognition is grounded in a deeper understanding of both the possibilities and limitations that affect individual and collective aspirations about solidarity and social praxis. Critical hope, then, entails an ethical and political responsibility for constant vigilance in the process of change and becoming. Creating pedagogical spaces for embracing critical hope in educational settings may therefore be seen as an act of ethical and political responsibility that has the potential to recover a lost sense of connectedness, relationality and solidarity with others.

Pedagogies of critical hope

In light of the above analysis of the notion of critical hope, the following key questions may be raised: What do pedagogies of critical hope look like, if a well founded and critical hope is to be nurtured and experienced by educators and students? In what ways can pedagogies of critical hope really make a difference in a world full of inequality and despair? The use of 'pedagogies' (in the plural) in this context does not signify classroom pedagogical practices; rather pedagogies are defined as the relational encounters among people through which unpredictable possibilities of connectedness, solidarity and action are created. There are three elements of pedagogies of critical hope that I want to discuss here; these elements are mutually constitutive and highlight the *affective*, *ethical* and *political* sensibilities that are involved in pedagogical efforts to nurture critical hope in schools.

First, just as critical hope is grounded in a committed and active struggle against inequality and despair, pedagogies of critical hope require certain affective commitments. Above all, educators need to be open to critique, ambivalence and uncertainty. This ambivalence implies a decentered, multiple, nomadic process by which belonging is defined. Thus, for example, if solidarity is an important aspect of a critical vision of hope, it is important to transgress traditional boundaries and norms by which belonging and otherness are constructed (e.g. nation-state norms). The nomadic character of this process can produce emotional resistance and uncertainty because of traditional feelings of belonging to a certain nation-state. The courage to pursue this ambivalent path and the solidarity to collectively struggle to change terms of community building in order to establish new forms of connectedness – on the basis of common vulnerability – are essential components of pedagogies of critical hope.

In other words, to engage in pedagogies of critical hope means asking students and educators to radically re-evaluate the affective economies in which they live. The re-evaluation of affective economies has the potential to constitute new binding affective forces (Thrift 2004) and new social imaginaries (Taylor 2004). For example, there are numerous instances in schools in which empathy and mutual understanding often go unnoticed on an everyday basis. These include friendships and relationships across racial, religious or other divides. It is important, therefore, that educators and students identify and nurture such instances and consider how these moments can become inspiring for social praxis. The politics of friendship should not be underestimated in the constitution of powerful affective communities (Gandhi 2006).

Furthermore, the mobilization of affects is a valuable element of the ethical and political components of pedagogies of critical hope. Pedagogies of critical hope are involved in the creative production of affects (e.g. compassion, kindness, solidarity) that provoke educators and students to participate in community struggles, which refuse to accept oppression, suffering, and exploitation. This issue points to the notion of pedagogies of critical hope being attentive to those affects that produce particular struggles and histories which offer hope for individual and collective transformation. Examining and encouraging affective relationality opens creative spaces for feeling the world differently and envisioning and enacting alternative affective communities. This is clearly not limited pedagogically to students exercising self-reflection, as Giroux (1997) rightly points out; rather, it includes the critical analysis of the diverse ethical, political and affective mechanisms through which subjectivities and collectivities are constructed and have certain consequences. For example, sustaining dichotomies between 'we' and 'they,' between citizens and non-citizens (e.g. migrants) creates particular relations governed by feelings of superiority and resentment. A critical ontology of one's collective self interrogates what one has become and refuses to submit to the categories, explanatory schemes, and norms according to which one should think and judge one's self and others. The process of sustaining we-and-they dichotomies and their critical interrogation are shown in practice in the vignette that follows next.

The challenge for pedagogies of critical hope is precisely to sustain the hope for keeping criticality alive through action. Action and hope "fuel and sustain each other," therefore, "critical hope entails persistence, resourcefulness, generosity, determination, responsibility, discipline, compassion, courage, patience, accountability, humility, collaboration, attentiveness, and flexibility" (Hytten 2009: 161). Pedagogies of critical hope, then, inform us about the limits and possibilities of the present and the practices that are necessary to enact such possibilities. Pedagogies of critical hope combine the affective, the ethical and the political through actions and practices that stress the contextual nature of issues yet they systematically link the individual with a collective sense of transformation. Also, pedagogies of critical hope highlight the view that politics is not only about power relations but also about affects and ethics, thus such pedagogies engage politics and ethics through powerful affective modalities. In other words, pedagogies of critical hope create a language of the 'not yet' by conceptualizing and nurturing the enactment of the affective commitment to goal-directed social praxis. Therefore, it is important to reiterate once again that the issue is not about "*combining* the discourse of critique and hope" (Giroux 2002: 104, added emphasis); rather, critical hope and its enactment is seen as a unified concept and pedagogical practice that re-territorializes hope by emphasizing action for social transformation.

To conclude, pedagogies of critical hope require that the pedagogical intervention needed to initiate individual and collective transformations can be nothing less than a radical subversion of the existing regime of truth. This process must, therefore, work simultaneously at several levels that identify and critique one's affective, ethical and political commitments and attachments. But the pedagogical challenge is not simply to identify and critique one's affective attachments to certain politics and ethics but to find ways to move beyond these attachments and establish new affective connections that are empowering for change. Pedagogies of critical hope, then, grow out of viewing the classroom as a space that is constituted through the establishment of strategic affective alliances. I now explore the notion of *critical emotional praxis* as a particular manifestation and a valuable pedagogical tool for developing and sustaining critical hope in schools.

The contribution of *Critical Emotional Praxis* in the formation of pedagogies of critical hope

In my previous work (Zembylas 2008, 2012), I theorized critical emotional praxis as a pedagogical tool that shows how emotions can be engaged as critical and transformative forces in education. As noted earlier, false or naïve hope would have us believe in individualized notions of suffering and success, but critical hope demands that we recover the lost sense of connectedness and solidarity, by struggling to combat oppression and social injustice alongside one another. While the emotions of suffering, injustice, and oppression are very real, and very devastating features of life in many societies, educators can work towards radical healing (Ginwright 2009) through devising pedagogies that do not remain stuck in misery (Duncan-Andrade 2009; Edgoose 2010). The prospects of critical emotional praxis as a pedagogical tool to teach about/for critical hope are shown below through one vignette from my on-going ethnographic research in my home country, Cyprus, a place in which discrimination and structural injustices against migrants have risen at alarming levels in recent years (ECRI 2011). In particular, this vignette shows how one teacher's use of critical emotional praxis in the classroom provided an informed insight into efforts with her students to promote critical hope and solidarity with dispossessed and marginalized migrants of their community.

Vignette[1]

Cyprus has traditionally been a country of out-migration throughout the twentieth century and especially after the 1974 Turkish invasion that divided Cyprus into its north part (still occupied by Turkey) and its south part (government controlled area). However, labor migration (mainly from Asia, the Middle East, and Eastern Europe) to the Republic of Cyprus started in the 1990s as a result of the relatively quick economic boom that has turned Cyprus into a host country for migrants. In recent years, a number of racist incidents (e.g. random attacks against migrants, especially those not considered to be white) have raised concerns whether Greek–Cypriots are xenophobic and discriminate against migrants. For instance, there have been research studies covering the Greek–Cypriot media and education that show the existence of discriminatory practices and the presence of strong negative stereotypes towards migrants – e.g. views such as "migrants take our jobs," "they threaten our national identity," and "they are usually criminals" (see Zembylas 2010; Zembylas and Lesta 2011). The situation is further complicated in the light of the unresolved political conflict between Greek–Cypriots and Turkish-Cypriots for the last fifty years. Greek–Cypriot teachers, in other words, have to negotiate a complex situation: on one hand, they have to deal with the increasing flow of migrants that changes Cyprus rapidly; on the other hand, they need to negotiate the challenges of co-existing with those many of them consider to be 'enemies' (i.e. Turkish Cypriots and Turks).

The present vignette draws from a case study that shows a Greek–Cypriot teacher, Maria, who struggled to enact critical emotional praxis, after attending a series of workshops on intercultural education at the Open University of Cyprus.[2] Maria was a white teacher at a multicultural urban school in Cyprus – a school that received an increasing number of migrant students (especially from the Middle East and North Africa) in recent years. Maria struggled since the beginning of the school year to formulate intercultural pedagogical practices that tackled discrimination and stereotypes against migrant students. Her use of critical emotional praxis aimed at challenging her students to examine their negative behaviors toward and emotions about migrant students and engage in specific actions to change those. Inevitably, issues of (critical) hope were raised in classroom discussions at two levels: at one level, students' feelings of despair about the impact of migrants on changing Greek–Cypriot culture and society and Maria's hopelessness about the possibilities to transform her students' feelings; and, at another level, feelings of hope that solidarity on the basis of common humanity and vulnerability could make small connections with migrants and their lives.

Feelings of despair and hopelessness

Maria taught Social Studies at a high school in which there was increasing hostility from local students (i.e. Greek–Cypriots) toward migrant students, with threats and fights taking place inside and outside the school on a weekly basis. Maria repeatedly expressed her passionate commitment about social justice in her teaching, so her primary goal was to help her students deal with the challenges of migration in critical, non-violent, compassionate and considerate ways. As she once said: "I am wholeheartedly committed to the values of social justice and so I object to any words or actions that discriminate against any student." However, the school authorities and the local community did not seem to share the same vision. My research team documented very negative attitudes and beliefs towards migrants on the part of Greek–Cypriot students and teachers alike; migrants, in general, were considered responsible for changing the cultural and ethnic character of Greek–Cypriot society, a situation with which Greek–Cypriot students and teachers felt very uncomfortable. Greek–Cypriot students often expressed feelings of despair because Cyprus was changing too rapidly and they felt that in a few years, they might become a minority in their own country. Also, Greek–Cypriot students and teachers linked migration with the ongoing military occupation of the northern part of Cyprus by Turkey; therefore, they viewed migration in the south part as another manifestation of Turkey's intentions to change the demographic character of the Greek–Cypriot society. As one student put this: "They [Turks] want to bring all these foreigners here because their ultimate goal is the Turkification of Cyprus."

Negative emotions about migrants in the context of larger societal norms were sparked in the daily exchanges among migrant students and Greek–Cypriot teachers and students. Maria had a vision of intercultural education that took into consideration the needs of migrant students and embraced them with love and compassion. However, she felt hopeless because there was no appreciation of multiculturalism by most of her colleagues and she became witness to several episodes of racist behavior against migrant students by Greek–Cypriot teachers and students alike. Known for her sensitivity to issues of migration and social justice, she was once told in the teacher lounge: "Migrant students are only creating troubles. Why do you care so much about them? Chill out! Hopefully, one day they will abandon our country and leave us alone." The emotions of self-doubt, confusion, and hopelessness were overwhelming to her. She felt that she had to fight forces (e.g. societal norms) that were far more powerful than her passion and commitment to social justice for all. As she admitted in one of our conversations: "Sometimes I feel so desperate [...] It seems that I am fighting against so much larger forces than what I can handle. Even if you manage to build up something good at school, the society out there destroys it."

Nurturing feelings of solidarity and connectedness

Despite her feelings of hopelessness, Maria systematically organized several activities to engage her students in investigating and recognizing the hardships of vulnerable people in their community, and particularly those of migrants and their families. To do this, she used literature and films, and arranged visits to local workplaces where migrants had made a major social contribution. For example, she showed the films *Hotel Rwanda* (2004), *Gran Torino* (2008), and *American History X* (1998), and assigned novels such as *The Boy in the Striped Pyjamas* (2006) and *To Kill a Mockingbird* (1960). Her approach in dealing with these novels and films was to provide first a list of focus questions that would guide students' viewing and then devote time to discussing the plot and its interpretations. Thus, issues of race, discrimination, hatred, stereotypes, and conflict were frequently at the centre of classroom discussions. As Maria explained in an interview: "My goal is to provoke them to consider the consequences of categorization, discrimination and hatred and relate those to their own lives and the lives of migrants and others in our society. It's not easy, but sometimes we manage to establish some interesting connections."

Another activity was to ask her students to interview one former Greek–Cypriot migrant and one migrant worker from other countries; in this way, Maria attempted to engage her students in examining the phenomenon of migration in general and realizing first-hand the implications of stereotyping the 'Other.' Initially, some of the students resisted the activity saying, "Why should I waste my time to talk to *them*? Don't we have something better to do?" When students conducted their interviews and brought their transcripts in the classroom, they were surprised how many similarities they identified in migrants' experiences. Notably, one of the students admitted: "I never really thought how I was making all these generalizations about migrant workers. Now I see that there is something bigger about the experience of migration that is common to all humans, regardless of their ethnic background."

On one occasion, Maria asked her students to consider a world based on the values of social justice, solidarity and respect. Several of her Greek–Cypriot students replied almost cynically that they could not imagine this world because part of their own country was occupied by Turkey. As one student pointed out: "How can you expect us to behave in a just manner towards migrants when we are the victims of injustice in our own country?" Maria was admittedly surprised at this response and asked for further explanations. In the exchange that followed, some students spoke extensively about their strong feelings of resentment, fear, and despair with increased migration in Cyprus. For example, one student suggested that, "As long as our country is occupied, I cannot turn my face away from my people and pay attention to them [migrants]. Frankly, we have our own problems. We don't need theirs too." It was generally acknowledged that their emotions were strong about this matter; the students also recognized that these emotions 'colored' their perceptions about migrants and all of those who were not Greek–Cypriots.

One audacious yet risky way with which Maria attempted to tackle Greek–Cypriot students' feelings of despair and resentment for the 'Other' and nurture solidarity with migrant students was to push Greek–Cypriot students to acknowledge some of their privileges. Many Greek–Cypriot students and teachers did not want to recognize that, in some ways, they were privileged compared to migrant students; for example, most Greek–Cypriot families at the school were middle-class and were doing fairly well, compared to the financial circumstances of migrant families in the community. However, the overwhelming majority of Greek–Cypriots' views were fixed to the unresolved political problem of Cyprus and their feelings of being the 'victims' of a great injustice; they refused to see that others also suffered in their lives – e.g. several migrant children were refugees from Iraq, Lebanon, Syria, Palestine and other conflict areas in the Middle East. Maria struggled with worry that this fixation on one's own concerns blinded Greek–Cypriot students from seeing the emotional difficulties others experienced as well. This reality struck sharply during a class discussion following a serious school incident in which migrant students were attacked and beaten at school by a group of Greek–Cypriot students. As Maria reflected on this discussion:

> It's so ironic because no matter what I do with native [Greek–Cypriot] students, they continue investing emotionally in the belief that they are 'victims,' and that this victimhood gives them the right to treat others with disrespect and resentment. As one of my students told me 'We, Greek–Cypriots, have the right to be racists because our country is occupied by Turkey. We always have to take a defensive position to save our country from all foreigners.'

Maria continued her efforts to encourage students to acknowledge not only the role of emotions in conflict and violence against migrants but also how reflecting critically on these emotions could instill some hope for change. As she told her students in class many times, "Other peoples and groups have been victimized in the world we live; recognizing their pain and suffering does not devalue our own pain and suffering as Greek–Cypriots." For this purpose, she led a series of lessons focusing on the ways different groups throughout history have stereotyped, abused, and oppressed others, often resulting in violent exchanges. She then asked students to consider the possibility of nonviolence based on the vision of a shared, common humanity and solidarity. After long struggles, towards the end of the school year, some Greek–Cypriot students admitted that, "We are all human. This is more important than what divides us." Although this acknowledgment did not solve any long-term, structural problems at the school, it was a small step towards recognizing the consequences of emotional divides and exclusions. Maria expressed some feelings of hope that, "If we manage to acknowledge some of the injustices and discriminations against migrant students and empathize with them, because we also experience similar feelings as a result of the ongoing Turkish occupation in north Cyprus, then we may have a point of departure to create a few small cracks to the system."

Conclusions and implications

The concept of critical emotional praxis acknowledges that emotions play a powerful role in either sustaining or disrupting hegemonic discourses about one's self, others, belonging and knowledge/truth. Critical emotional praxis is grounded in a psychoanalytic and socio-political analysis of emotion (Zembylas 2008, 2012) and provides a platform from which educators and students can critically interrogate their own emotion-laden beliefs. This analysis exposes privileged positions of psychic and socio-political power and moves beyond the comfort zones in which educators and students are usually socialized in a society.

Furthermore, critical emotional praxis recognizes the emotional ambivalence and ambiguity that often accompanies this process and thus creates pedagogical opportunities for critical inquiry into how emotions of uncertainty or discomfort, despite making the world seem ambiguous and chaotic, can restore humanity and encourage healing. Ambivalent emotions – for example, resentment and bitterness but also feelings of common vulnerability and empathy – emerge from teaching and learning that recognizes relationality, connectedness, and solidarity; that is, if we can narrate 'our' stories of suffering to ourselves and to those who have wounded us and listen to the narratives of those we have wounded, we might set up better conditions for imagining and enacting new political and ethical relations (Georgis and Kennedy 2009).

The ambivalence of emotion, then, highlights that positive and negative emotions are provisional readings and judgments of others that change, when there are opportunities to re-articulate the past in new ways (Chubbuck and Zembylas 2008; Zembylas 2009, 2010). Critical emotional praxis, therefore, offers opportunities to produce transformative action in pedagogies of critical hope, because educators and students can translate their hopes and emotional understandings into new ways of living with others.

The vignette contained in this chapter has shown how a high-school teacher used critical emotional praxis as a productive form of engagement with narratives of social injustice and discrimination in her classroom and how this process nurtures different manifestations of hope for herself and her students. In designing and implementing different activities for her students, Maria was purposely trying to engage students' emotions as critical and transformative forces. This effort was not always 'successful' of course; in fact, one could argue that most of the times, it was the opposite. And yet, the measure of 'success' has less to do with the number of minds that are changed by the end of the school year and more with the spaces and the openings that become available for the process of transformation. Maria's use of critical emotional praxis as a pedagogical tool, in my view, created spaces for critical hope along three important dimensions.

First, critical emotional praxis was grounded in and interrogated an historical and political understanding of the role of despair and hope in Maria's classroom and society at large. In other words, critical emotional praxis consists in the ability to question emotionally charged, cherished beliefs and hopes, exposing how privileged positions and comfort zones inform the ways in which one recognizes what and how one has been taught to see/act (or not to see/act), and empowering different ways of being with/for the other. In the vignette, Maria demonstrated this understanding by constantly examining the emotional implications of unjust systems and practices such as feelings of despair and resentment by native colleagues and students toward migrants. Engaging in this interrogation was not a liberatory act by itself, yet it began to challenge students' and teachers' interpretations of emotions (e.g. resentment, despair) and the ideologies in which they might be grounded (e.g. nationalism, racism). For example, it was shown that Greek–Cypriot students continued to express strong feelings against migrants, yet these feelings were accompanied by some ambivalence as indicated by some of the data generated.

The second dimension is that critical emotional praxis illuminated the transactional role of emotions in local contexts. That is, the specific context produces emotional responses such as hope or despair; at the same time, emotions shape the particulars of the context. This transaction can challenge or sustain just and unjust relations. An education which remains fixed on moral polarities ('good-us' vs 'bad-them'), and that privileges only good feelings about one's community and nation, for example, fails to recognize the place of racism, oppression and wrongdoing. The desire for pride and the repulsion of shame in almost all modern nation-states (and their educational systems) since the nineteenth century has become a major mechanism of self-affirmation. An opening to gain a renewed sense of passion, care and solidarity through questioning existing social inequalities cannot be achieved by good will alone, or by declaring that deep down 'we are all strangers.' We must acknowledge that we have a shared vulnerability, yet at the same time we also need to acknowledge how some have been systematically oppressed and recognized as 'stranger' than others and as non-members of the community (Ahmed 2004).

In this vignette, Maria was desperately trying to break down the 'us-and-them' mentality of native students, yet the results of this effort were mixed. The emotional basis of us-and-them categories was developed partly as a result of students' perceptions of themselves as 'victims' of the ongoing Turkish occupation and this was the hard reality that Maria had to work with. Instead of accepting this victimhood uncritically though, her effort was to show her students that others were victimized too and that recognizing this would not devalue the Greek–Cypriot experience of suffering and trauma.

And finally, the third dimension of critical emotional praxis refers to how these emotional understandings are translated into relationships, pedagogical practices, and policies that benefit social justice and instill critical hope as a sense of possibility that negates the conditions of misery. In the vignette, a key to constructing and sustaining some hope lay in Maria's efforts to engage her students into action that would initiate some changes in their everyday lives – e.g. through encouraging students to conduct real world analysis of the implications of migration; through highlighting the importance of justice in all aspects of classroom and school life; and through relating with migrant students in a more empathic manner. These pedagogic actions, which essentially attempted to *re-educate* her students' emotions, were important aspects of Maria's pedagogies of critical hope, because they uncovered and problematized the deeply embedded emotional dimensions that framed and shaped native students' daily habits, routines, and unconscious complicity with hegemony. By closely examining her students' emotional reactions and responses, Maria hoped to identify unconscious privileges as well as invisible ways in which the students complied with dominant ideology. The results were not always encouraging but students' ambivalent feelings in several occasions revealed that the pedagogic actions managed to problematize some ideas that were taken for granted.

All in all, pedagogies of critical hope make visible alternative ways in which educators and students as critical actors can be engaged in the production of social praxis. Again, this is not a vague utopian call for educators and students to simply 'change the world' and 'make it better.' Rather, it is a shared utopian agenda that sharpens action-oriented plans while deconstructing the powerful affective investments that normalize social orders. The role of educators and students should not be underestimated in producing powerful affective connections that create even small cracks to traditions of oppression and injustice. This means a forward pull to negate critically the conditions giving rise to present situations of oppression and injustice and thus pedagogies of critical hope refuse to degenerate into a form of empty utopianism.

In closing, I wish to reiterate that we need to acknowledge how the disruption of despair is certainly not an easy task for educators. Affective communities grounded in long-time emotions are not easily undone through an educational program in which ideas of critical emotional praxis and pedagogies of critical hope are somehow infused. It is, however, extremely important for educators to examine the interplay between critical hope and social justice by exploring what emotions *do* in everyday discourses and practices in relation to social justice and by finding ways to translate such analyses into critical emotional praxis and critical hope. Engaging in critical emotional praxis can evoke public and school pedagogies of critical hope that provide alternative ways of relating to others. A sustained endeavour to recognize social inequalities offers the potential to reinvent pedagogical spaces in which similarities and differences with others may be critically articulated and felt, toward constructing new shared possibilities for society.

Notes

1   The vignette that is presented here is based on ethnographic data that have been collected over the last five years. These data are part of a large project that explores, among other things, how school practices and discourses are entangled with emotion in relation to perceptions of race and ethnicity. The vignette narrated in this chapter is compiled from analyses of interviews, observations, and other data. All names used are pseudonyms.

2 These workshops are offered every year to a small group of educators who participate voluntarily. The workshops focus on how to develop intercultural pedagogies in the classroom and include: attending lectures from intercultural education experts, watching relevant movies and analyzing them, conducting small action research projects, and developing classroom materials.

References

Ahmed, S. (2004) *The Cultural Politics of Emotion*. Edinburgh: Edinburgh University Press.

Boler, M. (2004) 'Teaching for hope: The ethics of shattering world views'. In: D. Liston and J. Garrison (eds) *Teaching, Learning and Loving: Reclaiming Passion in Educational Practice*. New York: Routledge-Falmer.

Chubbuck, S. and Zembylas, M. (2008) 'The emotional ambivalence of socially just teaching: A case study of a novice urban schoolteacher', *American Educational Research Journal*, 45(2): 274–318.

Duncan-Andrade, J.M.R. (2009) 'Note to educators: Hope required when growing roses in concrete', *Harvard Educational Review*, 79(2): 181–94.

ECRI (European Commission against Racism and Intolerance) (2011) *ECRI Report on Cyprus*, Strasbourg: Council of Europe.

Edgoose, J. (2009) 'Radical hope and teaching: Learning political agency from the political disenfranchised', *Educational Theory*, 59(1): 105–21.

Edgoose, J. (2010) 'Hope in the unexpected: How can educators still make a difference in the world?', *Educators College Record*, 112(2): 386–406.

Freire, P. (1994) *Pedagogy of Hope: Reliving Pedagogy of the Oppressed*. New York: Continuum.

Georgis, D. and Kennedy, R.M. (2009) 'Touched by injury: Toward an educational theory of anti-racist humanism', *Ethics and Education*, 4: 19–30.

Gandhi, L. (2006) *Affective Communities: Anticolonial Thought, Fin-de-Siècle Radicalism, and the Politics of Friendship*. Durham, NC: Duke University Press.

Ginwright, S. (2009) *Black Youth Rising: Race, Activism, and Radical Healing in Urban America*. New York: Educators College Press.

Giroux, H. (1997) *Pedagogy and the Politics of Hope: Theory, Culture and Schooling*. Oxford: Westview Press.

Giroux, H. (2002) 'Educated hope in an age of privatized visions', *Cultural Studies/Critical Methodologies*, 2: 93–112.

Halpin, D. (2003) *Hope and Education: The Role of the Utopian Imagination*. London and New York: Routledge-Falmer.

Hytten, K. (2009) 'Cultivating hope and building community: Reflections on social justice activism in Educational Studies', *Educational Studies*, 46: 151–67.

Oliver, K. (2001) *Witnessing: Beyond Recognition*. Minneapolis, MN: University of Minnesota Press.

Taylor, C. (2004) *Modern Social Imaginaries*. Durham, NC: Duke University Press.

Thrift, N. (2004) 'Intensities of feeling: Towards a spatial politics of affect', *Geografiska Annaler Series B: Human Geography*, 86(1): 55–76.

Webb, D. (2008) 'Exploring the relationship between hope and utopia: Towards a conceptual framework', *Politics*, 28(3): 197–206.

Webb, D. (2010) 'Paulo Freire and "the need for a kind of education in hope"', *Cambridge Journal of Education*, 40(4): 327–339.

Weiler, K. (2003) 'Paulo Freire: On hope', *Radical Educator*, 67: 32–5.

Zembylas, M. (2007) *Five Pedagogies, A Thousand Possibilities: Struggling for Hope and Transformation in Education*. Rotterdam: Sense Publishers.

Zembylas, M. (2008) *The Politics of Trauma in Education*. New York: Palgrave MacMillan.

Zembylas, M. (2009) 'The politics of emotions in education: Affective economies, ambivalence and transformation'. In: E. Samier and M. Schmidt (eds) *Emotional Dimensions of Educational Administration and Leadership*. New York: Routledge.

Zembylas, M. (2010) 'Racialization/ethnicization of school emotional spaces: The politics of resentment', *Race Ethnicity and Education*, 13(2): 253–70.

Zembylas, M. (2012) 'Critical emotional praxis for reconciliation education: Emerging evidence and pedagogical implications', *Irish Educational Studies*, 31(1): 19–34.

Zembylas, M. and Lesta, S. (2011) 'Greek–Cypriot students' stances and repertoires towards migrants and migrant students in the Republic of Cyprus', *Journal of International Migration and Integration*, 12: 475–94.

2 Teaching for hope
The ethics of shattering worldviews[1]

Megan Boler

> Out beyond ideas of wrongdoing and right doing, there is a field. I'll meet you there. When the soul lies down in that grass, the world is too full to talk about. Ideas, language, even the phrase 'each other' doesn't make sense
>
> – Rumi

Every semester while teaching a required course in social foundations of education, I engage three categories of students. Firstly, there are those willing to walk down a path of critical thinking with me, who find their worldviews shattered, but simultaneously engage in creatively rebuilding a sense of meaning and coherence in the face of ambiguity. Secondly, there are those who angrily and vocally resist my attempts to suggest that the world might possibly be other than they have comfortably experienced it. Thirdly, there are those who appear disaffected, already sufficiently numb so that my attempts to ask them to rethink the world encounter only vacant and dull stares. While I should probably be most concerned about those with blank and vacant faces, I am given the hope and inspiration to go on by those who embrace the opportunity to rethink the dominant propaganda that has constituted the majority of their education thus far. However, it is often the case that the most intense emotions of suffering are experienced by both myself and the students who loudly resist having their worldviews challenged. How can educator and student make productive use of this suffering and discomfort? What role does compassion play in helping to negotiate the minefields of ambiguity and contradiction encountered when asked to rethink worldviews?

Those of us who teach any course that emphasizes critical thinking, especially if the content has to do with issues of race, class, gender, sexual orientation, or other cultural histories, will often find ourselves teaching students who may prefer to avoid thinking about social inequalities and institutionalized oppressions. Most US public schools will have exposed students to partisan histories well documented by such books as James Loewen's *Lies My Teacher Told Me* (1995). Steeped in these nationalist myths, students may cling to the myth of the American Dream, to individualism and to a faith in meritocracy as the arbiter of privilege. Attachment to these myths is not merely cognitive but deeply emotional: The American Dream may be a dream that offers students hope – for their own family, for themselves, or a naïve hope that others, less privileged than themselves, may improve their lot in life if they would only work hard enough.

Because the educational system does not systematically teach US citizens about the histories of disenfranchised groups, students encountering social justice curricula – reading, for example, Jonathan Kozol's scathing indictment of unequal education in *Savage Inequalities* – may well experience a shocking cognitive dissonance: Can it be that the world is not as I was taught to perceive and believe? For some students, such curricula do not threaten but rather validate a worldview that may have been missing from their official schooling. Students who are hungry for untold histories indeed do not find social justice curricula threatening, but rather find resources in the readings and discussions that help shape their sense of self in positive ways. On the other hand, there are many students who, as mentioned in the opening, vocally resist attempts to suggest that the world might possibly be other than they have comfortably experienced it.

An angry, defensive response to social justice and analyses of power and oppression signals someone who is struggling to maintain his or her identity in what feels like a threat of annihilation. On an emotional level, social justice courses can make some people feel like they are the bad guy, that they have no place of belonging. And those who respond in this manner are not only white males. Every semester I also encounter a woman and sometimes, though more rarely, a person of color who is angry and defensive, who is clinging tightly to a belief that sexism (or racism) does not exist, that everyone should stop whining because there is equal opportunity for all. To shatter worldviews – specifically, to suggest that some unfairly benefit from (white, or male, or heterosexual) privilege – can be emotionally translated into feeling one has no place of belonging. Often, angry protestations are the cries of someone trying to save him or herself from annihilation.

To develop compassion for those suffering from 'dominant cultural withdrawal,' as this might be termed, is a slippery slope: I do not feel that my responsibility as an educator committed to social justice is to pamper those who have experienced a life of privilege, nor to validate desires to cling to privilege and not recognize injustice. However, education is not effective if it is combative and alienating. The story I tell in this chapter reveals to me that compassion and offering hope are important complements to a pedagogy of discomfort.

In this chapter, I examine how a 'pedagogy of discomfort' engages critical inquiry regarding the emotional investments that shape both educators' and students' attachments to particular worldviews. Secondly, I define and explore what I call 'inscribed habits of emotional inattention,' which are revealed when a pedagogy of discomfort challenges one's usual beliefs and views. The focus of this chapter is to better understand the vocal and loud resistance to rethinking one's worldview and the suffering caused to the student and to the educator in this process of renegotiating understanding of how power defines social stratification. In relation to this edited collection, my focus on suffering and compassion suggests one model for understanding the dynamic relationships between educator and student. If education is a commitment to growth and change, then that change will require facing up to our investments and experiencing the discomfort of new thinking. I will discuss the kinds of compassion that are necessary to complement ethical approaches to a pedagogy of discomfort.

Before defining a pedagogy of discomfort and its emotional vicissitudes, I wish to foreground the comments of Buddhist psychologist Mark Epstein. In a book that analyzes the overlap of Freudian psychology and Buddhist philosophies, Epstein offers important insights into the contradictory and ambiguous terrain of emotions. His comments quoted here emphasize the necessity of moving beyond binaries and instead recognizing the ambiguities of experience and meaning.

> In Buddhist psychology, emotions are classified as 'skillful' or 'unskillful.' The 'afflicted' ones of anger, envy, pride, worry, agitation, and greed are opposed by their counterparts of love, compassion, humility, patience, tranquility, and generosity. The model is a simple one: two opposites cannot occupy the same psychic space. Anger impedes and occludes love and vice versa. Turn one down by cultivating the other. But there is another way of understanding this model, one that is more attuned to the ambiguities of contemporary psychoanalysis. In this view, these skillful and unskillful emotions are opposite because they are part of a single dialectic. Anger is a perversion of love, transformed in the crucible of frustration. Anxiety is restricted excitement. Envy is a contracted form of empathy, since both spring from the capacity to know another's experience.
> (Epstein 2001)

The dialectic model understands, then, that the angry resistance of those who feel threatened in our classrooms is also a complex cry for recognition and care. This highlights to me that suffering and compassion are not mutually exclusive. Specifically, in teaching, by 'following the affect' rather than the words people actually utter, one can begin to see how emotional investments reflect both individuals' willingness to grow as well as the embedded quality of dominant cultural values. Epstein emphasizes the value of becoming conscious of what I call 'inscribed habits of emotional inattention' as a means of creating 'space' where once there was rigid habit:

> [I]n our desire for freedom, we imagine that we have to eliminate unwanted aspects of ourselves. My understanding does not support such an approach. Change will happen naturally as we open to the truth. The more we bring our attachments into awareness, the freer we become, not because we eliminate the attachments, but because we learn to identify more with awareness than with desire. Using our capacity for consciousness, we can change perspective on ourselves, giving a sense of space where once there was only habit. Discipline means restraining the habitual movement of the mind, so that instead of blind impulse there can be clear comprehension.
> (Epstein 2001: 71)

Epstein's insight underscores a pedagogy of discomfort's key aim – to disrupt emotional habits and equilibrium in search of re-evaluating attachments to rigid notions of self and world. However, to engage in dissecting the comfort of a familiar worldview can involve a kind of 'shattering' emotional experience. Compassion may be called for as a crucial element of a pedagogy of discomfort so that students are able to move from fear and anger to what Epstein (2001: 71) described as "clear comprehension" – comprehension of the historical and cultural reasons for the attachments that one has to particular worldviews.

A pedagogy of discomfort

I now turn to define a pedagogy of discomfort that offers context for the story of conflict between myself and Sam, which shall follow. As its name suggests, a pedagogy of discomfort emphasizes the need for both the educator and student to move outside of their comfort zones. In the final chapter of *Feeling Power: Emotions and Education* (Boler 1999), I introduce the notion of a 'pedagogy of discomfort' to describe how I engage students in a process of critically analyzing cherished beliefs and assumptions such as that of the American Dream and pervasive individualism. In that work, I contrast 'spectating' versus 'witnessing' to outline how students can engage in critical reflection and take social responsibility in the act of reading texts and films and, more generally, in looking at the world.

The 'comfort zones' we inhabit are inscribed cultural and emotional terrains that we occupy less by choice and more by virtue of dominant cultural values, which we internalize as unconsciously as the air we breathe: "Hegemony refers to the maintenance of domination not by the sheer exercise of force but primarily through consensual social practices, social forms and social structures produced in specific sites such as the church, the state, the school, the mass media, the political system and the family" (McLaren 1989: 203). The comfort zone reflects emotional investments that by and large remain unexamined because they have been woven into the everyday fabric of what is considered common sense.

A pedagogy of discomfort recognizes and problematizes the deeply embedded emotional dimensions that frame and shape daily habits, routines and unconscious complicity with hegemony. The purpose of attending to emotional habits as part of radical education is to draw attention to the ways in which we enact and embody dominant values and assumptions in our daily habits and routines. By closely examining emotional reactions and responses – what we call emotional stances – one begins to identify unconscious privileges as well as invisible ways in which one complies with dominant ideology.

One should not make the mistake of assuming that a pedagogy of discomfort seeks only to destabilize members of the dominant group. A pedagogy of discomfort invites not only members of the dominant culture but also members of marginalized cultures to re-examine the hegemonic values inevitably internalized in the process of being exposed to curricula and media that serve the interests of the ruling class. No one escapes hegemony. Those born in the United States, as well as those who immigrate to the US, absorb, consciously or not, common sense beliefs about what it means to be an 'American.'

Of course, every individual will have their own idiosyncratic experiences of discomfort. Heterosexuals, for example, may as a group tend to experience discomfort when asked to think carefully about their views toward lesbian and gay people. White people may be more 'uncomfortable' discussing racism than are people of color. However, there are moments in which it is uncomfortable for a gay person to consider his or her own internalized homophobia or for a person of color to reflect on his or her own internalized racism. In short, no one escapes internalizing dominant cultural values despite the fact that these values take different forms in different individuals.

To engage students in sophisticated critiques of difference requires unlearning the myth of neutral education. As Donald Macedo writes in the Introduction to *Chomsky on Miseducation*:

> Given the tendency for humans to construct "satisfying" and often self-deceptive stories, stories that often damage themselves and their groups, particularly when these deceptive stories are rewarded by the dominant social order, the development of a critical comprehension between the meaning of words and a more coherent understanding of the meaning of the world is prerequisite to achieving clarity of reality. As Freire suggests, it is only "through political practice that the less coherent sensibility for the world begins to be surpassed and the more rigorous intellectual pursuits give rise to a more coherent comprehension of the world."
>
> (Macedo 2000: 10–11)

To gain a 'clarity of reality' requires particularly close attention to those stories that naturalize themselves through common sense or familiar cultural myth. The story I share below illustrates how a pedagogy of discomfort reveals what I am calling inscribed habits of emotional inattention. I believe that critical pedagogy benefits from attending to these emotional habits as a means to excavate the internalized effects of hegemony.

I propose *inscribed habits of emotional inattention* as a way to describe the embedded, cultural habits of seeing and not seeing. These habits come to feel like one's chosen self-identity, but are in fact as much social and cultural as they are personal. Habits of emotional inattention offer an explanatory concept that integrates the difficult notion of the 'unconscious' with the notion of hegemony. Such habits of belief – for example, a belief that each person is individually responsible for his or her own destiny – usually reflect dominant cultural ideology but are internalized by individuals and in turn become part of a person's sense of self. This process describes hegemony: Dominant ideology enforces itself, not necessarily through violent means, but through people's agreement to abide by and value a status quo that benefits institutionalized powers.

This emotional selectivity some philosophers call 'patterns of moral salience.' Like Aristotle, John Dewey analyzed 'selective emphasis' and argued for the ethical importance of seeing the 'whole context' (Garrison 1997: 109). To attend carefully to the relationships we create with our students as we each engage the painful process of recognizing habits is a process of encountering suffering and developing compassion we may not have known we had.

The emotional fallout of hegemony for those who do social justice education is that we encounter individuals who are so deeply invested in the dominant cultural values that these values have defined their sense of identity, and to question these values feels emotionally like an annihilation of self. Thus one faces loud and vocal resistance to rethinking the world as it is hegemonically constructed: 'But the American Dream does come true for some people, so it isn't a myth!' 'If those children just worked harder, or if their parents made an effort to help them more with their homework, they could get to college!' And sometimes the resistance is more than ideological: students denounce our courses, write bad evaluations, refuse to engage written work as assigned, become generally unhappy and angry in our presence – thus posing genuine challenges about how a pedagogy of discomfort requires compassion in order to recognize the suffering of some students and often of the educator, as I shall describe in what follows.

Impasse: Resistance and suffering

One of the results of this pedagogy is that I frequently have the opportunity to witness students' intense emotional reactions and resistances to rethinking cherished assumptions and worldviews. Lately, I have also been forced to re-evaluate the costs and benefits of my own emotional investments in students' willingness to change. I am learning to accept that *people will not go where they don't want to go*. For understandable reasons, students may not welcome the invitation to rethink their worldviews in ways that disrupt and shatter their comfortable status quo. Inevitably, each semester, I find myself encountering my own emotional investments and reactions to students who dig in their heels and blatantly refuse to engage in critical thinking. For example, my own serenity was 'shattered' by one particular student who, as a result of his vociferous resistance and the large amount of space he inhabited in our classroom expressing his anger, was, as they say, living rent-free in my head far too much of the time.

My irritation and obsession began during the fifth week of that semester when, at the end of a class in which we were discussing white privilege, the said student ended the class nearly shouting, and visibly shaking, proclaiming: 'My name is Sam [pseudonym]! I am a human being! I am an American! None of this history, race, or anything else has anything to do with my identity. The fact is the world is divided – someone has to clean the toilets!' I took a deep breath and asked, as calmly as possible, why it was that brown and black people are primarily the ones cleaning toilets? His face reddened and his body tensed with great physical agitation and anger, while the other 15 students squirmed uncomfortably in their seats in part because of their own discomfort with his emotion. He retorted in a loud and harsh tone, in clear defiance of the previous five weeks of reading and discussion, 'They *choose* to clean toilets! That is their *choice*!' These words shocked me. Somehow, despite the fact that I know that individualism and choice are perhaps the hardest discourses to critically challenge, to hear this explicit rationalization of social injustice took me aback. We had spent five weeks dissecting the myths of the American Dream, and most had been willing to engage and accept some of that critical thinking. The clock signaled the end of class, and I was left with a shattered sense of my own investment and vision of 'transformational educational process.'

Following this highly emotional and in many ways vulnerable and courageous expression of his visceral feeling that he does not possess white privilege – a sentiment no doubt shared albeit not voiced by some of his colleagues – I struggled with whether or not I should say something to him. What was the ethical response as an educator? Should I say, 'Thank you for being so bold and courageous, I appreciate your courage in expressing these views?' My worry was that if I said anything, I would be simply affirming and condoning his right to refuse to rethink his position of privilege. I did not want to say something that would give him the impression that his refusal to be open-minded is an acceptable educational stance. Nonetheless, from a 'caring' place, I was aware that he had made himself vulnerable, and that his expression reflected feelings and thoughts that others in the class likely shared.

After much internal deliberation, my lingering discomfort regarding the fact of his emotional outburst and, secondly, my concern to reiterate how white privilege is embedded in our society, pushed me to change the agenda slightly the next week. I began the subsequent class by acknowledging the courage it had taken to share such strong feelings. I reiterated that, while members of the class held very different opinions, I hoped that we (educator and student) could each listen with an open mind and that we would each make an effort to re-evaluate our views.

However, despite my best intentions, I actually believe that my having publicly acknowledged him in this way simply fuelled his fire. To address his insistence that we should all just be 'Americans,' I screened a 15-minute excerpt of a video called *The Colour of Fear*, which documents a group of nine men of Anglo, Asian, Black and Hispanic descent who, during a professionally facilitated weekend retreat, come together to challenge racist oppression and issues of internalized racism. The film portrays an unusually intimate and politically charged scenario, in which the viewer has the opportunity to witness emotionally harrowing and poignant conversations. The video has some very heated moments; in particular, one in which the most articulate man in the film, Victor, who is African American, confronts David, the quintessential "upper-middle class, white, heterosexual liberal." The heated exchange reveals David's privileged denial of racism. In effect, David's position as a privileged white male can be characterized as follows: 'I am not racist. I employ Mexicans; I am very friendly to them. I don't know why you coloured people are so angry. You should not be angry. The white man does not want to stand in your way. If you are having trouble making progress in the world, you are standing in your own way.' This video clip that I selected for class directly illustrates why it is difficult for persons from non-European or non-Anglo heritage to claim the identity 'American' in any simple way. The men of color in the video explain to the 'resistant' white man that because the dominant cultural norm of identity in 'American' culture is presumed to be a white Anglo-Saxon middle class male, and because being an 'American' in a melting pot requires assimilation, to identify oneself simply as 'American' is in many ways to 'pretend to be white.' In the video, the men of color express the profound frustration and anger they feel living in a racist society and the anger and frustration they experience precisely because white persons in this society can afford to be ignorant about the cost of assimilation for people of color.

During the discussion following this video excerpt, Sam proceeded to railroad the conversation with assertions that entirely missed the point voiced by the men of color in the video. When he began angrily demanding 'evidence' that he has 'white privilege,' I responded by shifting the class discussion to examine statistics I had prepared for our discussion about gender issues and education. The statistics detail degrees conferred nationwide and illustrate the radical gender disparities between fields such as engineering, which is predominantly male, and those such as education, nursing, and social work, in which women are overrepresented. My hope was that he would be able to translate this evidence of 'systemic inequality' of male privilege to understand white privilege as an interlocking system. It did not seem to work. Apparently, no amount of statistical evidence or rational persuasion is effective in the face of this particular kind of defense and angry investment and the fear of allowing one's worldview to be shifted.

I regret to report that my suffering regarding this student's anger continued throughout the term to take up far too much space in my own emotional world. I found myself describing the experience to friends and colleagues, clearly encountering my own experience of discomfort. The day after the class I have just described, I attended a remarkable lecture by a leading African-American female scholar. My students are required to attend cultural events during Black History month and Women's History month. The auditorium was packed full of students as well as community members, an unusual occurrence at this campus. During the first 45 minutes of the lecture, I found myself distracted, picturing whether or not my belligerent student might be convinced by this charismatic speaker. As she echoed what I had been teaching in my class – namely, that racism is alive and well and secondly that we all need to take responsibility for the contemporary privileges and costs of racism – I found myself obsessively wishing that the student could be hearing these words from someone other than myself, who might possibly push him to change his intransigent position. Ironically, 45 minutes after her talk had begun, I happened to see him walking into the auditorium. My heart leapt: I was at first thrilled to see him arrive. But then, I spent the last 15 minutes of her talk furious that he had disrespectfully missed the majority of her lecture and therefore missed the opportunity to be transformed. My obsession continued: I found myself thinking, when he turns in his two-page synopsis of the cultural events to receive his five points, why should I give him five points when he did not hear the whole talk? (And indeed, lo and behold, he turned in a most bizarre response in which he said, 'I have heard her speak before so I won't summarise. Let me just say how irritated I was during the talk that 50 students were going in and out of her lecture being disrespectful and distracting and not attending the whole event even though they will write up a report for credit.'!)

Suffice to say, my form of caring about his emotional and educational growth was not particularly effective. I began to think that it was not effective because I was the one who was suffering. And the suffering, while valuable for my growth, was showing me my own sites of attachment to another's change, which in fact is quite beyond my control. It is only months after this experience, as I reflect back on what occurred next between Sam and myself, that I also see that there is a need for compassion, a part of the pedagogy of discomfort. A particular compassion might be required for those who feel their 'self' is being annihilated and who are angrily protesting, not necessarily because they cannot see how power operates but because they need something to replace what I am threatening to take away from them.

An unexpected shifting

Toward the end of the semester, I happened to present an early version of this paper at the American Educational Research Association's Annual Meeting. During the discussion following our session, someone asked if I thought Sam would change. I answered unequivocally, 'I have no hopes that we will ever reconcile our differences nor that he will ever love me!'

One can imagine my surprise when, two days after having returned to campus, after our class he asked to meet me during office hours. I found myself quite fearful and left my office door open when he entered – even asking a colleague to keep an eye out, as I feared a belligerent exchange. Sam perched on a chair, clearly nervous and fearful. I began to invoke my compassion: I smiled and consciously breathed in and out, recognizing his discomfort and mindfully making myself present. He then blurted out an apology for his behavior throughout this semester. He had come to realize, he confided, that he was acting out his frustration with 'this system of oppression' on me, but that he realized his anger need not be directed at me. I took this information still smiling, trying to breathe deeply in the face of both of our discomforts.

Rather struck by what seemed a significant change of heart on his part, I asked him if there was anything about the class or my conduct that I might change to make students like him feel more engaged and less resistant to my curriculum. He told me that the material 'felt cold.' He said that he had also been upset because I did not seem to state in class that all these screwed up things in the world could possibly change. He said he wished I had told the class that 'just by virtue of you sitting in this class, things can get better.' I responded by thanking him for the feedback. I replied that perhaps I had not said that, because I do not necessarily believe that things will get better simply by people sitting in my classroom. I did reply that I would try to be more encouraging of the fact that I do believe people can choose to advocate for social change and can thereby make a difference.

Finally, he told me that the other action that had significantly changed his feelings was that when he came into my office, I had smiled at him. 'You don't smile a lot in class,' he reported.

In the ensuing months, I feel I have learnt quite a lot from Sam's two comments, the significance of which has taken time to settle into my consciousness. His first comment was that he wished I had told him that there was 'hope' – even though the world is so screwed up.

For those who do not feel threatened by the course content, reading about social inequality itself can offer a kind of hope or validation: their perceptions are perhaps being validated in many cases for the first time. But for people like Sam, who had held so desperately to an identity carved through illusions of 'we are the same' meritocracy, course content may well need to include clear delineation of what will replace the sense of a self lost. I detail some ideas on this replacement in the discussion of critical hope below.

Sam's second comment, that the simple act of my smiling when he came into my office enabled him to re-evaluate the appropriate object for his anger, makes me think about how compassion facilitates change. As discussed in this chapter, for those who feel significantly threatened by course content, something needs to be offered to replace what feels like loss or annihilation. Smiling is in part a way of recognizing the other as s/he is, of communicating a compassionate acceptance. I do not think this act need mean 'you can go ahead and refuse to rethink the world and maintain your privilege.' Rather, it means that compassion is especially crucial for those who feel they are out on a limb.

It is worth noting, considering issues of gendered emotional labor, that for a man to ask a woman to smile more is also a complicated request. In my office, I recall smiling at him quite intentionally, practising what Buddhists call *tonglen* and *maitri*, or loving kindness. I have, during the ensuing months following his comment, made an effort to smile more during engagements with students. I confess, I feel torn about the implied admonition to 'smile more,' because I have no doubt that part of the demand for this smile is a demand for a form of gendered labor. I am positioned by this young man as distinctly female, and his request for my smile is in part a request for a nurturing partner or mother. Is it the educator's duty to smile as part of the emotional work of seducing students into social change? Political analyses can indeed come into conflict with simple calls for compassion.

To return, however, to Sam's request that I tell him there is 'hope' when I am simultaneously asking him to recognize the rather overwhelming inequities of our society: rather uncannily, his comment about hope reflects something I had previously written about – critical hope versus naïve hope. It is only in the process of writing this chapter that I saw the connection between Sam's request for hope and my own previous intellectual analyses of critical hope.

Beyond discomfort: Critical hope

As one recognizes inscribed habits of emotional inattention and disrupts these tenacious habits, one may cry out for something new to hold on to. Between utter despair, which may come about with the dismantling of worldviews, and the denial that typifies hegemonic mystification is a middle ground. While 'shattering' may occur with a pedagogy of discomfort, one lifeline is to build 'critical hope.' Here I will describe first a framing of critical hope, drawing on concepts from Maxine Greene and Paulo Freire. I will then briefly suggest some specific curricular directions that might offer critical hope to someone like Sam.

What does Sam want when he asks me to tell him that "even though the world is screwed up, your being here in this classroom, Sam, will make a difference?" What I do not want to offer to this request is naïve hope, which stands in stark contrast to how I shall define critical hope. Naïve hope may be defined as those platitudes that directly serve the hegemonic interest of maintaining the *status quo*, particularly by espousing humanist rhetoric. These platitudes include the rhetoric of individualism; beliefs in equal opportunity; the puritanical faith that hard work inevitably leads to success; and that everyone is the same underneath their skin.

In contrast to naïve hope, critical hope recognizes that we live within systems of inequality, in which privilege, such as white and male privilege, comes at the expense of the freedom of others. A willingness to engage in in-depth critical inquiry regarding systems of domination needs to be accompanied by parallel emotional willingness to engage in the difficult work of possibly allowing one's worldviews to be shattered.

Critical hope entails a responsibility – a willingness to be fully alive in the process of constant change and becoming. Maxine Greene emphasizes this throughout her writings. "When habit swathes everything," she writes, "one day follows another identical day and predictability swallows any hint of an opening possibility" (Greene 1995: 23). In an astute description of the interrelationship between habit, sense of self, and what we do and do not wish to see or feel, John Dewey writes:

> Habit reaches […] down into the very structure of the self; it signifies a building up and solidifying of certain desires; an increased sensitiveness and responsiveness […] or an impaired capacity to attend to and think about certain things. Habit covers […] the very makeup of desire, intent, choice, disposition which gives an act its voluntary quality.
> (Garrison 1997: 139)

Critical hope directly challenges inscribed habits of emotional inattention and signifies a willingness to exist within ambiguity and uncertainty. One knows, for example, that there is no assurance of justice, but one is yet willing to fight for justice. As Greene notes, "There are always vacancies: there are always roads not taken, vistas not acknowledged. The search must be ongoing; the end can never be quite known" (1988: 15). Similarly, Freire writes, "What makes me hopeful is not so much the certainty of the *find*, but my movement in search" (1973: 106).

Freire's emphasis on process resonates with the Buddhist emphasis of the difficult process of change. One can see the distinct resonance between the two in the previously quoted excerpt from Epstein:

> Change will happen naturally as we open to the truth. The more we bring out attachments into awareness, the freer we become, not because we eliminate the attachments, but because we learn to identify more with awareness than with desire. Using our capacity for consciousness, we can change perspective on ourselves, giving a sense of space where once there was only habit.
> (Epstein 2001: 71)

The cliché that 'change is hard' is explained when one acknowledges that critical hope can only emerge from what Paulo Freire calls our 'incompleteness.' Rather than being absorbed by the myth that our world is static, unchanging, and complete, we recognize that we ourselves and our world are in a constant state of dynamic change. In recognizing the dynamic present, we also recognize that our relations to others and the form of reality itself can be other than they are. What Freire describes in terms of love and humility as central to dialogue, I have emphasized here as compassion. Sam asked me to tell him he can make a difference. My response is to outline critical hope: there is hope if we are willing to step beyond our known selves. The educator has a compassionate responsibility to show students others who have walked down this path.

Making up for the loss

If I am asking students in some sense to annihilate the self as they have known it, I must be able to meet their discomfort with compassion – and with resources to help them replace the lost sense of self. Most importantly, Sam's request for hope makes me think that critical hope requires a clear explication of what is lost and what might be gained through this suffering of loss. If a pedagogy of discomfort takes away someone's worldview, in compassion it needs to replace the vacuum with something else.

Productive 'replacements' for the loss might be found in the following focus of course content. First, one might engage discussions of how the construct of masculinity or white privilege, for example, also bears a cost to those who benefit (Sut Jhally's video *Tough Guise* addresses Jackson Katz's analyses of how violent representations of masculinity are damaging to men, for example). A second approach is to make use of the first-person accounts, such as Minnie Bruce Pratt's essay 'Identity: Blood Skin Heart' in which she describes her shift from not recognizing her complicity in white supremacy to becoming an antiracist activist. A third approach is historical, emphasizing social movement history in more detail, including histories of white Northerners who came to the South during the 1950s to help do such work as enlist black people to vote.

Critical hope requires seeing one's self within historical context, re-evaluating the relationship of one's privilege to others in the world. It entails as well seeing how these relations of power shift and change over time and in one's lifetime. This pedagogical relation is a negotiation of hegemonically constructed habits, internalized as attachments to particular beliefs and corresponding emotional reactions to change. But I wish to stress that this inquiry is a collective, not an individualized, process. Searching for freedom, as Greene notes:

> [N]ever occurs in a vacuum. Freedom cannot be conceived apart from a matrix of social, economic, cultural, and psychological conditions. It is within the matrix that selves take shape or are created through choice of action in the changing situations of life. The degree and quality of whatever freedom is achieved are functions of the perspectives available, and the reflectiveness on the choices made.
> (Greene 1988: 30)

This process of searching for freedom takes place as a collective process. Second, this process depends on learning to notice how our selves and perspectives are shifting and contingent. This collective process depends most centrally on the interpersonal relationships between educator and student and between students, interpersonal relationships shaped in a political context – in a sense, on teaching as a form of loving kindness. To unravel the complex emotional fabric of relationships, often fraught with heated differences of perspective, entails, as I have described, a particular compassion or loving kindness for the suffering that may be involved in this rethinking of oneself and the world.

In *Pedagogy of the Oppressed* (1973), Freire writes that dialogue requires love, faith, and humility. Humility is in part the ability to listen to others as we forge connections and the courage to recognize that our perspectives and visions are partial and striving and must remain open to change.

Conclusion

In this chapter, I have explored how a pedagogy of discomfort reveals one's inscribed habits of emotional inattention, a process that may cause disturbance for educator and student alike. By introducing critical hope, I have tried to outline how educators can take seriously the ethical implications of shattering someone's familiar and comfortable worldview. What can we offer to replace the sense of self and values that may be threatened and displaced through a pedagogy of discomfort?

I have suggested critical hope as an approach that takes the cry for help seriously and that recognizes with compassion the need for something to hold on to as the world is made to seem ambiguous and chaotic when learning to see differently. By recognizing the other's suffering with compassion, one is pushed to smile, even in the midst of conflict. One is pushed to offer blueprints for roads that lead to hope, 'even though the world is screwed up.'

Struggling for social justice is rarely easy work. Unlearning one's habits of being and thinking, and one's inscribed habits of inattention, can be painful labor as well. In the midst of this discomfort, compassion suggests an attitude of loving kindness. Compassion means developing a patience for my own shortcomings. It means developing patience and respect in the face of the other's suffering, no matter how painful it may feel to be the object of another's anger.

Rumi's words offer a description of the space of dynamic interaction that exceeds our words and thoughts in educational encounters: "Out beyond ideas of wrongdoing and great doing, there is a field. I'll meet you there. When the soul lies down in the grass, the world is too full to talk about." To meet the other in this field beyond ideas of right and wrong asks us to open ways of understanding that do not rely only on words. Compassion is one bridge between those suffering a pedagogy of discomfort and those who have invited new ways of being fully alive into a world replete with imperfections.

Note

1   This chapter has previously been published as Boler, M. (2003) 'Teaching for hope: The ethics of shattering world views'. In: D. Liston and J. Garrison (eds) *Teaching, Loving, Learning: Reclaiming Passion in Educational Practice*. New York: Routledge. (pp. 117–31). We have obtained permission from the editors to publish a slightly edited version of this chapter.

References

Boler, M. (1999) *Feeling Power: Emotions and Education*. New York: Routledge.
Bruce Pratt, M. (1984) 'Identity: Skin Blood Heart'. In: E. Bulkin, M. Bruce Pratt and B. Smith (eds) *Yours in Struggle*. New York: Longhaul Press. (pp. 11–63).
Epstein, M. (2001) *Going On Being: Buddhism and the Way of Change*. New York: Broadway Books.
Freire, P. (1973) *Pedagogy of the Oppressed*. New York: The Seabury Press.
Garrison, J. (1997) *Dewey and Eros: Wisdom and Desire in the Art of Teaching*. New York: Teachers College Press.
Greene, M. (1988) *The Dialectic of Freedom*. New York: Teachers College Press.
Greene, M. (1995) *Releasing the Imagination: Essays on Education, the Arts, and Social Change*. San Francisco, CA: Jossey Bass.
Loewen, J. (1995) *Lies My Teacher Told Me: Everything Your American History Textbook Got Wrong*. New York: New Press.
Macedo, D.P. (2000) 'Introduction'. In: N. Chomsky, *Chomsky on Miseducation*. Lanham, MD: Rowman & Littlefield. (pp. 1–36).
McLaren, P. (1989) *Life in Schools: An Introduction to Critical Pedagogy in the Foundations of Education*. New York: Longman.

3 A pedagogy of critical hope in South African higher education

Vivienne Bozalek, Ronelle Carolissen and Brenda Leibowitz

Introduction

Critical hope may be viewed as an appropriate antidote and action-oriented response to conditions of inequality. In this chapter, we build on the previous two contributions in which Zembylas and Boler outline their notions of critical and naïve hope. Here we explore possible avenues through which critical hope may be achieved in educational practice.

In the first two chapters of this book, Zembylas and Boler portray critical hope as an acknowledgement of the unjust and unequal societies in which we live, where privilege comes at the expense of other's abilities. They show how critical hope requires an analysis of the implications of how historical and material conditions have led us to our present positions. As Boler in Chapter 2 points out, 'critical hope directly challenges inscribed habits of emotional attention and signifies a willingness to exist within ambiguity and uncertainty' – this willingness includes changing our relationships with others with compassionate responsibility. Naïve hope, on the other hand, is what Boler regards as 'platitudes that directly serve the hegemonic interest of maintaining the status quo including the rhetoric of individualism; beliefs in equal opportunity; the puritanical faith that hard work inevitably leads to success; and that everyone is the same underneath the skin'. Zembylas notes that it is important to distinguish naïve hope – which is blindly optimistic – from critical hope – which calls on us to be reflexive and so leads to transformative action. Thus, we argue that in order to achieve critical hope rather than naïve hope, ongoing dialogue and reflexivity are a necessary part of educational practice to address what Boler refers to as 'inscribed habits of emotional inattention', by which she means embedded, cultural habits of seeing. It is also important to realize that dialogue and reflexivity may also unleash despair, however well intentioned the educators might be. In this chapter, we examine the potential of dialogue and reflexivity through an example of a teaching and learning project. Through this initiative we aimed to foster critical hope in students in higher education in a continuingly divided socio-political and material South African context. We begin by describing aspects of South African higher education before briefly describing the setting in which this study took place.

Apartheid-designed segregated higher education institutions continue to have a major influence on students and higher educators in South Africa. In spite of formal desegregation, an informal spatial segregation both between and within institutions, remains in South African higher education (Durrheim 2005; Erasmus 2006; Walker 2005). Furthermore, despite 19 years of democracy since the formal demise of apartheid in 1994, enormous disparities still persist within the South African education system, which includes the higher education sector (Bozalek and Boughey 2012). Historically white or advantaged institutions (HWIs or HAIs) continue to be the locations of choice for privileged middle class students who have had access to high schools that are likely to prepare them adequately for higher education. These social and economic disparities, as well as the social separation between differently placed institutions, are exacerbated by the paucity of examples of good curriculum and teaching practice at higher education level (McKinney 2004, 2007; Leibowitz 2012). Higher educators themselves are burdened by their own histories and prior experiences which influence their ability and preparedness to mediate dialogue on difference (Jansen 2009). Thus, the degree to which higher education institutions, their social make-up, ethos as well as curricula can contribute to social transformation of the sector and, more broadly, to society has been disappointing, as noted in the Ministerial Committee on Transformation and Social Cohesion (2008). This disappointment is rendered poignant by the expectations of what higher education should be able to contribute towards the transformation of South African society via its graduates and academics. This vision as expressed in the Education White Paper of 1997 for example, proposes that higher education should contribute to the 'socialisation of enlightened, responsible and constructively critical citizens' (p. 7).

It is within this context that we initiated a project that attempted to engage students at two higher education institutions (HEIs) in the Western Cape, South Africa. These two institutions reflect key aspects of the divisions and inequalities typifying higher education in South Africa. Stellenbosch University (SU) is a historically advantaged or historically white institution, one of the top 'research-led' institutions in the country, with a majority of white and middle class students and academic staff. It also has a history of support for apartheid in previous decades and is struggling hard at present to transform itself socially, culturally and in terms of its curriculum (see van Rinsum's chapter in this volume for a more elaborate discussion of the history of Stellenbosch University and its current emphasis on hope). The University of the Western Cape (UWC) is a historically disadvantaged or black institution, with a majority of black and working-class students. It has a history of anti-apartheid activism and in the present era is regarded as an 'engaged institution,' which still attracts poor students, and is simultaneously building its research profile. Both of these institutions, as different as they may be, are grappling with how to develop new and contextually relevant identities for themselves. Both refer to the notion of 'hope' in their institutional mission or vision statements, promotional literature and in senior executive talk and both stress the importance of social relevance and community engagement (Hope as Guiding Concept for Stellenbosch University

2011; HOPE Project: n.d.; University of the Western Cape website). We believe, however, that hope may remain at a rhetorical level unless specific institutional practices are altered, particularly those which pertain to teaching and learning and research. In order to develop a different model of teaching and learning, we conceptualized a project across these two institutions, which required students and academics to engage with difference across numerous boundaries.

The pedagogy of discomfort

The initiative on which this study is based drew on the notion of a 'pedagogy of discomfort' developed by Boler and Zembylas (2003) as a useful framework for understanding, teaching and learning about difference. This pedagogy invites students to critique their deeply held assumptions, and to destabilize their views of themselves and their worlds. The process is both painful, but contains the promise of hope for the future (Halabi 2004) by virtue of the opportunity to reconstruct previously held views and, by doing so, to move to new insights and dispositions. The 'discomfort' within this pedagogy impacts upon all members of a group, whether these are members of dominant or marginalized groups. Boler and Zembylas (2003: 115) note that 'no one escapes hegemony'. From this perspective, those positioned as dominant may be more uncomfortable discussing discrimination or oppression than marginalized groups. However, there are moments in which this is uncomfortable for individuals from any identity position, as all are impacted by dominant discourses.

Emotions are central to the pedagogy of discomfort and are conceptualized not as individualized or psychologized, but as relational and political (Zembylas 2007, 2008, 2010). Zembylas (2008: 3) writes that: 'the politics of affects and emotions matters in many aspects of social life, including education […] affects and emotions show us how power relations shape inclusion and exclusion boundaries between bodies – who should be on the *inside* and who should be *outside*.' Thus, questions of identity and agency are influenced by broader economic, cultural and socio-political forces that shape our society. For this reason, our view of a 'pedagogy of discomfort' is influenced by Fraser's (2008, 2009) trivalent view of social justice, which foregrounds three different dimensions: the economic, cultural and political. All of these dimensions would require social arrangements to be in place for participatory parity or interaction as social equals to occur. This would require simultaneous attention to a recognition of the attributes of all students, an equitable distribution of resources and equal political representation. This theoretical stance is valuable in that it provides educators and students with conceptual tools to reflect meaningfully on the educational process with specific reference to difference and social justice. This view calls on educators to strive towards participatory parity in the classroom by being mindful of the way in which a learning opportunity is structured and the way resources are allocated in a course. It serves a cautionary function, in reminding educators that there are larger material and structural forces in society, which influence the final outcome of what students may take away from a learning opportunity.

The community, self and identity project

The course began with educators from both institutions feeling frustrated with conditions in both institutions. We hoped to explore ways to connect with others who wanted to achieve change with regard to teaching and learning and to work collaboratively across institutions, disciplines and social identities. The research team comprised six educators from the disciplines of social work, occupational therapy, psychology and teaching and learning in higher education (for more information about the team and its aspirations, see Leibowitz et al. 2012). We shared concerns regarding the cultural encapsulation perpetuated by the separation across historically advantaged and disadvantaged institutions. We set out to develop strategies in the curriculum that would allow students and higher educators to re-evaluate their own positions in relation to implicit and explicit disciplinary knowledge, institutional and social identities. We ourselves needed to develop our own skills and dispositions in order to exercise the kind of pedagogic expertise and leadership required to develop meaningful dialogue across difference – what Burbules (2006) refers to as a 'third space dialogue' – and to forge a curriculum that crosses boundaries of social identities, discipline and institution. In doing this, we were creating different learning spaces in which we as educators and the students may have the opportunities to engage in dialogue and reflexivity as a catalyst for critical hope.

The Community, Self and Identity (CSI) course was conceptualized as one in which students and higher educators from historically differently placed institutions and disciplines would work together to critically interrogate concepts that could be regarded as core to human service professionals. Key to the course objectives was for students to learn together across the boundaries of race and social class, institution and discipline. We believed that this was essential in order to foster critical hope. Learning in isolated bubbles would not grant students the opportunity to test their own epistemological and ontological assumptions in relation to those with differing life experiences and disciplinary backgrounds. Herein lay the challenge: to work with appropriate levels of comfort/discomfort, depth and intensity. To engage with difference in a superficial or simplistic manner could encourage at best, false optimism, and at worst, despair. Jones, for instance, writes from the Australian perspective: 'It is undeniably the case that fantasies and acts of shared communication are preferable to fantasies and acts of ignorance and separation. However, desires for shared communication must be mediated more by cautious critique and limited expectations than by urgent and ultimately self-defeating optimism' (Jones 2005: 66–7).

Also from the Australian context, Sonn (2008: 164) writes about the challenges of engaging students on issues of difference: "This process is not necessarily smooth and unproblematic, and while students do become aware of whiteness and the heterogeneity of whiteness, they also struggle to know its workings and often re-engage in oppressive relations." Other dangers inherent in diversity work with students are that it can lead to resistance and defensiveness, as has been pointed out in the South African context (McKinney 2004, 2007).

Diversity work can also further silence the marginalized, as highlighted in the context of the USA (Blackwell 2010). Burbules (2006) warns against unmediated spaces for dialogue that unwittingly disadvantage some and advantage others, and place heavy burdens on participants to manage the reciprocal interaction. Leonardo and Porter (2010) challenge the idea of a 'safe space' in public dialogue about race, pointing out how black students' views are silenced in dialogues on diversity, as they are fearful of genuinely expressing what they feel – therefore a safe space cannot be assumed. We thus need to see the classroom as a place of potential discomfort rather than necessarily a safe space.

In order to develop the possibility for a structured interchange to encourage students to engage in a pedagogy of discomfort, we needed to find techniques which would require emotional as well as cognitive labor to negotiate issues of difference. We thus looked for methods which could cumulatively create what Burbules refers to as 'third space dialogues'. These dialogues are those: "[w]hich are problematic and problematizing moments, risky and as prone to chaos or even heightened conflict, as to producing new understandings [...] where contending parties meet – and sometimes are also linked to specific practices, even rituals, that establish an unusual place and time" (Burbules 2006: 114).

We anticipated that our chosen methods would lead to this kind of space and to new understandings as well as emotional engagement. Furthermore, the methods used in the project were intended to enable students to share their lived political, social and economic experiences and to challenge taken-for-granted-knowledge in relation to the concepts of community, self and identity. Such methods included participatory learning and action (PLA) and narrative techniques, blended learning and the use of guest speakers and literature which presented notions of identity as complex, fluid and non-essentialized (for more details regarding these methods see the article on the pedagogy of hope by Carolissen *et al.* 2010 and Bozalek and Biersteker 2011).

A range of participatory techniques, blended learning, critical reading, theatre, art, film, workshops and presentations were used to support students to explore their own, and their colleagues' personal, social and professional identities. Although the course was evaluated, reflected on and adapted after each year, the following basic structure was followed every year: there were three face-to-face workshops, interspersed with a number of online or virtual interactive exercises over a period of seven weeks.

Each course started with the first face-to-face workshop at UWC. Approximately 95 students from SU and UWC took part on an annual basis, incorporating the disciplines of Social Work, Psychology and Occupational Therapy. At the initial workshop, students were allocated to groups comprising six students from the different institutions and disciplines. A facilitator from one of these disciplines or a course designer was assigned to work with a particular small group for the duration of the course. The course began with an introduction to PLA techniques. PLA techniques are group-based, open-ended, flexible visual methods that are used in the learning process (Bozalek and Biersteker 2010; Chambers 2007). The specific PLA techniques that we utilized were community mapping and rivers of life.

Table 3.1. Demographic distribution of students who completed the course between 2006 and 2008

	Year	2006	2007	2008	Total	%
Discipline	Psychology	41	14	13	68	24.1
	Social work	50	44	54	148	52.5
	Occupational therapy	N/A	44	22	66	23.4
Gender	Female	78	93	77	248	87.9
	Male	13	9	12	34	12.1
Race[1]	African	19	30	36	85	30.1
	Coloured	43	58	35	136	48.2
	White	29	14	6	49	17.4
	Indian	–	–	2	2	0.7
	Not specified	–	–	10	10	3.6
Language	African	17	30	30	77	27.3
	Afrikaans	46	22	16	84	29.8
	English	28	50	41	119	42.2
	Other	0	0	3	3	1.1
Total		91	102	89	282	–

For the community mapping exercise, students were asked to draw a picture/map of their homes and neighborhoods including the resources that they identified as being available. They were then asked to identify and label three things that they wished to change (which were identified as being physical or related to attitudes and/or social issues). Finally, they were asked to prioritize these issues and rank them from most to least important. After the drawing and ranking exercise they were requested to explain their pictures and the identified changes they wished to make in their environments with other members of their small groups. Figures 3.1 and Figures 3.2 provide two examples of community maps.

The second PLA technique employed was the river of life (Figures 3.3–5). In this exercise students drew the rivers of their lives that had brought them to their current choice of profession/discipline. They examined different periods in their lives, by going back to the source of the river (their early years). Students could use structural aspects of rivers such as ebbs and flows to symbolize quiet, peaceful times (smooth flow) or wild, difficult times (waterfalls, rough water). They introduced detail such as tributaries and different colours to illustrate important events and moods, which impacted on their lives.

We chose to use these PLA techniques for a number of reasons. Firstly, they provided an excellent visual medium for differently positioned students across institutions to introduce themselves to each other. The techniques mediated an in-depth and meaningful interaction around student experiences of community, self and identity. The drawings – and discussion which ensued – ensured a powerful means of eliciting self depictions and perceptions of privilege and disadvantage. The third reason for using these techniques was that students across the institutions and disciplines were differently placed in relation to academic

46 *Vivienne Bozalek et al.*

Figure 3.1 Example of community maps drawn by students.

Figure 3.2 Example of community maps drawn by students.

discourses, and the visual medium provided a way of leveling the playing fields and valuing subjugated knowledge. In this way, we designed the curriculum so that students who had had less access to traditional academic resources would be able to contribute confidently to the debates (Bozalek and Biersteker 2010). Finally, these techniques provide channels for engaging emotionally with issues of difference, whilst simultaneously enabling participants to distance themselves from their experiences depicted in the drawings.

The drawings were photographed and uploaded onto an e-learning platform. In the virtual space, students could see only the work of those students in their own groups. This facility provided an opportunity for further virtual interaction within small groups around issues of community, self and identity. At this stage, critical literature was introduced to facilitate further interrogation of their initial communication around these concepts.

After engaging with each other and the literature in a series of online activities, students met for a second face-to-face workshop at UWC. During this second workshop, various guest speakers were asked to reflect on their experiences of community, self and identity. Guest speakers included Berni Searle, an acclaimed South African artist, who through her video installations explores issues of racialized, gendered and classed identities. The Remix theatre group of differently able-bodied dancers was another example of performance related to difference to which the students were exposed. Students also were given the opportunity to work in their small groups to prepare presentations of their own understandings

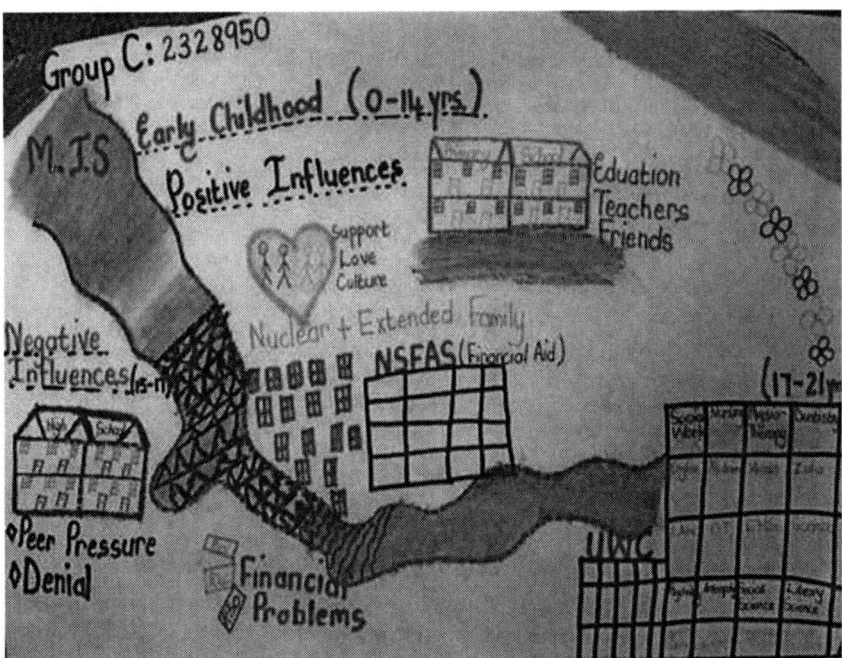

Figure 3.3 Example of rivers of life drawn by students.

48 *Vivienne Bozalek et al.*

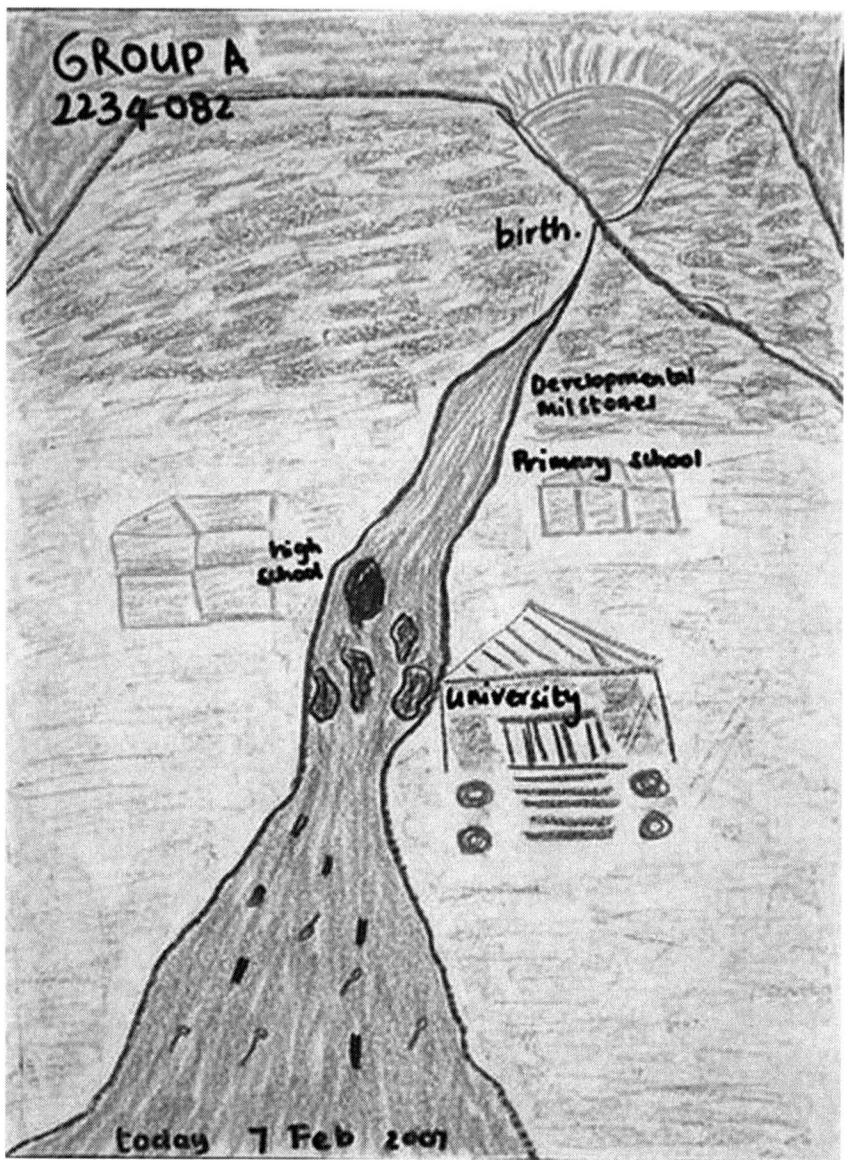

Figure 3.4 Example of rivers of life drawn by students.

of community, self and identity for the third face-to-face workshop held at SU. At this workshop, students presented their work in their small groups to an audience of their peers, facilitators and invited guests. This was the final encounter which the students had with each other. At this workshop the course was evaluated by the students. The final online assignment that was required was an

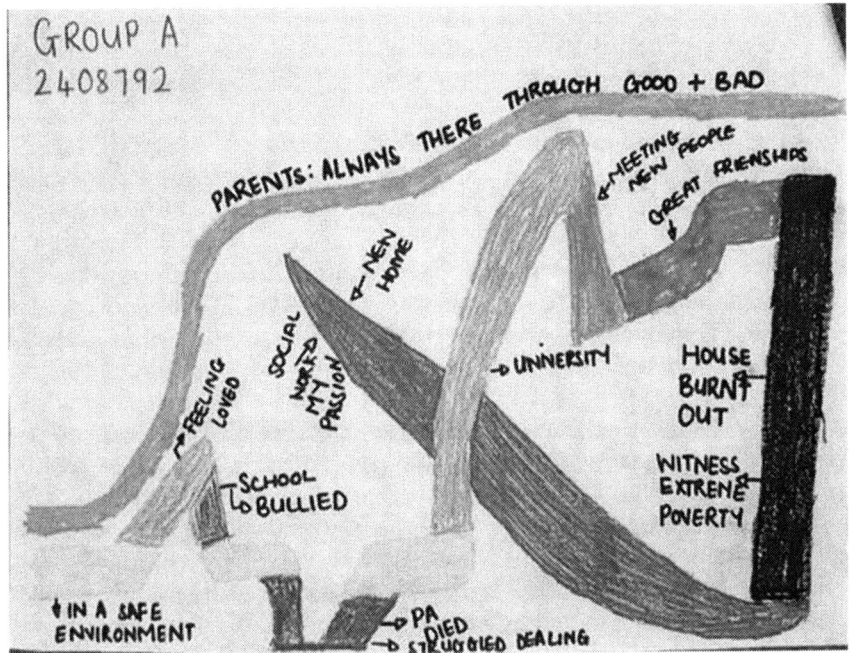

Figure 3.5 Example of rivers of life drawn by students.

integrative essay reflecting on how the readings influenced their learning experiences in the course. They specifically had to think about how the readings, in conjunction with their experiences, impacted on their understanding of notions of 'community,' 'self' and 'identity.' Finally, they wrote a reflective essay in which they considered whether their learning in this course differed from previous learning about notions of community, self and identity.

Student responses

Although 97 percent of the students each year reported that they appreciated the course, an analysis of the reflective essays written by students in the 2006 course revealed that the teaching methodology we employed was successful in providing an opportunity for all students to engage with issues of difference.

An analysis of student reflective essays revealed that engaging in a pedagogy of discomfort requires a cognitive as well as an affective dimension. The cognitive dimension involved working with the prescribed texts and with concepts about society and the past, which are salient in the South African post-apartheid public discourse:

> The term 'community' to me meant a common group of people who were of one race and culture. I always tried to avoid the political aspect of how

> communities were formed as it tends to 'bring back memories' of the past and how it affected people of colour.
>
> (Samantha,[2] UWC)

The affective dimension involves moments of gratification and resolution as well as moments of despair, fear and anger. The affective dimension was noted in student accounts; for example, Terry, a white SU student, says the following:

> I feel like I have been deeply challenged to become more proficient in other languages besides English. I can see that if I wish to practice in diverse communities then I will need to learn another language, despite my fear of this.

Although all students learnt something, for many, the learning remained at a superficial level while, for others, the learning was deep and engaged (Leibowitz et al. 2010). How much students learnt depended partly on their prior learning and experience. We found via a longitudinal study conducted for the project that for some of the students who participated in the course, it had a deep and lasting impression and informed their reflective engagement with their professional work after they had graduated (Carolissen 2012).

There were many instances of students seeming to develop a sense of reflexivity and agency through the course, as one of the students wrote in her reflective essay towards the end of the course. Berenice, a colored student from UWC, said:

> What I found so fascinating about it was that we had to sketch figures which affected our 'smooth life flow'. These included factors which were considered negative influences in our lives which caused obstruction of our life flow and were represented by either driftwood or rocks. I found this assignment particularly beneficial as we really got to know not only our group members better but I personally feel we learnt a lot about ourselves. We were discussing this as a group and came to the conclusion that neither of us really acknowledged how many obstacles we came across to be where we are today and really felt pleased with ourselves.

According to Halabi (2004: 8), dialogue 'between groups is painful, because it involves letting go of a familiar situation and a stable, clear reality, however dreadful; but it is also full of hope for a better future.' The process students were required to undergo involved learning as well as unlearning:

> For the first time in my life, I was the so-called 'odd one out', since I was the only white girl and I also come from a more privileged background than the other group members. I think that maybe the most valuable lesson that I have learnt is the feeling of the possibility of rejection and 'standing out'. It is important to note that my group members' reactions and behaviour

honestly did not contribute to this experience, but even so I felt that my appearance and background separates me from them and that they look at me as an outsider [...] As a community psychologist I will often work with races other than my own and therefore this is an important realization for me for my future work.

(Alan, SU) (Quoted in Leibowitz *et al.* 2010: 90).

As Leonardo and Porter (2010) note, it is important to work through, rather than avoid, the discomfort associated with the dialogue around issues of difference. Thus the route towards a critical hope is an ongoing and cyclical process of dialogue leading to disruption, reflexivity, and possible reconfiguration of previously held positions. It is also one which might involve elements of despair along the way. When reflecting on one's positionality regarding privilege and discrimination, despair might appear to be a legitimate and necessary response. Obviously, the pedagogical intention is not to produce situations where students remain mired in despair, defensive, closed to dialogue and unable to see alternative and constructive forms of thought or action. On the contrary, it is hoped that they should move on to positions of critical hope. From the various student responses we analyzed, it would appear that most, but not all, of the students who participated in the project felt that they had undergone a valuable and productive learning experience.

Final thoughts about the course

A number of factors contributed to enactments of critical hope in this project. Bringing people together where they had the opportunity to interrogate concepts of community, self and identity and their associated feelings provided a platform for deep engagement about difference. The use of PLA techniques as an alternative and inclusive method allowed engagement that went beyond pure 'contact.' Performances by guest speakers stimulated spontaneous engagement and reactions. Students were able to share intimate details about their lives, providing challenging as well as more empathic engagements around humanity and the pain of their life stories. Telling their own stories provided students with the opportunity for reflexivity in relation to professional practice. Some students learnt what sharing personal details were like for 'clients.' Sharing their own experiences allowed them to see the 'other' as human beings rather than reified objects, thus connecting with each other's humanity (Bozalek 2011). Working in pre-structured groups across disciplines and institutions, with a final joint presentation in mind, forced students to engage with each other collaboratively. Furthermore, the tasks that were set for students were specifically designed to elicit discussions about difference and community.

There were also factors that engendered elements of despair on the part of the educators in their roles as curriculum designers. Despair was evident in some instances, for example, when the course appeared to consolidate prejudice or defensiveness for some students. In some cases preconceived ideas about difference between disciplines and institutions were also entrenched. However, it is important for educators to realize that the shift towards new ways of thinking may sometimes happen after the end of the course.

Despair on the part of the educators related to the disparities in marks. Stellenbosch students performed better than UWC students on the whole and in so doing symbolically contributed to maintaining preconceived views of who is competent. In addition, material differences among students were not altered; in fact, students' knowledge of their own material positions was highlighted when, for example, UWC students saw the elaborate student center (cafeteria/mall) at Stellenbosch University. Despite this engagement, some Stellenbosch students maintained patronizing and missionary attitudes. Similarly, many UWC students accepted the assumed competence of some Stellenbosch students by, for example, proposing that SU students do PowerPoint presentations for the group, thus re-enacting the stereotype of SU students as academically 'superior.' There were thus several aspects of the course that could be redesigned to ameliorate some of the elements which detracted from the success of the course, the principal one being its short duration. However, others are more systemic and contextual, and are beyond the scope of the course designers.

The course designers are currently working with the pedagogy of discomfort and the development of critical hope with higher educators across institutions, rather than working directly and exclusively with students. We see this shift in focus as a way of addressing the sustainability of such endeavors in South African teaching and learning.

Conclusion

This chapter focuses on critical hope, both conceptually and practically, in the South African higher education context. Our discussion foregrounds the complexity of the development of critical hope through engaging in discomforting dialogues. We provide one possible way of conceptualizing critical hope as an iterative, ongoing process that has no end. The infinite nature of critical hope is crucial as it assumes that critical hope is a *process* associated with practices that are constantly reviewed and revised as a result of reflexivity and dialogue. We have used a concrete example of a teaching and learning project to illustrate the processes involved in designing a curriculum which contained opportunities for engaging in 'third space' dialogues across difference. The pedagogy of discomfort makes such a conceptualization of critical hope possible and serves as a guiding theoretical framework for our work on critical hope. In order to facilitate opportunities for the development of a critical hope, educators themselves need to be reflexive and continually vigilant regarding their own preparedness to reconfigure or reconstruct their own frameworks. This, as our project indicated, needs structured facilitation of dialoguing across difference, rather than leaving students to engage in open-ended conversations.

Notes

1 We use the South African terms for race found in most policy and census documents, i.e. African, Coloured, Indian and White.
2 Pseudonym.

References

Blackwell, D.M. (2010) 'Race ethnicity and education sidelines and separate spaces: making education anti-racist for students of color', *Race, Ethnicity and Education*, 13(4): 473–94.
Boler, M. (1999) *Feeling Power: Emotion and Education*. New York: Routledge.
Boler, M. and Zembylas, M. (2003) 'Discomforting truths: The emotional terrain of understanding difference'. In: P. Trifonas (ed.) *Pedagogies of Difference: Rethinking Education for Social Change*. New York: Routledge-Falmer.
Bozalek, V. (2011) 'Acknowledging privilege through encounters with difference: Participatory learning and action techniques for decolonizing methodologies in Southern contexts', *International Journal of Social Research Methodology*, 4(6): 465–80.
Bozalek, V. and Biersteker, L. (2010) 'Exploring power and privilege using participatory learning and action techniques', *Social Work Education*, 29(5): 551–72.
Bozalek, V. and Boughey, C. (2012) '(Mis)framing higher education', *Social Policy and Administration*, 46(6): 688–703.
Bozalek, V., Carolissen, R., Nicholls, L., Leibowitz, B., Swartz, L. and Rohleder, P. (2011) 'bell hooks and the enactment of emotion in teaching and learning across boundaries: A pedagogy of hope', *South African Journal of Higher Education*, 25(1): 157–67.
Carolissen, R. (2012) 'Student experiences of the CSI module'. In: B. Leibowitz, L. Swartz, V. Bozalek, R. Carolissen, L. Nicholls and P. Rohleder (eds) *Community, Self and Identity: Educating South African University Students for Citizenship*. Cape Town: HSRC Press.
Chambers, R. (2007) 'From PRA to PLA and pluralism: Practice and theory', *IDS Working Paper 286*. University of Sussex: Institute of Development Studies, Brighton.
Education White Paper 3 (1997) *A Programme for Higher Education Transformation*. Online. Available HTTP: <http://www.info.gov.za/whitepapers/1997/educ3.pdf> (accessed 4 June 2009).
Durrheim, K. (2005) 'Socio-spatial practice and racial representations in a changing South Africa', *South African Journal of Psychology*, 35(3): 444–59.
Erasmus, Z.E. (2006) 'Living the future now: "Race" and the challenges of transformation in higher education', *South African Journal of Higher Education*, 20(3): 413–25.
Fraser, N. (2008) 'Reframing justice in a globalizing world'. In: K. Olson (ed.) *Adding Insult to Injury: Nancy Fraser Debates Her Critics*. London and New York: Verso.
Fraser, N. (2009) *Scales of Justice. Reimagining Political Space in a Globalizing World*. New York: Columbia University Press.
Halabi, R. (2004) *Israeli and Palestinian Identities in Dialogue: The School for Peace Approach*. New Brunswick, NJ: Rutgers University Press.
Jansen, J. (2009) *Knowledge in the Blood; Confronting Race and the Apartheid Past*. Cape Town: UCT Press.

Jones, A. (2005) 'Talking cure: the desire for dialogue'. In: M. Boler (ed.) *Democratic Dialogue in Education: Troubling Speech, Disturbing Silence*. New York: Peter Lang.

Leibowitz, B. (2012) 'Understanding the challenges of the South African Higher Education Landscape'. In: B. Leibowitz, L. Swartz, V. Bozalek, R. Carolissen, L. Nicholls and P. Rohleder (eds) *Community, Self and Identity: Educating South African University Students for Citizenship*. Cape Town: HSRC Press.

Leibowitz, B., Bozalek, V., Rohleder, P., Carolissen, R. and Swartz, L. (2010) '"Ah, but the whiteys love to talk about themselves": Discomfort as a pedagogy for change', *Race, Ethnicity and Education*, 13(1): 83–100.

Leibowitz, B., Bozalek, V., Carolissen, R., Nicholls, L., Rohleder, P. and Swartz, L. (2012) 'Educating the educators: Creation of a powerful learning environment'. In: B. Leibowitz, L. Swartz, V. Bozalek, R. Carolissen, L. Nicholls and P. Rohleder (eds) *Community, Self and Identity: Educating South African University Students for Citizenship*. Cape Town: HSRC Press.

Leonardo, Z. and Porter, R.K. (2010) 'Pedagogy of fear: Toward a Fanonian theory of "safety" in race dialogue', *Race, Ethnicity and Education*, 13(2): 139–57.

McKinney, C. (2004) '"A little hard piece of glass in your shoe" – Understanding student resistance to critical literacy in post-apartheid South Africa', *South African Linguistics and Applied Language Studies*, 22(1+2): 63–73.

McKinney, C. (2007) 'Caught between the "old" and the "new"? Talking about "race" in a post-apartheid university classroom', *Race, Ethnicity and Education*, 10(2): 215–231.

Ministerial Committee (2008) *The Report of the Ministerial Committee on Transformation and Social Cohesion and the Elimination of Discrimination in Public Higher Education Institutions*. Pretoria: Government Gazette.

Norton, B. (2000) *Identity and Language Learning: Gender, Ethnicity and Educational Change*. London: Pearson.

Sonn, C. (2008) 'Educating for anti-racism: Producing and reproducing race and power in a university classroom', *Race, Ethnicity and Education*, 11(2): 155–66.

University of Stellenbosch, HOPE Project (no date) 'About the Hope Project'. Online. Available HTTP: <http://thehopeproject.co.za/hope/Pages/default.aspx> (accessed. 28 March 2103).

University of the Western Cape website http://www.uwc.ac.za/searchcentre/pages/Results.aspx?k=hope (accessed 28 March 2013).

Walker, M. (2005) 'Rainbow nation or new racism? Theorizing race and identity formation in South African higher education', *Race, Ethnicity and Education*, 8(2): 129–46.

Zembylas, M., (2007) *Five Pedagogies, A Thousand Possibilities: Struggling for Hope and Transformation in Education*. Rotterdam: Sense Publishers.

Zembylas, M. (2008) *The Politics of Trauma in Education*. New York: Palgrave MacMillan.

Zembylas, M. (2010) '"Teachers" emotional experiences of growing diversity and multiculturalism in schools and the prospects of an ethic of discomfort', *Teaching and Teachers: Theory and Practice*, 16(6): 703–16.

Zembylas, M. and McGlynn, C. (2010) 'Discomforting pedagogies: emotional tensions, ethical dilemmas and transformative possibilities', *British Educational Research Journal*, 38(1): 41–59.

Part II
Critical hope and a critique of neoliberalism

4 "That's scary. But it's not hopeless"
Critical pedagogy and redemptive narratives of hope

Gustavo Fischman and Eric Haas

> I appreciate your efforts [...] Now at least I know what Neoliberalism is, how it operates, and how it affects my personal and professional life [...] I don't think that I am a naïve teacher that doesn't know about exploitation, racism and oppression [...] and also the criticisms that should be made to bad schools, but [...] after reading and discussing all these books, I don't know, but I am feeling sad. I am feeling that no matter what, we cannot win.

These were the thoughts and emotions that Nancy, a Doctoral student in a seminar on 'Curriculum and the Politics of Education,' shared with the class during the final meeting. The first person in her family to attend college, a proud Mexican-American, and self-described "progressive, caring and competent" fourth grade mathematics teacher, Nancy had consistently expressed a tremendous sense of pride about her work in an urban school in Phoenix. At the age of 32, she was a straight 'A' student, easily open and assertive about her difficulties and disagreements with some of the texts we read. Defending what she called "the perspective of the teachers in the trenches," Nancy's opinions were very important to the students in the class. And for the first time this semester, she had concluded, "we cannot win."

For Dr Fischman the course instructor, a former grass-roots educator, this was not how he expected the class would conclude the course. Having worked with poor communities in popular education projects before moving into formal education and the world of schools, he was familiar with the anger and frustration that occur when trying to transform 'oppressive' situations, classrooms, and schools. In all of these experiences, although he had continually looked for ways to incorporate what he saw as the necessary criticisms of the functioning of schools, administrators and teachers with ideas that will aid educators and communities to change schools, he recognized that some things might scare them away. Yet, he was ill prepared for Nancy's response, not least because she voiced some of his own deep-seated fears and concerns.

The class remained silent after Nancy spoke. He looked around the room in vain for a student who could add another perspective to Nancy's reflections, but the class appeared to avoid his attempts to make eye contact. The silence was a deafening indication that the students shared Nancy's opinions.

A feeling of despair and self-doubt began to overwhelm him. Dr Fischman counted to 60, then to 100 before asking: "I have the impression that reading and discussing Freire and Critical Pedagogy had the emotional effect of creating a sense of despair and hopelessness in the group. Am I right?" Several in the group nodded their heads in agreement. Paula, one of the youngest in the group and usually reticent about sharing her thoughts, said with a laugh, "Don't worry you didn't 'Ellsworthize' us ... well, maybe a little, but not too much and we can handle it."[1] There was general laughter in the class, and, in my case at least, a small sense of relief. Then Paula added: "You have to acknowledge that we made a lot of progress since the beginning of the seminar. Many of us have had to overcome many challenges to sit in your class [...] We were not used to the language and the critical perspective [...]." By now the whole group appeared re-energized and several parallel dialogues were initiated. Vera raised her voice over the others while waving a few pages. "This is perfect. I remembered it when Nancy talked and you asked the question about hope. Can I read it to the group? We discussed it before."

> [I]magine having as your central professional message [as a teacher educator] that schools are lousy places to work, young people are alienated, and the curriculum is fundamentally and perhaps fatally flawed! True or not, a year is a long time to endure such fare, and perhaps even a longer time to push it.
> (Bullough and Gitlin 1995: 8)

Vera's statements refocused the class' attention, and a vivid exchange followed. Some contended that the situation of schools was dire and our critical discussions only reflected 'reality.' A few others tried to recover some of the concepts of the class – like 'resistance' and 'agency' – and insisted on the possibility of Freire's conscientization. It did not look like the group would approach consensus, but the noise and debate felt a lot better than the silence of only three minutes before. After a few exchanges, Nancy's words once again grabbed the group's attention:

> I would like to say something. I don't want to be misunderstood. No, I don't feel hopeless. I don't think that you hammered us with the 'bad schools-oppressive teachers' message, or 'Ellsworthized,' or even tried to 'Freireize,' or 'brain-wash' us [...]

> I've been thinking about this since the beginning of this class, but I didn't have the words to express myself. I said that we couldn't win. I was sad, but that is not all. It was also [...] I was ashamed [...] it is just that I realized that my hopes, were 'easy hopes,' kind of 'Hello Kitty hopes' [...] and then [...] working with all of you I have to give up the idea that by being the 'super-caring-knowledgeable-efficient' teacher – and you know that I am all of that – I was going to first, fix my grade, then my school, later the district and so on. Please, don't laugh [...] that may have been unrealistic but it was my dream. That was my goal [...] I was sad not because I felt hopeless about

what we can do as teachers. I think that I was sad because I realized I was trying to convince myself that teachers can win without pissing off people, without making enemies [...] I was sad of letting my 'Hello Kitty hopes' go. That is sad [...] That is scary. But it's not hopeless.

The class was silent, and Dr Fischman could not tell if the final silence was an expression of respectful agreement with Nancy or a general disagreement with what she said. Either way, things that had seemed clear were suddenly fuzzy.

This chapter begins with this recollection, not because testimonies hold some sort of magical power, or because we think that this example illustrates that we are effective 'critical' educators. On the contrary, we share Nancy's reflections and reactions because we think that her words and thoughts point to the limits of redemptive progressive pedagogical discourses, when in an effort to empower, develop consciousness, or create counter-narratives in the struggle against oppressive educational systems, they often cannot recognize the limitations and contradictions of their own narratives.

In order to better understand the dilemmas inherent in the positioning and use of narratives that negate the complex web of factors in contemporary teaching and learning we argue that the viability of progressive pedagogies as educational–political discourses depends upon the articulation of discourses of hope that go beyond notions of individual 'superteachers' and 'narratives of redemption' to implementing pedagogical practices that both recognize and support educators as committed intellectuals.

Progressive pedagogies: Beyond the narrative of redemption

We will refer to progressive pedagogies as a conglomerate of broadly connected perspectives, that have 'empathy' as their most important guiding value. As George Lakoff describes:

> Behind every progressive policy lies a single moral value: empathy, together with the responsibility and strength to act on that empathy. Never forget 'responsibility and strength,' because there is no true empathy without them. During the conservative reign we have seen what Barack Obama has called an empathy deficit – a failure to care, both about others and each other. Caring is not just feeling empathy; it is taking responsibility, acting powerfully and courageously. You have to be strong to care, and to act on that care with success.
>
> (Lakoff 2008: 47)

Deweyan, Freirean, Feminist(s), critical, anti-racist, and popular education are all progressive pedagogies[2] articulated as what it 'should be' – an abstract construction, a guiding model that points to goals that could be achieved by the social practices of teaching/learning in relation to processes of social transformation

(Apple 2006; Kincheloe 2007). In this orientation towards the future, most progressive pedagogies establish a direct connection with the ideals of the Enlightenment. In the words of Peter McLaren:

> First of all schooling should be a process of understanding how subjectivities are produced. It should be a process of examining how we have been constructed out of the prevailing ideas, values, and worldviews of the dominant culture. The point to remember is that if we have been made, then we can be "unmade" and "made over".
>
> (McLaren 2003: 92)

These progressive pedagogical discourses share the general goals of working with the society as a whole, while focusing on a particular sector (such as the oppressed, poor, working class, women, indigenous) in order to help in the construction and organization of transformative social and political movements aimed at the construction of real democracies.[3]

One of the strongest claims of progressive pedagogies is that the concrete results of schooling are deeply connected with the possibilities of achieving the goal of democratizing societies. That is, the results of schooling and democracy are intertwined and constructed in and through people's linguistic, cultural, social, and pedagogical specific interactions, which both shape and are shaped by social, political, economic, and cultural dynamics. From this perspective, societies, communities, schools, teachers and even students engage in oppressive practices, and those understanding those practices need to be connected with transforming them.

The connection of awareness to pedagogical transformation, we believe, is an important distinguishing feature of progressive pedagogies, not only as a theoretical standpoint but also as a model of action that advances an agenda for educational change; it forces educators to understand their practices in broader socio-political contexts. By emphasizing the importance of understanding-transforming pedagogical-social realities, *Progressive Pedagogies* also point to the intrinsic relationship between educational and social transformations, keeping in constant view new means of breaking down all forms of oppression.

A second strong claim of progressive pedagogies, dating back to Dewey's (1956; 1966) perspectives, is that educators have a central, but not exclusive, role in maintaining and challenging educational systems. For example, building upon a Gramscian concept of praxis (Gramsci 1971) and a Freirean notion of concientization (Freire 1989, 1997a, 1997b), Giroux (1993: 138) has extensively discussed the possibility of teachers becoming "transformative intellectuals." Giroux contends that teachers need to engage in debate and inquiry in order to open the spaces for taking critical stances towards their own practice and the practice of others. Through these activities, educators could begin to reflexively and actively shape their curricula and school policies. Transformative intellectuals are aware of their own theoretical convictions and are skilled in strategies for translating them into practice (Giroux 1993, 2002).

Giroux's perspective is widely embraced by those associated with *Progressive Pedagogies* (Darder 2002; Giroux 1993; McLaren 2003). The social and political dimensions of schooling, the need to understand and transform schools and society, and the key role that educators in these processes play are core themes shared by many critical educators (Darder *et al.* 2003; Fischman *et al.* 2005). Although it is hard to quantify or even qualify the influence of progressive pedagogues in the USA, it would be hard to deny that, as a collective movement, it has produced one of the most dynamic and controversial educational schools of thought of the twentieth century (Apple *et al.* 2009). Nonetheless, it is also hard to deny that there are many educators like Nancy who react to the proposals of progressive pedagogies with great skepticism and despair.

We contend that a good deal of those reactions are related to progressive pedagogies' use of a *narrative of redemption* when arguing in favor of educational change. Narratives of redemption involve a quasi-schizophrenic perspective in which schools are presently horrible and schools can be beautiful. The link between the horrible present and the beautiful future is the narrative of redemption with the superteacher as its hero. This is a common depiction in discourses about teachers in teacher education programs, but it is also especially strong in popular culture (Kincheloe 2004).

Narratives of redemption provide the basic discursive structure of most Hollywood characters from the films *To Sir with Love*, *Dangerous Minds*, and *Stand and Deliver* and the teachers of television's *Boston Public*. Narratives of redemption work when an individual teacher overcomes all the systemic failures through the sheer force of his or her heroic and 'organic' consciousness and deeds. When others follow the lead of the superteacher, the class or school as a larger system is redeemed. This process follows the biblical tradition of sin-crisis-failure-trauma and finalizes with archetypal myths of redemption-absolution-success-recovery.[4] If accepted, the redeeming vision will, after the defeat of the enemy, create the ideal school, in which the perfect teacher and the model student will learn in individual harmony, separate from the chaos of the surrounding educational and social system.

The redemptive narrative is often used indiscriminately by both supporters and opponents of progressive pedagogies, and one of its distinctive markers is that teaching appears as both the target of harsh social criticisms and the last space of hope. In that critical juncture of society's imaginary about teachers, they become the makers of terrible presents and hopeful futures. Further, the use of narratives of redemption in the teaching of progressive pedagogies also contributes to the proliferation of gloom and doom. In fact, it often does so quite well. The references to Ellsworth (1989) and to Bullough and Gitlin (1995) by the students in the seminar are illustrative of the complexities of the tasks ahead. For these three scholars and for many teacher educators, there is a sense that *Progressive Pedagogies* can be a self-defeating endeavor, in part because the rationalist assumptions and difficulties in analyzing power imbalances between progressive pedagogues and their students. Critique of public schools, and of our own roles as teachers and teacher educators, is an essential aspect of *Progressive*

Pedagogies, but critique can become debilitating, we believe, when it is structured by overwhelming narratives of redemption.

A remarkable characteristic of narratives of redemption is the normative presentation of conflicts and struggles as expressions of hope in connection with educational and social change (Fischman and Diaz 2012). Yet, only within the redemptive mythology of heroic teachers and students is it possible to find 'hope' inherent in racism, poverty, discrimination and other conflicts, for to do so requires one often to minimize or ignore the real-life risks and suffering associated to those struggles.

We do not see any 'natural connection' between struggle and hope, or even between schooling and hope. Our position is to recognize that conflicts and struggles are part of the everyday life of schools and societies, sometimes explicit and clear, often implicit and confusing, but always anchored in complex manners and expressing multiple dynamics of class, race, sexuality, language, and ethnicity. It is by understanding that educational conflicts are unavoidable that committed teachers "must speak for hope, as long as it doesn't mean suppressing the nature of the danger" (Williams 1989: 322). It is for these reasons that we find the intersection of progressive pedagogies with the narrative of redemption as expressed in Nancy's 'Hello Kitty'[5] hopes to be counterproductive for the development of critically aware teachers who are effective in developing socially just school reform.

What we want to contend is that the concrete results of schooling, as understood through the lived experience of the pedagogical relationship between teachers and students, cannot be reduced to absolute and universal terms of complete failure or total success. For Nancy and for countless teachers, assessing the results of their/our pedagogical interventions is constrained by conflictive relationships and the ways in which each of us, as members of multiple and specific social groups, recognizes, perceives, believes, and acts upon complex and contradictory realities. We contend that this "lived irreducibleness" (Freire 1989) of most educational processes confronts teachers and students with unavoidable tensions that need to be understood in their complexities and not reduced to binary oppositions and assessed as simplistic barriers to the realization of pedagogical conscientization.

We propose that schools do not need superteachers or progressive superconscious "organic intellectuals" (Gramsci 1971). Instead, schools need teachers that can recognize their intellectual function and can then assume the role of "committed intellectuals" (Fischman 1998). Commitment to the idea of educational change, born out of indignation when witnessing injustices or suffering them very likely precedes or at least develops with conscientization (Fischman and McLaren 2005) and, in that sense, the notion of teachers as committed intellectuals is more of an orientation or a process than a final state of being. As Freire (1989) wrote: "Conscientization is not exactly the starting point of commitment. Conscientization is more of a product of commitment. I do not have to be already critically self-conscious in order to struggle. By struggling I become conscious/aware" (p. 46). In other words, an educator who is a committed intellectual is sometimes critically self-conscious and actively engaged in social networks, but at other times is confused, or even unaware of his or her limitations or capacities to be an active proponent of social change. Educators will continue to be both oppressed and oppressor, even as they struggle to become less of both. Teaching aimed at democratizing education needs commitment, but not in abstract terms, because having a deep understanding of the complex processes of oppression and domination is not enough to guarantee personal or collective praxis. As Daniel Schugurensky clearly notes, "More democratic, effective and enjoyable schools require teachers who are generous, committed, democratic, and knowledgeable and who do not dichotomize cognition and emotion" (2011: 134).

The type of commitment that we are proposing begins here and now, and it is not guaranteed forever because, as Shor cleverly noted, "this kind of project is no different from other exercises in social change, which begin from the concrete they are destined to erase" (1980: 269).

Commitment is central, but the commitment to struggle against injustice is not 'organic' and is more natural for some people than for others (Fischman and McLaren 2005). Further, this commitment is not just to an individual struggle, but also to a developing community of similarly committed fellow activists. Only by developing an understanding that is born of a commitment to social justice in cooperation with others can such an understanding lead to both the type of conscientization and the counter-systemic networks necessary to challenge the hegemonic structures of domination and exploitation. The inequities of the globalization of capital can be challenged and even defeated, but not simply by understanding its formation and toiling individually; rather, it requires developing the will and the courage – the commitment – to struggle against it in cooperation with others.

The notion of the teacher as a committed intellectual is exactly the opposite of the teacher as the super-agent of educational change, where s/he is able to accomplish heroic tasks and thus everything is possible. Following Badiou, we assume that the accomplishments of the committed intellectual will be a lot more humble:

> The conception of politics that we defend is far from the idea that 'everything is possible'. In fact, it is an immense task to try to propose a few possibles, in the plural – a few possibilities other than what we are told is possible. It is a matter of showing how the space of the possible is larger than the one we are assigned – that something else is possible, but not that everything is possible.
> (Badiou 2001: 115)

We contend that potentially all teachers could be committed intellectuals, based on the functions that they perform and not on any essential virtue or personal characteristic that will explain their vocation or destiny. We are convinced that teaching is an intellectual activity, but do not think that educators' 'commitments' can be reduced to merely rational positions. On the contrary, in our experience most teachers are committed to the well-being of their students, believe in the importance of democratizing societies,[6] and are more likely than others to 'feel' in their guts that it is not enough to understand how the multiple forms of exploitation are affecting their students, their families and communities. Most teachers also feel the need to act in their classrooms (and beyond) as one of the focal points to transform the world. As Foucault convincingly indicates:

> The essential political problem for the intellectual is not to criticize the ideological contents supposedly linked to science, or to ensure that his own scientific practice is accompanied by a correct ideology, but that of ascertaining the possibility of constituting a new politics of truth. The problem is not changing people's consciousness—or what's in their heads—but the political, economic, institutional regime of the production of truth.
> (Foucault 1980: 133)

Many teachers have experienced firsthand how the Freirean notion of praxis and the capacity to engage in critical self-consciousness are not enough to transform both the repressive and integrative functions of any hegemonic order. Moreover, most teachers know that their actions do not compare well with the extraordinary heroic actions of fictional characters. As researchers and educators, we are convinced that most of us know rather well that we cannot transform the world through schooling, but nevertheless some of us also feel the commitment to intervene, most likely in non-extraordinary ways, pretty often in quite simple and less than awe-inspiring forms, just to maintain for ourselves the possibilities for transforming the world.[7]

Contrary to the rational Cartesian super-conscious teachers of so many progressive accounts, and the all-powerful 'heroic-teacher' or the all-knowing 'super-conscious progressive-teacher' of the narratives of redemption some teachers can be seen as intellectuals committed to their particular students, oriented by goals of educational and social justice without succumbing to essentialist positions or easy rhetorical discourses of good versus evil, populist nostalgia, possessive parochialism, or militant cultural particularism (Glass 2004). As Friedrich *et al.* expressively note:

> No matter how your ideal educational institution compares to currently existing ones, it will still fail to be democratic, if we follow Rancière's political theory—that is, if we understand democracy not as a form of government or a set of rules on how to live a moral life, but as a political act of subjectification, as a challenge to the distribution of the sensible, to the ways in which the world is perceived, thought and acted upon.
> (Friedrich *et al.* 2010: 572)

Concluding ideas

A few months ago, Nancy called Dr Fischman to tell him that she decided to leave her school, to become a 100 percent 'Chicana activist/intellectual' working for social transformation in a place that makes her happy. She said:

Don't feel sad. I am continuing to be committed to my kids, but as we discussed in class, schools are not the only places where education happens, or transformation begins and besides [...] How can I say this to you? Don't laugh, but I'm feeling with a renewed sense of hope [...] Yeah perhaps a little bit 'Hello-Kitty-ish', but it feels cool and good [...].

Dr Fischman assured Nancy that he was very happy for her and was not laughing, but asked her why she thought that he was going to laugh. After a few seconds of hesitation, Nancy laughingly told him in Spanish:

I know you, you hate 'Hello Kitty' but what can I do, I am who I am, and my mom always told me that "Hope is the last thing to lose." I know that one day, you will start liking 'nice and cute' things, like Hello Kitty.

At the end, Dr Fischman and Nancy were both laughing.

Hope for a better and fairer future for our schools and societies is not problematic *per se*, as long as we can work with our students and colleagues in teacher education to distinguish between wishful optimism based on narratives of redemption and forms of "critical situated hope" (Rivers 2011).[8] Recognizing the problems, understanding the risks, while also avoiding despair, is required to respond creatively to the conflicts happening in our classrooms. But it is only when the creative response draws on the educational community's resources and traditions that we can avoid the spiral of apathy and educational despair, which is today the mark of too many US schools.

However, a sense of hope that relies on a redemptive narrative of individual superteacher heroism, whether wrapped in naïvely hopeful rhetoric or critical discourses, is ineffectual hope. Learning from Nancy's example implies the recognition that our classrooms must offer not only consistent theoretical analyses informed by lofty progressive ideals, but also concretely value and recognize the importance of the lived experiences of our students, even in their multiple identities with all the contradictions that may generate in the teachers, because:

It is a condition of being modern that our double or triple identities look weird from the outside but are the only kinds that feel authentic from the inside. The passionately nationalist Québecois who listens exclusively to Metallica and AC/DC; the Muslim fundamentalist with the satellite dish – from outside, we wonder how they reconcile the contradictions. But they don't have to reconcile the contradictions in order to cope with reality. The contradictions are themselves the form that a reconciliation with reality takes.

(Gopnik 2009: 78)

Freire (1997a) believed that hope is an historical and ontological need and not an external characteristic of the pedagogical situation, alien to the daily struggle of teachers and students. Progressive pedagogues have developed a great repertoire of concepts and practices that are presumed to offer a realistic and feasible alternative to oppressive educational systems, but in order to be effective, *Progressive Pedagogies* should recognize that the starting point of many teachers is similar to Nancy's original Hello Kitty hopeful attitude: a sense of love, a sense of commitment and, thus a sense of responsibility.

Freire, vehemently stated, "Just to hope, is to hope in vain" (1997b: 9). Nancy's initial hope was very close to the perspective criticized by Freire and many in the progressive pedagogies but her notion should not be dismissed as merely romantic, and naïve, nor should it be accepted uncritically as unchangeable. It is simply, perhaps, a good place to start. It is also where we must start. Nancy's hope, we will argue following Hannah Arendt, is also a responsible perspective as opposed to a cynical or merely ironic standpoint. As Hannah Arendt noted, "education is the point at which we decide whether we love the world enough to assume responsibility for it and by the same token save it from that ruin which, except for renewal, except for the coming of the new and young, would be inevitable" (1968: 196). Nancy assumed her responsibilities and contributed to the process of renewal; our commitment and hopes are to work with as many Nancies as possible.

Notes

1 Elizabeth Ellsworth's 'Why doesn't this feel empowering' was one of the required readings for the class. Considered one of the most poignant criticisms of the theory and practice of critical pedagogy, Ellsworth concludes that far from providing a discourse of hope and transformation and the abilities needed to make reforms, CP makes things worse. "When participants in our class attempted to put into practice prescriptions offered in the literature [of CP] concerning empowerment, student voice, and dialogue, we produced results that were not only unhelpful, but actually exacerbated the very conditions we were trying to work against, including Eurocentrism, racism, sexism, classism, and banking education [...] Far from helping to overcome relations of oppression in the classroom, the "discourses of critical pedagogy [...] had themselves become vehicles of repression" (1989: 298).

2 It is important to stress that it is not our intention to caricaturize these perspectives nor ignore the key differences among them, but to point out to the commonalities that are applied in educational courses.

3 In the Deweyan sense of real democracy as "a name for a life of free and enriching communion" (Dewey 1954: 184) and: The devotion of democracy to education is a familiar fact. The superficial explanation is that a government resting upon popular suffrage cannot be successful unless those who elect and who obey their governors are educated. Since a democratic society repudiates the principle of external authority, it must find a substitute in voluntary disposition and interest; these can be created only by education. But there is a deeper explanation. '*A democracy is more than a form of government; it is primarily a mode of associated living, of conjoint communicated experience*' [italics added]. (Dewey 1956: 87, in Vinson *et al.* 2001: 7.)

4 This semantic chain was cleverly summarized by the prominent philosopher Mortimer Adler (1939: 141) "Crisis is a turning point. In pneumonia, it is the point at which the patient gets either better or worse. But the present crisis in education is different. Things can't get worse. They can only get better. We have reached an extreme in the swing of the pendulum."

5 'Hello Kitty' 'is a fictional character produced by the Japanese company Sanrio, first designed by Yuko Shimizu. She is portrayed as a female white Japanese bobtail cat with a red bow http://en.wikipedia.org/wiki/Hello_Kitty
6 With regards to the question of the relationship of education and democracy we agree with Friedrich *et al.* that "Rancière's thought is helpful in exposing the deeply problematic link present in the notion of 'democratic education.' Democracy requires an uncertainty that seems to be antithetical to education, an uncertainty regarding not only the results of education (something many pedagogues propose as a better method), but an impossibility of any kind of plan or vision of the future regarding the social order, an acceptance of dissensus at the core of society, in ways that make any consensus fall into policing" (2009: 9).
7 We acknowledge that the labor-capital antagonism is a fundamental dialectical contradiction within capitalist society, but reject as self-defeating the reduction of educational conflicts to simplistic binaries such as evil Neoliberalism versus good social democracy.
8 Melissa Rivers developed the notion of 'situated hope', borrowing from Lave and Wenger's (1991) concept of situated learning. For Rivers "Situated hope in teacher education is located in social contexts, is connected to personal beliefs and attitudes, the activities of teaching, including curricular and pedagogical decisions, and is influenced by outside contexts including public, policy, departmental and other regulatory factors" (2011: 131).

References

Adler, M.J. (1939) 'The crisis in contemporary education', *The Social Frontier*, V(42): 140–5.
Apple, M.W. (2006) *Educating the "Right" Way: Markets, Standards, God, and Inequality*, 2nd edn. New York: Routledge.
Apple, M.W., Au, W. and Gandin, L.A. (eds) (2009) *The Routledge International Handbook of Critical Education*. New York: Routledge.
Arendt, H. (1968) *Between Past and Future: Eight Exercises in Political Thought*. New York: Penguin Books.
Badiou, A. (2001) *Ethics: An Essay on the Understandings of Evil*. London: Verso.
Bullough, Jr, R.V. and Gitlin, A. (1995) *Becoming a Student of Teaching: Methodologies for Exploring Self and School Context*. New York: Garland Publishing, Inc.
Darder, A. (2002) *Reinventing Paulo Freire: A Pedagogy of Love*. Boulder, CO and Oxford, UK: Westview Press.
Darder, A., Baltodano, M. and Torres, R. (eds) (2003) *The Critical Pedagogy Reader*. New York: Routledge-Falmer.
Dewey, J. (1956) *The Child and the Curriculum/The School and Society*. Chicago, IL and London: University of Chicago Press. (Original works published 1902 and 1899.)
Dewey, J. (1966) *Democracy and Education: An Introduction to the Philosophy of Education*. New York: Free Press. (Original work published 1916.)
Ellsworth, E. (1989) 'Why doesn't this feel empowering? Working through the repressive myths of critical pedagogy', *Harvard Educational Review*, 59: 297–324.
Fischman, G.E. (1998) 'Donkeys and superteachers: Popular education and structural adjustment in Latin-America', *International Journal of Education*, 44: 191–213.
Fischman, G.E. and Diaz, V. (2012) 'Education without redemption: Ten reflections about the relevance of the Freirean legacy', *International Journal of Education for Democracy*, 5.

Fischman, G.E. and McLaren, P. (2005) 'Rethinking critical pedagogy and the Gramscian legacy: From organic to committed intellectuals', *Cultural Studies Critical Methodologies*, 5: 425–47.

Fischman, G., McLaren, P., Sünker, H. and Lankshear, C. (eds) (2005) *Critical Theories, Radical Pedagogies and Global Conflicts*. Lanham, MD: Rowman and Littlefield.

Foucault, M. (1980) *Power and Knowledge: Selected Interviews and Other Writings*. New York: Pantheon.

Freire, P. (1989) *Education for the Critical Consciousness*. New York: Continuum.

Freire, P. (1997a) *Pedagogy of Hope: Reliving the Pedagogy of the Oppressed*. New York: Continuum.

Freire, P. (1997b) *Pedagogy of the Heart*. New York: Continuum.

Friedrich, D., Bryn J. and Popkewitz, T. (2010) 'Democratic education: An (im)possibility that yet remains to come', *Educational Philosophy and Theory*, 42: 571–87.

Giroux, H.A. (1988) *Teachers as Intellectuals: Toward a Critical Pedagogy of Learning*. New York: Bergin & Garvey.

Giroux, H.A. (1993) *Border Crossings: Cultural Workers and the Politics of Education*. New York: Routledge.

Giroux, H.A. (2002) 'Rethinking cultural politics and radical pedagogy in the work of Antonio Gramsci'. In: C. Borg, J. Buttigieg and P. Mayo (eds) *Gramsci and Education*. Lanham, MD: Rowman & Littlefield.

Gopnik, A. (2009) 'The trial of the century. Revisiting the Dreyfuss affair', *The New Yorker* (28 September 2009).

Glass, R. (2004) 'Moral and political clarity and education as a practice of freedom'. In: M. Boler (ed.) *Democratic Dialogue and Education: Troubling Speech, Disturbing Silence*. New York: Peter Lang.

Gramsci, A. (1971) *Selections from the Prison Notebooks*. New York: International Publishers.

Kincheloe, J.L. (2004) *Critical Pedagogy Primer*. New York: Peter Lang.

Lave, J and Wenger, E. (1991) *Situated Learning: Legitimate Peripheral Participation*. Cambridge: Cambridge University Press.

McLaren, P. (2003) 'Critical Pedagogy: A look at the major concepts'. In: A. Darder, M. Batodano and R.D. Torres (eds) *Critical Pedagogy Reader*. London: Routledge.

Rivers, M. (2011) 'Situated hope: Understanding teacher educators' notion of hope', unpublished thesis, Arizona State University.

Schugurensky, D. (2011) *Paulo Freire: A Triangle of Transformation for the Twenty-First Century*. New York: Continuum.

Vinson, K., Gibson, R. and Ross, E.W. (2001) 'High-stakes testing and standardization: The threat to authenticity', Progressive Perspectives, Monograph Series, vol. 3, no. 2, John Dewey Project on Progressive Education Winter.

Williams, R. (1989) *Resources of Hope*. New York: Verso.

5 Plasticity, critical hope and the regeneration of human rights education

André Keet

Introduction

This chapter offers a plastic reading of 'critical hope' as a 'left over' form of a radical and transformative human rights education that has not yet materialized. The premise of my argument is that generally human rights education has, despite its 'explosive reserves,' developed into an unproductive and declarationist pedagogy that works against the 'critical.' Using Malabou's concept of 'plasticity' which follows, in my logic, from Derrida's deconstruction, a case is made that the regeneration of human rights education can best be conceived of on the level of 'left over' forms. This line of reasoning advances from an engagement with the concepts of 'plasticity' and 'deconstruction,' linked to a critique of human rights education. It provides the basis to argue that 'critical hope' is both a 'left over' form of current conceptions of human rights education and is constitutive of its radicalization.

Human rights education is currently one of the most dominant pedagogical formations within the cluster of peace, democracy and citizenship education. This dominance is derived from the ascendancy of the human rights language within the global geo-political discourse of the United Nations and the ensuing human rights standards. The massive injection of resources that has gone into the explosion of human rights education over the past 30 years (see Suarez 2006; Suarez and Ramirez 2004), contributed, as Honig (2006: 170) argues with reference to the analyses of Mouffe, Brown, Butler, Rancière, Derrida and others, to the "deadening effects of rights-centered constitutionalism on spontaneous political action." Honig (p. 169) argues for a kind of rights that continuously agitates against even the very laws within which they are inscribed. This agitation should have been a function of a radical human rights education within which political action could take rational form. The absence of such radicalism is a consequence of the deadening effects of which Honig speaks, constituted, in part, by an unproductive and uncritical human rights education. Human rights education is in need of regeneration and such regeneration, to my mind, can best be conceptualized within the scheme of 'plasticity.'

Critical hope is encrypted into the aspirational logic of human rights that permeates human rights education (see Lynch *et al.* 1992; Andreopoulus and

Claude 1997; Flowers 2004; Bajaj 2011). Therefore, in this instance, it has to protrude as that which is 'left over' from a demand for a radical human rights education that did not materialize over the past 20 years (see Keet 2010, 2012). Non-materialization of this kind takes shape against the backdrop of massive social pathologies as the canvas on which 'hopelessness' adopts a variety of meanings. One of these relates to a growing acknowledgement that current forms of human rights education do not match up to the hope on which the dominance of the human rights discourse is found. In fact, over the past decades, human rights education, in general, steps forth as a *conservative* and *declarationist* educational formation that works against the 'critical' (see Keet 2010). The regenerative human rights education that I propose has the constitution of the critical and the radical as one of its main objectives.

I use the term critical in this chapter to refer to the necessary distance between human rights education and human rights universals that allows for a reflexivity which is capable of questioning, from a social justice perspective, the assumptions, premises and suppositions of human rights itself and how and why these are exported into the praxis of human rights education in the way that they are. The critical is regenerative aimed at perpetual transformation of, in this case, human rights education. Furthermore, the concept of 'critique,' following Delanty's (2011) analysis, has four dimensions, two of which apply to the use of the concept in this chapter:

> Firstly, critique takes as its starting point a sense of a problem or crisis in the objective order of society [...] The second level of critique has a stronger interpretative dimension to it but may be termed reconstructive critique in that its aim is to reconstruct the immanent possibilities in a given situation [...].
>
> (Delanty 2011: 88–9)

A critical human rights education thus constructs a relationship of 'questioning' between itself and the human rights universals that it is tasked to legitimate. Such questioning will uncover the 'explosive reserves' of human rights education to resist and rebel against the domination of power in pursuit of social justice. This is the radicalized version of human rights education that has not yet materialized. This conception of the critical and critique gives meaning to the critical in 'critical hope' as an 'educated hope.' As will be discussed later, I conceive of critical hope as the 'straining forward movement' toward the 'event,' as Derrida would have it, or toward the "immanent possibilities in a given situation" as Delanty argues in the passage quoted above. These potentialities are dependent on the 'regenerative' which can, in turn, best be rethought on the level of the left over. That is, regeneration requires a de-layering movement that can excavate what is left over from the promising inscription of 'critical hope' into human rights education. From this plane, a transformative reconstitution of human rights education can be launched which both perpetually regenerates itself and continually renews critical hope within its own inscription. These are the explosive reserves that Malabou (2011: 85) may have in mind for human rights education. That is, to 'repair' or to 'recover,' are most productive on the level of the left over as a transformative dialectic steered by plastic reading.

The left over is given shape by the notion of plasticity which can only become intelligible in conversation with deconstruction, which in turn has *logocentrism* as its main focus of critique according to Mikics's (2009) intellectual biography of Derrida. Human rights were not spared this critique. Thus, even though deconstruction's battle with *logocentrism* as a 'metaphysics of presence' is not the main focus of this chapter, its critique of human rights invites plasticity as a conceptual frame for, at least, considering the future pedagogical viabilities of a critical hope as the left over form of a radical human rights education that never came into being.

Plasticity, Malabou (2010: 52) argues, is the "shape or form of that which remains or survives in the wake of deconstruction." In the case of human rights education, critical hope, I suggest, is inscribed in these left over shapes. Stated differently, it was there already as a *kernel*. Likewise, associated pedagogical formations such as democracy and citizenship education are simultaneously fashioned on critical hope on the one hand, and driven by explicit aspirational standards and hopeful content on the other. No doubt, scholars of Dewey and Freire will argue that these connections are historically common within critical pedagogies. The point here is that these relatively new pedagogical formations owe their very architectures to a certain 'idea of hope' that is converted into and reduced to human rights standards.

In most instances critical hope is perceived as having disappeared ironically under the weight of the standards which aim to express it, while there is a dominant view that human rights education potentially is the most productive pedagogical formation in relation to critical hope. This is underscored by the adoption of the United Nations Declaration on Human Rights Education and Training (UNDHRET) on 19 December 2011 (resolution 66/137), a landmark moment in the history of human rights education. The attraction of human rights education in relation to critical hope lies in it being able to conceive of critical hope in an integrated and relational genre, cutting across the various foci of and approaches to human rights education, and straddling moral, legal, social and political conceptions (Roux 2012). Herein rests the potential productivity of human rights education in developing holistic notions of critical hope as pedagogical principles that can respond to the overwhelming pessimistic élan of despair.

Plasticity and the 'left over' forms of human rights education

> Human rights education and training comprises all educational, training, information, awareness-raising and learning activities aimed at promoting universal respect for and observance of all human rights and fundamental freedoms and thus contributing, inter alia, to the prevention of human

rights violations and abuses by providing persons with knowledge, skills and understanding and developing their attitudes and behaviours, to empower them to contribute to the building and promotion of a universal culture of human rights.

(Article 2, UNDHRET)

Following this definition of human rights education, article four of UNDHRET provides that human rights education should be based on the "principles of the Universal Declaration of Human Rights (UDHR) and relevant treaties and instruments" (GA 66/137). This refers to more than 200 human rights instruments. Official United Nations documents describe human rights as rights inherent to all human beings as expressed in "treaties and other sources of law at the national, regional and international levels" which go under the collective term of "international human rights instruments (treaties, declarations, principles, recommendations, guidelines, etc.)" (UN NGLS 2008: v).

The overproduction of human rights instruments and the standards that constitute them has its roots in the 1940s and continues up to this day, with the one which 'declarationized' human rights education itself, UNDHRET, recently being adopted. Just in terms of sheer numbers and range, the business of rights enunciations has dominated, and continues to dominate, the international agenda and relations amongst nations and peoples (Knowles 2004: 133). We are, without doubt, in an age of rights (Baxi 2008), paradoxically as the inverted hope against the human suffering that is endemic to the world. On the back of these developments, human rights education has become an emerging field of inquiry (Tibbitts 2002: 160); its prevalence is closely tied to the proliferation of international and regional human rights instruments and standards and accompanied state legitimation (Suarez 2006). Studies in human rights education also increased in number and frequency (Suarez 2006). More recently, Bajaj (2011: 481–2) argues that over "the past four decades, human rights education has become a greater part of international discussions of educational policy, national textbook reform, and the work of non-governmental organizations (NGOs) ... [it also emerged] on its own as a field of scholarship and practice." Further, she (p. xx) reflects on the definitional trends within human rights education as inclusive of education *about* human rights (cognitive); education *through* human rights (participatory methods that create skills for active citizenship); and education *for* human rights (fostering learners' ability to speak up and act in the face of injustices). Bajaj's work suffers from the most common of seductive forms of oversimplification in the human rights education field. First, she provides an oversimplified version of human rights; which, second, becomes the mainstay of an oversimplified version of human rights education. This allows for 'naïve hope' to undercut the transformative potential of what should be one of the most powerful pedagogical endeavors in contemporary times. The perceived legitimacy of human rights universals constructed human rights education free from the demand of *pedagogical justification*. Consequently, because it could not set up and maintain the necessary critical distance between rights and its educational form, human rights education became the legitimating extension of human rights itself. It thus aided in what Slaughter (2007: 2) describes as a human rights that has reached rhetorical, juridical and political hegemony. This makes critical deconstructive analyses of human rights education toilsome, partly because a morally and diplomatically legitimated set of human rights standards have layered the possible *kernels* of the *radical form* of human rights education to such an extent that careful 'excavations' are required. Nevertheless, such analyses have been and are important because they may just be the most productive movement in the reconstitution of human rights education, especially in exploring the conditions that allowed such layering to materialize in the first place. It is to this possibility that I now turn my argument by risking a discussion on deconstruction and plasticity in relation to the *regenerative* options available to human rights education.

Derrida (1998: 27) argues that deconstruction "undeniably obeys an *analytic* exigency, at once critical and analytic" and always steering towards "*undoing, desedimenting, decomposing, deconstituting* sediments, *artefacta*, presuppositions, institutions [...]" This unbinding insists on the "irreducibility of difference" and the possibility and desire to recapture "the originary."

> Very schematically: an opposition of metaphysical concepts (for example, speech/writing, presence/absence, etc.) is never the face-to-face of two terms, but a hierarchy and an order of subordination. Deconstruction cannot limit itself or proceed immediately to a neutralization: it must, by means of a double gesture, a double science, a double writing, practice an overturning of the classical opposition and a general displacement of the system [...] Deconstruction does not consist in passing from one concept to another, but in overturning and displacing a conceptual order, as well as the nonconceptual order with which the conceptual order is articulated.
> (Derrida 1982: 329)

In an intricate series of studies by Derrida (see Mikics 2009), deconstruction has the metaphysics of presence and logocentrism as its target. The overturning and displacement of this system invokes its de-constitution. From this basis, deconstruction's movement of decomposing structures and practices establishes the referral to difference and otherness as an "asystematic reserve, a non-present remainder or heterogeneous other which exceeds all structures and systems even while making them possible [...] Deconstruction affirms an inappropriable difference, or the repressed other [...]" (Wortham 2009: 38). The asystematic reserve, though repressed, constitutes in part, the privileged centre of meaning. Thus, Taylor (2004) writing for the *New York Times*, suggests that the "guiding insight of deconstruction is that every structure [...] that organizes our experience is constituted and maintained through acts of exclusion."

Applying this reading to human rights education will inevitably lead to questioning the privileged centre of meaning-making that is based on what I refer to as 'an epistemology of diplomatic consensus.' That is, the truth indices of rights reside in the trade-offs of the diplomatic processes of the United Nations in Geneva and New York. Moreover, human rights education uncritically imports 'diplomatic truths' to frame the real-life experiences of individuals and groups in the image of such truths. But, such authority of truth can be overturned. For instance, refugee rights, instead of a *humanitarian* reading, may be interpreted as attempts at justifying the governance of the 'foreign' body within the logic of the nation state. For this reason, Soguk's (1999) *States and Strangers: Refugees and Displacements of Statecraft* offers a great example of a deconstructive reading in the field of human rights. The international construction of *refugee rights* can thus be shown to disclose the asystematic reserves of the inappropriable differences that it represses, and the violence that it allows, theoretically and materially. Privileging and repression, in this sense, serve the purposes of a discursive regime such as law and human rights to "constitute and regulate, imagine and test, kinds of subjects, subjectivities and social formations" (Slaughter 2007: 8). Similarly, Brown (2002: 459) argues that human rights "produce and regulate the subjects to whom they are assigned." In this scheme, human rights education is the major conduit through which the strategies of regulation are legitimized. Even in this troubling example of refugee rights, there are left over forms after deconstruction. Other examples may also be offered.

Tie (2009: 88), in response to the dislocations of human rights ensuing from deconstructive and 'postmodern' readings, suggests that such movements may close the possibility of the political commitments that accompany human rights. Taking issue with Ignatieff's (2004, cited in Tie 2009) argument that human rights allow for "the betrayal of liberty in the name of its defence" and Douzinas's (2000, cited in Tie 2009) "analysis of the complicity of human rights in the centralization of political power," Tie (2009: 89) argues that human rights may incite political contest with the "express purpose of giving effect to the materiality of the representations through which observing subjects encounter violations of human rights." How such materiality is uncovered is, of course, not this straightforward; neither is the claim that human rights can give effect to a materiality that is suffocated by standards. However, the possibility of the claim resides in plasticity, *after* the de-layering of standards. That is, the 'left over' forms of the political commitments of human rights may be re-activated by deconstructive readings and regenerated by a plastic reading.

What would be regarded as the substantive shifts between deconstruction and plasticity? I will limit my argument here to 'form,' a concept which seems to signify one of the major movements from Derrida's deconstruction to Malabou's plasticity. The metaphysics, against which Derrida battles, refers, in his understanding, to "the search for an essence behind or above sensible appearances" (Mikics 2009: 1). The task of a deconstructive reading is to show that such essences do not exist as privileged centres of meaning-making. Form, for Derrida, has such an intonation of 'essence.' He thus opts for 'trace' and argues that trace dissociates itself from form. The key to tracing the 'trace' resides in Derrida's treatment of the 'sign' in writing (Wortham 2009: 229–30):

> If every sign acquires its value only on the strength of its difference from other signs, nevertheless other signs leave their trace in the sense that they are constitutive of the difference that maintains the sign's identity. Every sign bears the traces of the others from which it differs, but to which it also defers in order to receive its value as a (differential) sign. The trace is thus not reducible to the sign, nor can it be turned into a sign.

The trace does not present itself as an essence or an originating kernel of meaning, because it can be substituted by other concepts such as *différance* or *supplement*. It appears as 'presence' with the traces of others that are 'absent' and thus escapes the metaphysical binary of presence/absence. However, the location of trace outside of metaphysics also places it outside of 'metamorphosis,' outside of 'transformation.' Therefore, deconstruction may limit the transformation it aspires to, given the rejection of form. 'Inconvertible,' is how Malabou (2010: 47) describes the trace's relationship to form: the trace cannot be converted to form since "the graphic element (of otherwise than Being) – namely the trace – definitely dissociates itself from the plastic element (of Being) – namely form." But one "must be in good shape to welcome the trace" argues Malabou (2010: 49), and thus she does not "believe in the absence of form or in a possible beyond of form [...] Form is the metamorphizable but immovable barrier of thought." The shift from deconstruction to plasticity now emerges as plasticity retains the transformable form that deconstruction rejects as metaphysical, even though the trace, as Malabou has showed, requires a 'shape' to welcome it. This explains plasticity's focus on the 'left over forms and shapes' in the wake of deconstruction. It is thus possible, and it is towards this possibility that I am now directing my attention, to argue that these forms are productive elements of and the necessary requirements for metamorphosis, transformation, change and regeneration.

Malabou's (2005) *The Future of Hegel* re-introduces the concept of plasticity to mean "the capacity to receive form and the capacity to produce form" (p. 9). Plasticity also refers to a philosophical attitude that Hegel described as a "sense of receptivity and understanding on the part of the listener" (p. 10) which Malabou (2005) paraphrased as the reader and interlocutor being "receptive to the form, but they in their turn are led to construct and form what they hear and read." She interprets Hegel's dialectic as a process of plasticity, "a movement where formation and dissolution, novelty and anticipation, are in continual interplay" (During 2000: 191). Hegel's dialectic does not lead, as generally interpreted, to a closure, but to a future that is open (p. 192). Steering away from 'transcendentalist' readings of Hegel, Malabou (2011: 65) insists that plasticity is "not an empty, transcendental instance." Rather, plastic reading is a "new, transformed type of structural approach" that "moves beyond what might appear to be the decisive limitations" of the deconstructive readings inaugurated by her teacher, Derrida (James 2012: 84). In essence, plasticity is the "shape or form of that which remains or survives in the wake of deconstruction," a "movement or passage between the formation and dissolution of form" (James 2012: 84).

The dialectic is regenerated as a forward movement because of its plasticity (Crockett 2011: xii) and therefore 'plasticity' might "power social, economic, political and personal transformation" (Shread 2010: xxx). On the *regenerative* inscription of transformation into dialectic, Malabou (2011: 88) suggests that "regenerative plasticity [does] ... speak to us of [...] regeneration without sublation," without *Aufhebung*. In this instance, Malabou writes about plasticity in relation to the neurobiological sciences via the plasticity of the brain; the insights from regenerative medicines; and the biological capacities for regeneration in, for instance, the salamander (Malabou 2011). Thus, in terms of analytical productivity, 'regenerative plasticity' without total negation or sublation surpasses the analytical movement of the 'deconstruction of form.' Here, human rights and human rights education are provided with *a way out*. It may reconstitute, transform and regenerate itself around the left over shapes in a plastic movement *after* deconstruction.

How may human rights education go about these transformative movements as located within plastic reading? Human rights education has to live the deconstruction of human rights, and thus its own. It must resist resisting deconstructive analyses to excavate its radical potential which has been suffocated by the massive off-load of human rights standards onto the principle of rights. Baudrillard (1999: 273–4) would have argued that these standards have expelled human rights from its own principle. There is a case to be made for a strangled or expelled principle (see Baxi 2008, 2009) if the dominant moral, political, juridical and rhetorical language of our time itself dissolves into the social pathologies it has to address. This, I contend, seems to be the case with human rights, and HRE. Nevertheless, plasticity would suggest that the left over form of the principle of rights can be regenerated so as to result in a metamorphosis of human rights itself.

Douzinas's (2006: 626) excursion has shown that the collapse of human rights into legal rights resulted in human rights forfeiting the critical distance necessary for "dissent, resistance, and rebellion against the domination of power, the oppression of wealth and the injustice of law." Human rights were thus already conscripted into serving the domination of power. Douzinas's deconstructive reading follows from Derrida's *Force of Law* (1992) in which his "primary concern in relation to justice is to distinguish between law and justice, to 'insist right away on reserving the possibility of a justice, indeed of a law that not only exceeds or contradicts 'law' (*droit*) but also, perhaps, has no relation to law, or maintains such a strange relation to it that it may just as well command the '*droit*' that excludes it" (Briggs 2012: 257–8; Derrida 1992: 5–6). Again, here, there is a law by the name of 'justice' that exceeds law (*droit*) as dependent on enforceability and, as such, is located beyond the limits of law itself (Borradori 2003: 164). This justice may mandate the very law that excludes it. The implications for human rights education should be shattering-transformative. Collapsing human rights into legal rights combines them into *droit* with the possibility of placing *justice* outside the operational horizons of human rights itself. Human rights education is therefore pre-determined by the institution of human rights as *droit* and suffers law's resistance towards deconstructive analysis which renders a 'plastic transformative' reading challenging.

Critical hope and the regeneration of human rights education

As a professional field with its associated discourses, a conscious movement towards deconstructive readings seems to me the only option viable to regenerate HRE. Nothing, in this context, would be closer to inertia and self-annihilation if our field does not respond to this challenge. This would simply be a first step to allow plastic readings. Following Malabou, there will be a 'left over' form of HRE after deconstruction which I chose to name 'critical hope' as that what which I regard to be an originary inscription into human rights education. In what follows, I link critical hope to the 'political' to remain consistent with Malabou's materiality of form, the materiality of plasticity and her aversion to a 'transcendental' interpretation and a *beyond* of form.

Benhabib (2011: 2), in *Dignity in Adversity: Human Rights in Troubled Times*, engages with the complexities of a human rights disclosed by deconstruction where her brand of cosmopolitanism does not denote "a privileged attitude but rather, a field of unresolved contrasts." This kind of cosmopolitanism is required because our times are "inhospitable to the practice of critique – especially self critique; ... [the] resignation to the contracting space of possibilities" (Kompridis 2006: 247) is palpable. With the dissolution of these possibilities, the future "may no longer to be open to us, no longer welcoming" (Kompridis 2006). This confirms the earlier analysis of human rights and HRE. That is, it is a symptom of total skepticism and despair to have an overload of human rights standards in the midst of unproductive social action, or inaction, against the human rights violations that are littering our social landscape. To counter this, Benhabib (2011: 192), following Bloch (1986), calls for the "revitalization of a utopian tradition for without hope alternative politics becomes impossible."

In Zournazi's (2002: 122) *Hope: New Philosophies of Change*, Mouffe and Laclau tie hope to "the passions that make up our everyday reflections on the world, and to our political activities." The short supply of hope, for Rorty (1999), is linked to the positioning of the philosophy of language and the foci on 'identity' and 'difference' which seem to "result in a loss of hope" or an "inability to construct a plausible narrative of progress" (p. 232). Hope, in the context of a Deweyan social democracy, is for Rorty located in a utopia in which the "moral identity of every human being is constituted in large part [...] by his or her sense of participation in a democratic society" (p. 238). I am, limitedly so, uneasy with the concept of hope as linked to *utopia*, that is so say, "that which can never be real" (Cheah and Guerlac 2009: 23). Derrida (Cheah and Guerlac 2009) argues that utopia "can too easily be associated with dreams" whilst the 'im-possible' is a "movement to desire, action, and decision: it is the figure of the very real. It has its hardness, closeness, and urgency."

In his engagement with Marxism, via *Specters of Marx* (1994) and *Ghostly Demarcations* (1999), Derrida also frames the messianic as referring to "the coming of the eminently real, concrete event [...] [a] straining forward toward the event" which makes it "inseparable from a promise and an injunction that call for commitment without delay" (Derrida 1999: 248–9). Here, Derrida's formulations of 'im-possibility' and the 'messianic' are associated with the political conception of 'critical hope' which takes on a 'material dimension' through plastic reading.

I align myself with conceptions of critical hope that are tied to Derrida's 'straining forward toward an event;' works within Benhabib's cosmopolitanism; are rooted in Mouffe and Laclau's understanding of hope as located in the political; aims at developing Rorty's plausible narrative of progress; and which is inseparable from Derrida's insistence on a commitment without delay. This framing of 'critical hope' can seamlessly transfer to the critical pedagogies of Freire (1995, 2007) and McLaren (2000). Freire is an obvious candidate for a conceptual rooting of 'critical hope' and, as Burawoy and Von Holdt (2012: 111) argue, he "is much more optimistic than Bourdieu, for he sees within the psyche two selves, the humanistic individual and the oppressor; the true self and the false self." Freire thus substitutes Boudieu's socioanalysis with a "heavy dose of psychoanalysis" (ibid.). It is the 'humanism' of Freire, which anchors his 'pedagogy of hope' (1995). Further, Freire's later collaborator, Giroux (2009: 3), thinks of 'educated hope' in an instructive and productive manner:

> Hope, [...], is the precondition for individual and social struggle, the ongoing practice of critical education in a wide variety of sites [...] But hope is also a referent for civic courage and its ability to mediate the memory of loss and the experience of injustice as part of a broader attempt to open up new locations of struggle.

Giroux's educated hope has to be integrated with the moral imperatives of hope within Rorty's analyses, and the Derridean ethical commitment towards the other without delay, which is a 'straining forward movement.' A human rights education that has this kind of hope inscribed in its make-up will be transformative. Critical hope, as argued, is, in the case of HRE, the name given to the left over form *after* deconstruction. A human rights education that lives the deconstruction of human rights can regenerate itself around the left over form in a plastic movement of a dialectic that is infinitely transformative and affirmative. Douzinas may then see human rights education as that which pedagogically develops the activist and social justice qualities of human rights *per se*. The dissent, resistance, and rebellion against the "domination of power, the oppression of wealth and the injustice of law" (Douzinas 2006: 626) may well turn out to be *the* new thickness around the left over form and *kernel* of human rights education. Plasticity suggests that this thickness will continually be the subject of a transformative dialectic.

Conclusion

The social theoretical argument that I pursue in this chapter has a simple aim and attempts a modest contribution. The following claims are made. First, human rights education is constituted by and constitutes the élan of despair that has paralyzed its potential as a radical pedagogical form. Second, human rights education has evolved into a conservative educational form with an uncritical relationship with human rights universals and law. Third, human rights education is meant to be radical simply in terms of the purpose historically assigned to human rights as the counterpoint of the domination of power. Fourth, human rights education pedagogically failed to nurture the radical possibilities of human rights and has contributed to its sterility and that of its own. Fifth, the massive project of human rights standards generation provided human rights education with a legitimacy that had the consequence of layering imprisonment. That is, human rights education became the pedagogical arm of human rights in a relationship of reciprocal legitimization, with negative consequences for its self-radicalization. Sixth, human rights education must live its own deconstruction and that of human rights to disclose its own 'left over' form that goes by the name of 'critical hope,' and which was originally etched into its logic and purpose. Seventh, plasticity enters *after* deconstruction to provide human rights education with the conceptual architecture to regenerate and re-constitute itself around the left ove' form of 'critical hope' as a process of radicalization to be infinitely moderated by a plastic reading of transformative dialectics. Eighth, human rights education has to recover the hospitality of critique whose absence is precisely one of the symptoms of the loss of critical hope.' That is, the very critical distance between human rights education and the universals that it is mandated to teach is an additional space for encrypting critical hope that makes 'resistance' and activism possible.

References

Andreopoulous, G.J. and Claude, R.P. (eds) (1997) *Human Rights Education for the Twenty-First Century*. Philadelphia, PA: University of Pennsylvania Press.

Bajaj, M. (2011) 'Human rights education: Ideology, location, and approaches', *Human Rights Quarterly*, 33: 481–508.

Baudrillard, J. (1999) 'The perfect crime'. In: O. Savic (ed.) *The Politics of Human Rights*. London: Verso.

Baxi, U. (2008) *The Future of Human Rights*, 3rd ed. New Delhi: Oxford University Press.

Baxi, U. (2009) *Human Rights in a Posthuman World*. New Delhi: Oxford University Press.

Benhabib, S. (2011) *Dignity in Adversity: Human Rights in Troubled Times*. Cambridge: Polity Press.

Bloch, E. (1986) *The Principle of Hope*. Cambridge, MA: MIT Press.

Borradori, G. (2003) *Philosophy in a Time of Terror*. Chicago, IL: University of Chicago Press.

Briggs, R. (2001) 'Just traditions? Deconstruction, critical legal studies, and analytic jurisprudence', *Social Semiotics*, 11: 257–74.
Brown, W. (2002) 'Suffering the paradoxes of rights'. In: W. Brown and J.E. Halley (eds) *Left Legalism/Left Critique*. Durham: Duke University Press.
Burawoy, M. and Von Holdt, K. (2012) *Conversations with Bourdieu*. Johannesburg: Wits University Press.
Cheah, P. and Guerlac, S. (2009) *Derrida and the Time of the Political*. Durham: Duke University Press.
Crockett, C. (2011) 'Foreword'. In: C. Malabou (ed.) *Plasticity at the Dusk of Writing*. New York: Columbia University Press.
Delanty, G. (2011) 'Varieties of critique in sociological theory and their methodological implications for social research', *Irish Journal of Sociology*, 19: 68–92.
Derrida, J. (1982) 'Signature Event Context', trans. A. Bass, *The Margins of Philosophy*. Chicago, IL: University of Chicago Press.
Derrida, J. (1992) 'Force of law: "The mystical foundation of authority"'. In: D. Cornell, M. Rosenfeld and D.G. Carlson (eds) *Deconstruction and the Possibility of Justice*. New York: Routledge.
Derrida, J. (1994) *Specters of Marx*. London: Routledge.
Derrida, J. (1998) *Resistances of Psychoanalysis*. Stanford, CA: Stanford University Press.
Derrida, J. (1999) 'Marx & sons'. In: M. Sprinker (ed.) *Ghostly Demarcations*. London: Verso.
Douzinas, C. (2000) *The End of Human Rights: Critical Legal Theory at the Turn of the Century*. Oxford: Hart Publishing.
Douzinas, C. (2006) 'Left or rights?' In: T. Campbell (ed.) *Review of Rights: A Critical Introduction, Journal of Law & Society*.
During, L. (2000) 'The future of Hegel: Plasticity, temporality, dialectic', *Hypatia*, 15: 196–220.
Flowers, N. (2004) 'How to define human rights education? A complex answer to a simple question'. In: B.B. Georgi and M. Seberich (eds) *International Perspectives in Human Rights Education*. Gutersloh: Bertelsmann Foundation Publishers.
Freire, P. (1995) *Pedagogy of Hope*. New York: Continuum.
Freire, P. (2007) *Pedagogy of the Oppressed*. New York: Continuum.
Giroux, H. (2009) *The Audacity of Educated Hope*. Online. Available <http://www.counterpunch.org/2009/01/23/the-audacity-of-educated-hope/> (accessed 2 October 2012).
Honig, B. (2006) 'Dead rights, live futures'. In: L. Thomassen (ed.) *The Derrida-Habermas Reader*. Chicago, IL: University of Chicago Press.
Ignatieff, M. (2004) *The Lesser Evil: Political Ethics in an Age of Terror*. Edinburgh: Edinburgh University Press.
James, I. (2012) *The New French Philosophy*. Cambridge: Polity Press.
Keet, A. (2010) *Human Rights Education: A Conceptual Analysis*. Saarbrücken: Lambert Academic Publishing.
Keet, A. (2012) 'Discourse, betrayal, critique'. In: C. Roux (ed.) *Safe Spaces: Human Rights Education in Diverse Contexts*. Rotterdam: Sense Publishers.
Knowles, D. (2004). *Political Philosophy*. London: Routledge.
Kompridis, N. (2006) *Critique and Disclosure*. Cambridge, MA: MIT Press.
Lynch, J., Modgil, C. and Modgil, S. (eds) (1992) *Human Rights, Education and Global Responsibilities*. London: Falmer Press.

McLaren, P. (2000) *Che Guevara, Paulo Freire and the Pedagogy of Revolution*. Lanham, MD: Rowman & Littlefield.
Malabou, C. (2005) *The Future of Hegel: Plasticity, Temporality and Dialectic*. London: Routledge.
Malabou, C. (2010) *Plasticity at the Dusk of Writing*. New York: Columbia University Press.
Malabou, C. (2011) *Changing Difference*. Cambridge: Polity Press.
Mikics, D. (2009) *Who Was Jacques Derrida?* New Haven, CT: Yale University Press.
Mouffe, C. and Laclau, E. (2002) 'Hope, passion, politics'. In: M. Zournazi (2002) *Hope: New Philosophies for Change*. Annandale: Pluto Press.
Rorty, R. (1999) *Philosophy and Social Hope*. London: Penguin Books.
Roux, C. (ed.) (2012) *Safe Spaces: Human Rights Education in Diverse Contexts*. Rotterdam: Sense Publishers.
Shread, C (2010) 'Translater's note'. In: C. Malabou (ed.) *Plasticity at the Dusk of Writing*. New York: Columbia University Press.
Slaughter, J.R. (2007) *Human Rights Inc.: The World Novel, Narrative Form and International Law*. New York: Fordham University Press.
Soguk, N. (1999) *States and Strangers: Refugees and Displacements of Statecraft*. Minneapolis, MN: University of Minnesota Press.
Suarez, D. (2006) *'Creating Global Citizens? Human Rights in Latin America and the Caribbean*. CA, USA: Stanford University.
Suarez, D. and Ramirez, F. (2004) 'Human rights and citizenship: The emergence of human rights education'. In: *Working Papers, Number 12*, Center on Democracy, Development, and the Rule of Law, Stanford Institute for International Studies.
Taylor, M.C. (2004) *The Real Meaning of Deconstruction*. Online. Available HTTP: <http://www.nytimes.com/2004/10/14/opinion/14iht-edtaylor.html?pagewanted=all&_r=0> (accessed 2 October 2012).
Tibbitts, F. (2002) 'Understanding what we do: Emerging models for human rights education', *International Review of Education*, 48: 159–71.
Tie, W. (2009) 'Beyond the dislocation(s) of human rights', *Social and Legal Studies*, 18: 71–91.
United Nations Non-Governmental Liaison Service (NGLS) (2008) *The United Nations Human Rights System: How To Make It Work For You*. United Nation: Geneva.
Wortham, S.M. (2009) *The Derrida Dictionary*. New York: Continuum.
Zournazi, M. (2002) *Hope: New Philosophies for Change*. Annandale: Pluto Press.

6 Critical hope
Deconstructing of the politics of HOPE at a South African university

Henk van Rinsum

Introduction

This chapter examines the HOPE project at the University of Stellenbosch, a former predominantly Afrikaner, and Afrikaans-speaking, university.[1] The HOPE project was initiated by the Professor Russel Botman, the rector of the university who assumed office in 2007 after an unsettled period during which the university was entangled in heated discussions about its institutional identity. Botman began his rectorship by introducing the concept of the pedagogy of hope. The chapter attempts to deconstruct the HOPE project by exploring a number of elements associated with the concept of critical hope.

The notion of critical hope stems from the book, *Pedagogy of Hope* (1992) by the educator Paulo Freire, which reflects on Freire's life and writings more than two decades after his world-famous *Pedagogy of the Oppressed* (1970). Freire suggests that radical transformation requires both hope for change and a struggle. The adjective *critical* is essential in this respect. As such, critical hope can be seen as part of an encompassing critical theory. Referring back to Horkheimer, critical theory seeks "to liberate human beings from the circumstances that enslave them" (Horkheimer 1982: 244). Critical theory has three components: it explains, it provides norms, and it initiates action. It explains the predicament the modern world finds itself in and the consequent suffering people have to endure, and based on norms of humanity it calls for human action to put an end to suffering.

The chapter begins by placing the HOPE project in a historical context by presenting it as a phase of the institutional history of the University of Stellenbosch. It then elaborates on the instruments of critical hope theory in a bid to deconstruct the work that took place. In particular, it theorizes about the concept of 'diversity,' which played a central role in the heated discussions on institutional identity referred to in the introduction. This is achieved with the assistance of reference to critical theory literature, particularly literature on critical diversity. The literature is used to show the deeper layers of the HOPE project. The chapter argues that the project offers an interesting example of a modern and visualized translation of a university's corporate social responsibility. However, the translation is one that fails to examine critically its own institutional culture, which still bears the demographic marks of a non-diverse university.

Stellenbosch University: Kraamsaal van Apartheid (Nursery of Apartheid)

To arrive at a proper analysis of the HOPE project, it is essential to provide a brief genealogy of the University of Stellenbosch. During apartheid, the South African system of higher education was shaped along the lines of racial segregation. Segregation had developed from the end of the nineteenth century, but reached its ideological peak between 1948 and 1990, when the higher education system acquired the 'classic' apartheid features. Apartheid required the development of three types of universities (see, for example, Vale 1997). The first type encompassed white Afrikaans-speaking universities, including the University of Stellenbosch, and was characterized by a conservative Afrikaner identity. Afrikaans was the exclusive and excluding language. The intricate relationship between Afrikaner professors, administrators, state officials and church leaders was couched in a semi-secret conservative Afrikaner society, the Broederbond, which strove to preserve and foster the unity of the Afrikaner people.[2] The second type comprised predominantly white English-speaking universities. Although also financially favoured by successive apartheid governments, these universities generally took a more liberal position, such as regarding the admission of black students. The third type was made up of black universities established during apartheid for the main black ethnic groups, such as Xhosa, Zulu, Sotho and Venda, as well as for the Indians and Coloureds. One exception in the latter category was the University of Fort Hare, which was established before the apartheid era. These 'bush colleges' embodied the system of apartheid in higher education. Mostly located in peripheral areas, they were understaffed as well as underfunded. Bozalek and Boughey (2012) conclude that these racially informed policies continue to have an impact on the system of higher education in South Africa.

Thus, the University of Stellenbosch was one of the historically advantaged universities. It was founded on the existing Stellenbosch theological seminary and the Stellenbosch Gymnasium, institutions created in the middle of the nineteenth century.[3] The gymnasium was transformed into Victoria College in 1887. In 1913, the Victoria College Council published a memorandum written by three influential Afrikaners, among them Daniël Francois Malan, who became the first Prime Minister of South Africa in 1948. The 1913 memorandum played an important role in persuading the South African government to establish an independent university in Stellenbosch and in shaping the identity charter of the future university. It reads as follows:

> This [i.e., Stellenbosch] is the place from which the *Afrikaner volk* [Afrikaner people] can best realize its ideals and exercise the largest influence in South Africa. It is the best realization the *volk* has yet found of a deeply-felt need. It stands for an idea! That's why it became, not merely an educational

institution, but the symbol and guarantee of its own powerful, growing, and expression-seeking, national life. [Translation by the author] (Thom *et al.* 1966: 65).

The memorandum clearly expresses the ideology and intimate connections between the institution and Afrikaner identity. In 1916, Victoria College was upgraded to the Universiteit van Stellenbosch. From then on, the University of Stellenbosch came to play a pivotal role in the development of an Afrikaner intelligentsia closely connected to the politics of Afrikaner nationalism and apartheid. Many prominent apartheid politicians, including four prime ministers (D.F. Malan, H.F. Verwoerd, B.J. Vorster and P.W. Botha) were linked closely to the University of Stellenbosch, whether as student, professor, or chancellor. However, the university was also home to more 'verligtes' (enlightened) and critical Afrikaner intellectuals, such as the philosopher, Johan Degenaar, who questioned the apartheid system (Nash 2009; see also Esterhuyse 2012). Chris Brink, Rector of the University of Stellenbosch from 2002 until 2007, stated that the university was referred to as the 'kraamsaal van apartheid' (nursery of apartheid) (Botha 2007). From its inception, the university became intimately connected to Afrikaner nationalism and apartheid, the Dutch Reformed Church (Nederduits Gereformeerde Kerk), and the National Party.

Confronted with the legacies of racial segregation in higher education after 1994, the new African National Congress (ANC) government embarked on a project of radical reform. The government wanted to redress the situation in higher education in which:

> There is an inequitable distribution of access and opportunity for students and staff along lines of race, gender, class and geography. There are gross discrepancies in the participation rates of students from different population groups, indefensible imbalances in the ratios of black and female staff compared to whites and males, and equally untenable disparities between historically black and historically white institutions in terms of facilities and capacities.
> (Department of Education 1997: 1.4)

The ANC government urged the universities, including the University of Stellenbosch, to engage in a process of transformation that would place them in line with the new post-apartheid era of "ensuring that the composition of the student body progressively reflects the demographic realities of the broader society" (Department of Education 1997: 2.24).

Strategic framework 2000: Inventing a new idea (of excellence, diversity and legacy)

As a former Afrikaner historically advantaged institution, the University of Stellenbosch had to cope with the loss of the prominent position it had held during the apartheid era and the legacies of its intimate links to the apartheid regime. It was forced to reformulate its ideological charter and to transform its identity into a post-apartheid society. At the same time, it needed to reposition itself as an institution of higher education in a period in which the predicament of universities globally had become the subject of debate caused by a neoliberal political and economic regime in Europe and the USA.

In 2000, a document entitled *Strategic Framework for the Turn of the Century and Beyond* was formally approved, in which the former Afrikaner university tried to reposition itself in a post-apartheid South Africa (University of Stellenbosch 2000). The document defined the university at three interrelated levels. Firstly, it observed the imperative of a global playing field for South African universities. The dominant paradigm on this playing field is the university as a market-oriented, entrepreneurial institution. *Excellence* was the nucleus of this narrative. Secondly, there was the new national South African political theatre to which Stellenbosch was forced to connect. The key words were *diversity* and *access*, a favoured concept that related strongly to the ideology of a new post-apartheid era in South Africa in which people from different backgrounds and of different colours should have access to the material and intellectual resources in society, including higher education. And thirdly, there was the predicament of an increasingly fragmented community that shaped the university, the community of the Afrikaners. In the Strategic Framework, we read: "The university acknowledges its historical ties with the people from whom and communities from which it arose [...] [T]herefore the University commits itself to be language-friendly, with Afrikaans as the point of departure." The Strategic Framework thus tried to combine excellence, diversity and recognition of its own legacy. The document gradually evolved into a new charter for the University of Stellenbosch.

Rector Chris Brink: 'Anatomy of a transformer'

During the rectorship of Chris Brink – not born and raised in the Stellenbosch 'Matie community'[4] – from 2001–2007, Stellenbosch was involved in tense discussions about its institutional identity, focusing on the issue of diversity and language, with the central question being whether Stellenbosch should remain an essentially Afrikaans-speaking institution of higher education with Afrikaans as the default medium of instruction or whether it should develop into a dual medium institution to accommodate students from different backgrounds.

Rector Brink unmistakably put his personal 'transformational' stamp on the debate about the implementation of the Strategic Framework. For him, the concept of transformation was connected closely with diversity. However, his rectorship was marred by the tensions between the imperatives to reposition the university and the inexorable institutional genealogy of Stellenbosch. Brink observed that Stellenbosch had become a place where two different constituencies were claiming ownership of the university. The first constituency was a primarily Afrikaner community; the other was a broader university community for whom Stellenbosch had to serve both Afrikaans and non-Afrikaans speakers – a community extending not only across language boundaries, but also across color and religious boundaries (Brink 2006: 91). The language debate about the default position of Afrikaans, thereby especially excluding black students and staff for whom Afrikaans was not their mother tongue, was the decisive element in the discussions. However, Afrikaans in this debate was not merely a language of communication but a marker of identity (for a personal account of the debate, see Van Niekerk 2012).[5]

Chris Brink left office – quite unexpectedly – in 2007, only one year after the beginning of his second term. He did not succeed in his attempts to implement a (critical) diversity concept. This was reflected in some of the conclusions of the Higher Education Quality Committee (HEQC) of the Council on Higher Education, following its audit of the university, published in January 2007. The report states: "The HEQC recommends that Stellenbosch University conduct a rigorous review of its access model in order to identify the reasons for the slow transformation of the institution's student profile particularly at the undergraduate level." The report further notes that "interviews conducted with staff and students suggest that there is a deeply ingrained conservatism in institutional structures, especially in relation to student services and residences." Accordingly, it recommends "that Stellenbosch University develop a comprehensive strategy to transform its institutional culture" (Council on Higher Education 2007).

HOPE project: Rebranding Stellenbosch

Brink's successor, and former vice-rector, Professor Russel Botman, began his term of office with a speech invoking the alluring idea of Stellenbosch becoming "a multicultural university with a pedagogy of hope for Africa."[6] The text of his speech was made available on the university's website (Botman 2007). He commenced his installation speech with a reference to the Strategic Framework. According to the new rector, the new institutional commitment was to achieve "equity, in terms (inter alia) of the bringing about of a corps of excellent students and academic and administrative staff members that is demographically more representative of South African society." Botman acknowledged the dilemmas of the university, including "credibility, relevance, student success, people management and Afro-centricity." Therefore, in Botman's own words, the university needed "to understand the core of [its] own institutional strength and establish a new pedagogical framework – a Pedagogy of Hope" (Botman 2007).

In explicitly bringing up the concept of Afro-centricity, Rector Botman made a reference to a meeting of Commonwealth Education Ministers in 2006 in Cape Town. One of the meeting's conclusions was that the African university required a closer connection to the international development agenda and, more specifically, "that the Millennium Development Goals will only be achieved in Africa, and elsewhere in the world, if there are flourishing systems of tertiary education." Thus the concept of the pedagogy of hope was connected with the Millennium Development Goals (MDGs). Botman also stressed the concept of Stellenbosch as a "multicultural place: a home for everyone, a home where cultures meet," and acknowledged the "need to welcome more black people here, in their full diversity." Botman connected the Afrikaans language, an essentially contested element in the diversity discussion on campus, with the pedagogy of hope.

> I believe we have for too long emphasized the pain of Afrikaans. And this is understandable. But what about the hope of Afrikaans? Afrikaans is the hope for a better life for a very large number of people across our country. As a developed academic language it also represents hope for the development of all our other indigenous languages.
>
> (Botman 2007)

Botman clearly wanted to mark a break with the past:

> The transformation of the university has been going through different phases. I take responsibility for the third phase. My two immediate predecessors, Profs. Andreas van Wyk and Chris Brink, formulated the University's Strategic Framework and led the subsequent phase of self-examination respectively. But the University has now done enough navel gazing. The phase during which I take over the leadership will lead us to the implementation of self-renewal.
>
> (Botman 2007)

This pedagogy of hope gradually developed into the new 'idea' of the university and replaced the notion of institutional transformation. The idea had to be marketed in what was called 'the HOPE project.' With the help of Ogilvy South Africa,[7] a big advertising company, the University of Stellenbosch launched the HOPE project on 21 July 2010. The three years that elapsed between the installation speech and the launch of the HOPE project, were labeled by Botman as the silent phase of the HOPE project. In his speech in which he launched the HOPE project, Botman explained what it represented. He mentioned three responsibilities central to the university. First of all, "given our history, we have a moral responsibility to the poor, to rural communities and to the diversity of individuals in our country." The second responsibility was the "historical responsibility to face up to the lingering burdens of the 20th century." The third was "to embrace the challenges of the 21st century." Therefore, the HOPE project envisaged three objectives for the University of Stellenbosch: to be of service to society; to be the best university it could possibly be for a new generation; and to galvanize others into joining the university in its quest to help make the world a better place (Botman 2010).

In this speech, Botman repeated the commitment initiated in the Strategic Framework to change the institution in terms of equity and service, but stressed the HOPE project's role in achieving the practical realization of this commitment. He stated that "We [i.e. the whole university] are the HOPE Project." Based on the MDGs, the university formulated five development themes, namely the eradication of poverty and related conditions; the promotion of human dignity and health; the promotion of democracy and human rights; the promotion of peace and security; and the promotion of a sustainable environment and a competitive industry.[8]

The essential part of the HOPE project as formulated by the rector during its launch was a large fundraising campaign. The goal was to raise funds of at least ZAR 1.75 billion (USD 200 million) by 2015. Botman ended his speech with a reference to the positive contribution the FIFA World Cup™ being held in South Africa made to the country and to the continent's image and self image. This opened "African eyes to Africa's potential. It united the people of this continent like never before – not around political slogans and aid programmes but around pride in our own achievements." With the help of Ogilvy South Africa, a website was developed to present the HOPE project to a larger audience. Under the website's main banner, the five MDGs are presented. Connected with these goals are different initiatives by the faculties listed on the website (every initiative has a tag for more information and how to donate). If one clicks on the tag of the HOPE project it says: "True builders of Hope [...] At Stellenbosch University, we believe that we are true builders of hope on the African continent." The website also presents in key words *Vision 2015*. This vision has the following objectives:

> establishing a new and future aligned niche in science; – being a pioneer in technology-driven learning and research; – developing (building) a new generation of academics, geared to tackling the challenges of a future knowledge economy – training new generations of graduates that have the flexibility to adapt to future careers, – establishing community interaction driven by development, – creating sustainable scientific solutions to meet Africa's challenges.
>
> (University of Stellenbosch, HOPE Project: n.d.)

In the subheading, 'Campaign Leadership,' an advisory committee is mentioned. This committee consists mainly of "notable South African entrepreneurs, business leaders and philanthropists who advise, advocate and guide the strategy of SU's [Stellenbosch University's] HOPE Project." Among the members are several chief executive officers (CEOs) of industrial firms, including Remgro Limited, Exceed Group, Buildman, PSG Group Limited, RGS Reinsurance Company and Santam Limited, Naspers Limited, Cluver Wines, Steinhoff International, and Rootstock Investment. Part of the fundraising campaign is the establishment of a "Friends of Stellenbosch University Foundation" and a Stellenbosch University SA Foundation UK[9] (University of Stellenbosch, HOPE Project: n.d.).

Ambiguity and deconstruction: A theoretical perspective

Ambiguous concepts that play a crucial role in discussions related to the HOPE project demand some deconstruction. The first one of these is 'diversity;' the second is 'corporate' – not explicitly used but, as the chapter will argue, highly relevant in the deconstruction of the HOPE project and a concept that may afford an alternative view from the perspective of critical hope. Both concepts can have different meanings in different discourses. In deconstructing these concepts and their context by making use of the academic work of Stellenbosch's own scholars, reference is made to the work of Johan Degenaar, a highly respected Afrikaner who taught in the Department of Political Philosophy from 1949 until 1991. Although highly respected, Degenaar was also a controversial person considered suspicious by university authorities during the days of apartheid because of his open mindedness and critical nature. Degenaar was the protagonist of what Andrew Nash has labeled the 'Socratic dialectical tradition' in a hostile environment of the University of Stellenbosch during the apartheid years. Degenaar advocated 'oop gesprek' (open discussion) as being imperative in the academic sphere. He introduced the concept of 'second reflection' (Van der Merwe and Duvenage 2008). First reflection is regarded as the most common form of reflection, in which we take concepts, terminology, language and the words we use for granted. This is how we are programmed to think and act. Second reflection is the Socratic discussion in which participants stand back and reflect critically on what they thought was already known and systematically defined without taking a stance. This second reflection leads to fundamental questions rather than to answers. It is a form of deep reflection in which participants are prepared to question their own way of thinking, their own knowledge system. Implicit presuppositions that we were unaware of will be unmasked and new vistas will open. It is precisely this second reflection that the chapter employs in analyzing some of the concepts used in the discussion about the institutional identity of the University of Stellenbosch. This discussion resembles the questions that Van der Waal posed in his article on diversity and language at the University of Stellenbosch (Van der Waal 2002).

Diversity: From easy pluralism to critical diversity

In this section I want to use the case study of the HOPE project at the University of Stellenbosch to engage in a critical approach of the concept of diversity. Management of diversity in the domain of higher education has been high on the agenda of administrators for many years now, especially at American universities. Many diversity experts are more than willing to assist in training courses on how to become 'diversity sensitive.' It is not without reason that one finds many references to a multimillion dollar 'diversity industry.' Diversity management has become an important feature of American university bureaucracies. This diversity concept celebrates the benefits of an increasingly diverse labor force, as was predicted in the *Workforce 2000 Report* published in 1987 by an American conservative non-profit think tank, the Hudson Institute. The report indicated that a more diverse workforce would yield more resources and skills than a homogeneous workforce. This diversity concept included not only gender and ethnicity but also categories such as age, sexual orientation, and disability (Cavanaugh 1997: 40). This non-critical diversity "is welcoming, inclusive, embracing; like international or pluralist or ecumenical, it [suggests] a largeness of conception, a transcendence of sectional interest, an openness to the variety of human pursuits and achievements" (Caws 1994: 381, cited in Cavanaugh 1997).

This 'easy pluralism' – colour-blind diversity – was expressed in what Elaine Swan called the "image of the diversity as a mosaic" (2010: 82). Swan also referred to Prasad *et al.* (1997), who talked about metaphors such as the melting pot, the patchwork quilt, and the mosaic (Swan 2010: 82). Visual elements, including websites, can help to celebrate and thereby strengthen the 'easy pluralism' diversity paradigm.

Unlike this 'easy pluralism' diversity concept, however, critical diversity examines all forms of social inequality, oppression and stratification that revolve around issues of difference. "A theory of critical diversity includes an analysis of exclusion, discrimination, and it challenges hegemonic notions of colorblindness and meritocracy" (Henderson and Herring 2012: 632). Zanoni *et al.* (2010: 13–14), in their critique of the diversity literature, formulate three points. First of all, the diversity literature conceptualizes identities as ready-made, fixed, clear-cut, easily measurable categories. Secondly, diversity literature, dominated by socio-psychological approaches, tends to downplay the role of organizational and societal contexts in shaping the meaning of diversity. Thirdly, it tends to neglect power dynamics.

These points of criticism can be found in a contribution by Cavanaugh in *Managing the Organizational Melting Pot* (1997), entitled '(In)corporating the Other? Managing the Politics of Workplace Difference' (Cavanaugh 1997: 31–53). Cavanaugh focuses on "diversity's metaphoricity, its capacity to connote multiple images to different people." He differentiates between the instrumental and symbolic workings of the use of the concept of diversity. "I also suggest that although diversity may not always appear to 'work' at one level (the instrumental), it can still be understood as smoothly operating on quite another (the symbolic)." In particular, Cavanaugh is interested in "diversity's rhetorical contribution to the reproduction of organization." Cavanaugh characterizes diversity as a "conceptual quick fix that repositions the status quo. Diversity 'management' may have more to do with affirming the given than changing it." It bears the connotation of an 'easy pluralism.' According to Cavanaugh, "the diversity discourse remains excruciatingly silent on the enduring 'demographic characteristics of those in positions of power'." In other words, the easy pluralism discourse will sustain, rather than remove, the inequality structures within an organization.

Corporate social responsibility

The (non-critical) diversity paradigm is part of what has been labeled corporate social responsibility, also referred to as corporate social investment. Generally, corporate social responsibility revolves around the relations between business and society. These relations are defined in terms of the different types of responsibility that firms have with regard to society at large (see, for example, the Kentucky Fried Chicken project of *Wall of Hope* mentioned in note 7).

In most theories, the concept of corporate social responsibility relates to private business organizations. However, it can also be applied to public organizations, and more specifically, to universities. When looking at universities, the adjective *corporate* has an ambiguous meaning, relating as it does to two ideal types of universities. This ambiguity can even result in what Shore has labeled the schizophrenic university (Shore 2009). One interpretation is of corporate as 'business-like,' where the university is managed as a business, sometimes referred to as the McUniversity (Parker and Jary 1995). Universities are increasingly positioning themselves as businesses. When analyzing mission statements of universities – cloaked in well-designed websites – one comes across quite different interpretations of the concept of social responsibility. Often, teaching and research itself are seen as making an important contribution to society. Universities educate students in ways that qualify them to take up responsibilities in society, and universities are engaged in research ranging from the sort referred to as 'blue sky' or cutting edge to commissioned research aimed at helping to solve social problems. Universities are understood as institutions of public good that have a (corporate) social responsibility to the society in which they operate. And, in the course of history, the meaning of 'society' has changed from a local town to a global world.

The other interpretation of corporate, although admittedly the less likely one in present-day usage, relates to a sense of community, of corporations as a kind of guild, in this case a guild of academics and students, the '*universitas magistrorum et scholarium*,' the corporation of teachers, scholars and students, as it was called in the early history of universities. Stellenbosch philosopher, Johan Degenaar, wrote an article entitled "Education for this time and place: Education is assistance towards fully becoming human," published back in 1982. Corporate then means "a corporation of lecturers and students communicating in a rational search for truth" (Degenaar 1982: 21). Here, he referred to the work of Jürgen Habermas who distinguishes three categories of cognitive interests, namely technical, practical (or communicative) and emancipatory. Degenaar – following Habermas as part of the critical theorists – was of the opinion that emancipatory interest is the most basic form of rationality. Therefore, he argues that:

> education can be described as the process of liberation through rationality which does not accept uncritically the shared meanings and values of a society but questions them on the basis of the criterion of emancipation to determine whether they mirror oppression (of any kind what so ever) or whether they constitute a non authoritarian way of life.
> (Degenaar 1982: 11)

According to Degenaar, the search for truth "should not remain a mere regulative idea for criticism. It must be translated into reality for in the long run it is only an emancipated society which can guarantee distorted communication" (Degenaar 1982: 14). In this way, the elements of the critical theory, explanation, norms, and action need to be strengthened.

When analyzing the concept of CSR within the universities, Kunal Basu and Guido Palazzo argue that the study of CSR is not so much about content as about "internal institutional determinants, such as the mental frames and sense making processes" within the organization (Basu and Palazzo 2008: 123). They define "sense making" as "a process by which individuals develop cognitive maps of their environment" (Basu and Palazzo 2008: 123). In the case of Stellenbosch, we need to analyze the relationship between internal institutional determinants – the handling of the legacy of apartheid at Stellenbosch; and the outcome of the CSR activities – the principles of the HOPE project.

Discussion

On 6 August 2012, a young Stellenbosch student, Pieter Odendaal, posted an open letter to Rector Botman in the *Vrye Student* blog. Odendaal referred to the legacy of Stellenbosch as a university that was closely connected to South Africa's apartheid regime. He argued that one has to acknowledge the institutional culture of this heritage while at the same time stressing the need to follow the path of a structural and true transformation for the institution. Odendaal identified three barriers to transformation that were preventing the influx of black students to Stellenbosch. The first was language, with Afrikaans as an excluding language. The second was the residence culture on campus. With one-third of students living on campus in residences, allegations had arisen of discrimination in some of these residences, which were said to promote a dominant white male, heterosexual identity, excluding students who do not fit. The third was the sustained occurrence of incidents of discrimination. At the end of his open letter, Odendaal made a reference to the rebranding of the university through the use of the HOPE project. He concluded by imploring Botman "to stop saying idealistic things and to start doing them" (Odendaal 2012).

Professor Botman commented on Odendaal's open letter on 4 September 2012. He confirmed that in his second term he wanted to focus "on the continuation of the diversity endeavour at all levels of the university [...] By working together and joining hands on the road ahead, our transformation endeavours will gain content and significance that will make SU a proud beacon of unity in our diversity." Botman also pleaded for "a little bit more understanding that a large vessel such as SU, with its complicated history, takes a bit longer to turn" (Botman 2012).

The open letter to Botman was not the first time that doubts had been voiced about Botman's pedagogy of hope. Van Louw and Beets, quoting Paulo Freire, who first conceptualized the pedagogy of hope, note that hope "as an ontological need, demands an anchoring in practice" (Van Louw and Beets 2011: 181). Van Louw and Beets argue that: "if SU does not ensure fearlessly that both formal and epistemological access is the privilege of everyone at the institution, the Pedagogy of Hope will be in danger of sinking into just another exclusive pedagogy for those who are epistemologically prepared, causing others to despair" (Van Louw and Beets 2011: 180). When analyzing the institutional developments at the University of Stellenbosch, one may argue that the HOPE project has more or less depoliticized the transformation process that Stellenbosch has undergone since apartheid's demise. The HOPE project, visualizing the pedagogy-of-hope ideology of the current rector, offers an image of a university that has left the phase of painful discussion behind and is heading towards a new post-conflict position. The phrasing found on the HOPE project website has a strongly positive connotation. Even John Lennon's song, *Imagine*, is present on a screen behind an image of the rector giving a speech ("You may say I'm a dreamer, but I'm not the only one. I hope someday you'll join us. And the world will live as one ...").[10] The HOPE project seems to serve as a modern visualization of a business-like CSR ideology. Pictures on the HOPE website and the connected blogs present a well thought-out mosaic image. Elaine Swan stresses the importance of visual imagery in diversity management, for example, through the mosaic metaphor presenting a 'happy diversity' model. A striking example of this mosaic metaphor is the front page of the magazine, *Matieland*, (2010: 1), which is entitled '*Jy is die HOOP Projek*' (*You* are the HOPE Project).

Eight vertical columns and eleven horizontal rows feature images of people from the University of Stellenbosch, including the rector, the vice-rectors and the deans, a mix of sexes, colours and ages, offering a celebration of diversity and inducing a personalized responsibility for the HOPE project. Notice also a quote from an interview with Rector Botman as published on the HOPE website, in which he says "Every time that a black student from a poor environment proudly enters the professional world as a Stellenbosch alumnus, it is hope that is at work." This is an example of how a critical diversity notion is depoliticized, for instance, regarding the demographic distribution on campus. Of course there is no denying that hope is at work when a black student from a poor environment proudly enters the professional world as a Stellenbosch alumnus. However, from a critical diversity perspective a fair question would be "but how many times will a black student from a poor environment proudly enter the professional world as a Stellenbosch alumnus, compared to students from a more wealthy rich white background?" From this perspective, the HOPE project can also be interpreted as a "rhetorical contribution to the reproduction of an organization" (Cavanaugh 1997).

As discussed, the audit report by the Higher Education Quality Committee of the Council on Higher Education stated that the University of Stellenbosch needed "to identify the reasons for the slow transformation of the institution's student profile particularly at the undergraduate level." If one analyses the figures of the *Fact Book 2011, Part 1: Students Enrolments 2011*, published by the university's Division of Institutional Research and Planning, the slowness of this transformation is still visible. The number of black undergraduate students was 617 in 2006 versus a total of 11,167 white undergraduate students. In 2011 the number of black students doubled to 1,297, but this still formed only 10 per cent of the number of white undergraduate students (University of Stellenbosch 2011). For the mainly English-taught postgraduate programmes, the transformation profile is more positive.

Even more striking is the head count of personnel with permanent appointments (University of Stellenbosch 2011). The percentage of black personnel in Category 1 Personnel (Instruction/Research) was only 4 per cent in 2011. The percentage of white C1 personnel remained above 80 per cent from 2002–2011. The number of personnel with a Coloured background rose from 6 per cent in 2002 to 12 per cent in 2011. The percentage of Coloureds in Category 2 Personnel (Administrative and technical personnel) rose from 23 per cent in 2002 to 39 per cent in 2011 and in Category 3 (Service workers), where people from a Coloured background have an overwhelming majority of 90 per cent.

Textual and visual analysis indicates that the HOPE project works as a metaphorical discourse carrying a positive and celebrating connotation while at the same time stressing its CSR in South Africa and in Africa at large. As such, it is an example of a deliberate policy – in the words of Cavanaugh, a pre-emptive ideological project – of the management of meaning through institutional accounts on the part of the university authorities. The HOPE project is part of a modern development to demonstrate publicly the CSR of organizations, including public organizations such as universities. As such it combines the celebratory concepts of 'excellence' and 'accountability' without involving a fundamental and critical analysis of the organization itself. As Cavanaugh states, "Otherness is, in effect, dissolved by rising above differences and joining together in the solidarity of a common purpose, the organization's success" (Cavanaugh 1997).

Conclusion

This chapter is a contribution to the further development of theoretical perspectives on critical hope. It does not concern critical hope in the actual educational practices. Rather, in adopting Degenaar's concept of the second reflection, it attempts to critically engage the work of the HOPE project at Stellenbosch University by asking a number of fundamental questions. It argues that the HOPE project is an example of a business-like branding of a modern organization, in this case a modern university, stressing its CSR. However, at the same time, this modern university is still caught up in the struggle to overcome its apartheid legacy. The HOPE project attempts to invoke the image of a modern university stressing a 'happy' diversity culture, thereby covering up some of the lasting and damaging elements of the apartheid legacy.

The HOPE project of the University of Stellenbosch can only be a true HOPE project fostering critical hope education if it serves the emancipatory interest in education, and if it combines this with critical self-examination at every level of the institution. The HOPE project can only be a *critical* HOPE project if it combines hope, struggle and criticality in its educational practices.

Notes

1 People claiming to be *Afrikaners* were mobilized around the idea of being an ethnic group in South Africa that descended from Dutch, French, and German settlers. Their native tongue is Afrikaans. Afrikaans derives primarily from seventeenth-century Dutch, as well as from other languages. South Africans of British descent can be seen as a separate ethnic group from Afrikaners. Their first language is English.
2 For an excellent introduction to the Afrikaners, I refer to Hermann Giliomee's *The Afrikaners* (2003).
3 For an (uncritical) early history of the University of Stellenbosch, see Thom, H.B. et al. (eds) *Stellenbosch, 1866–1966; Honderd Jaar Hoër Onderwys* (1966).
4 Matie is the collective name given to Stellenbosch University students. In a broader sense, Matie – which is probably derived from the word 'maat' (buddy, mate) – serves as an indication of the university's intimate academic culture.
5 South Africa has 11 official languages: Afrikaans, English, Ndebele, Northern Sotho, Sotho, Swazi, Tswana, Tsonga, Venda, Xhosa and Zulu. Recent figures from South Africa's Census 2011 (Census in brief) show that the most common first language spoken by South Africans is Zulu (23 per cent), followed by Xhosa (16 per cent), and Afrikaans (14 per cent). Afrikaans is spoken not only by a majority of whites but also by 90 per cent of Coloured people.
6 Russel Botman is Rector and Vice-Chancellor of the University of Stellenbosch. Coming from the former Coloured University of the Western Cape, he joined Stellenbosch University in 2000 as Professor in the Faculty of Theology. In 2002 he was appointed Vice-Rector. Botman is an internationally known theologian. He has served as President of the South African Council of Churches.
7 Ogilvy is a large marketing communications network with offices in many countries. On its website, Ogilvy South Africa writes: "Established in 1984, Ogilvy South Africa has been one of the largest leading advertising and communications groups in South Africa for over 25 years. […] Ogilvy South Africa clients include a mix of local and multinational companies. The mission is to build magnetic brands – which in turn help clients build their businesses. The Brand Liberation philosophy of using breakthrough ideas to release the potential that exists in brands is Ogilvy's raison d'être, and is the cornerstone of the agency."
Online. Available HTTP: <http://www.ogilvy.co.za/news/ogilvy-continues-winning-streak-at-adfocus/>. Ogilvy assisted the South African brand of KFC in launching a *Wall of Hope* campaign in 2009 as part of the corporate social investment strategy. Part of the campaign was to develop a new website with a donation mechanism in order to raise more money towards hunger relief. Online. Available HTTP: <http://www.ogilvy.co.za/2011/06/kfc-wall-of-hope/>.
8 The MDGs are eight international development goals for 2015 that were officially established following the Millennium Summit of the United Nations in 2000. The goals are (1) eradicating extreme poverty and hunger; (2) achieving universal primary education; (3) promoting gender equality and empowering women; (4) reducing child mortality rates; (5) improving maternal health; (6) combating HIV/AIDS, malaria, and other diseases; (7) ensuring environmental sustainability; and (8) developing a global partnership for development.
9 It is interesting to note that the University of Stellenbosch has a long tradition of binding CEOs of commercial conglomerates to the academic community of Stellenbosch by awarding them honorary doctorates. Examples include Paul Cluver (of Paul Cluver Wines) in 2000; Ton Vosloo (of Naspers) in 2001; Johann Rupert Junior (of the Rembrandt Group and since 2009 Chancellor of the University of Stellenbosch) in 2004; Karel Bos (of BOSAL) in 2005; Bill Gates (of Microsoft) in 2006; Wendy Luhabe (a leading business women) in 2006; Koos Bekker (of Naspers) in 2007; Peter Wallenberg (of the WallenbergGroup) in 2009; G.T.

Ferreira (of the FirstRand Group) in 2011; and Roelof Botha (a leading investor in South Africa) in 2012.
10 The image can be found on the HOPE project's website at <http://thehopeproject.co.za/hope/HOPE Week/galageleentheid(5).jpg>.

References

Basu, K. and Palazzo, G. (2008) 'Corporate social responsibility: A process model of sensemaking', *Academy of Management Review*, 33(1): 122–36.
Blowfield, M. and Frynas, J.G. (2005) 'Setting new agendas: critical perspectives on corporate social responsibility in the developing world', *International Affairs*, 81(3): 499–513.
Botha, A. (2007) *Chris Brink: anatomy of a transformer*. Stellenbosch: Sun Press.
Botman, R.H. (2012) 'Rector responds to Dagbreek apology and open letter about transformation', University of Stellenbosch, *News*, 4 September. Online. Available HTTP: <http://blogs.sun.ac.za/news/2012/09/04/rector-responds-to-dagbreek-apology-and-open-letter> (accessed 11 December 2012).
Botman, R.H. (2010) 'Public launch of Stellenbosch University's Hope project', 21 July. Online. Available HTTP: <http://www.sun.ac.za/university/Management/rektor/docs/HOPE_Project.pdf> (accessed 11 December 2012).
Botman, R.H. (2007) 'A multicultural university with a pedagogy of hope for Africa', Speech on the occasion of his installation, 11 April, Stellenbosch University. Online. Available HTTP: <http://www.sun.ac.za/university/Management/rektor/docs/russelinstallation speech.pdf> (accessed 11 December 2012).
Bozalek, V. and Boughey, C. (2012) '(Mis)framing higher education in South Africa', *Social Policy & Administration*, 46(6): 688–703.
Brink, C. (2006) *No Lesser Place: The Taaldebat at Stellenbosch*. Stellenbosch: Sun Press.
Cavanaugh, J.M. (1997) '(In)corporating the Other? Managing the politics of workplace difference'. In: P. Prasad, A.J. Mills, M. Elmes and A. Prasad (eds) *Managing the Organizational Melting Pot: Dilemmas of Workplace Diversity*. Thousand Oaks, CA: Sage.
Council on Higher Education (2007) *Executive Summary Audit Report on Stellenbosch University, Report of the HEQC to Stellenbosch University*. Online. Available HTTP: <http://www.che.ac.za/auditing/instaudited/reports/Audit-Report_SUN_Jan2007.pdf> (accessed 11 December 2012).
Degenaar, J.J. (1982) 'Education for this time and place: Education is assistance towards fully becoming human', KwaDlangezwa: University of Zululand.
Esterhuyse, W. (2012) *Eindstryd: Geheime Gesprekke en die Einde van Apartheid*. Cape Town: Tafelberg.
Freire, P. (1992) *Pedagogy of Hope: Reliving Pedagogy of the Oppressed*. New York: Continuum.
Freire, P. (1970) *Pedagogy of the Oppressed*. New York: Herder and Herder.
Giliomee, H. (2003) *The Afrikaners: Biography of a People*. London: Hurst and Company.
Henderson, L. and Herring, C. (2012) 'From affirmative action to diversity: Toward a critical diversity perspective', *Critical Sociology*, 38(5): 629–43.
Horkheimer, M. (1982) *Critical Theory*. New York: Continuum.
Nash, A. (2009) *The Dialectical Tradition in South Africa*. New York: Routledge.

Odendaal, P. (2012) *Open Letter to Rector Botman*, 6 August. Online. Available HTTP: <http://vryestudent.com/profiles/blogs/open-letter-to-professor-botman-vice-chancellor-and-rector-of1> (accessed 11 December 2012).

Parker, M. and Jary, D. (1995) 'The McUniversity: Organization, management and academic subjectivity', *Organization*, 2(2): 319–38.

Prasad, P., Mills, A.J., Elmes, M. and Prasad, A. (eds) (1997) *Managing the Organizational Melting Pot: Dilemmas of Workplace Diversity*. Thousand Oaks, CA: Sage.

Shore, C. (2009) 'Beyond the multiversity: Neoliberalism and the rise of the schizophrenic university', *Social Anthropology*, 18(1): 15–29.

South Africa, Department of Education (1997) *Education White Paper 3: A Programme for the Transformation of Higher Education*. Pretoria: Government Printer.

Swan, E. (2010) 'Commodity diversity: Smiling faces as a strategy of containment', *Organization*, 17(1): 77–100.

Thom, H.B. *et al*. (eds) (1966) *Stellenbosch, 1866–1966: Honderd Jaar Hoër Onderwys*. Cape Town: Nasionale Boekhandel Bpk.

Turner, T. (1993) 'Anthropology and multiculturalism: What is anthropology that multiculturalists should be mindful of it?' *Cultural Anthropology*, 8(4) 411–29.

University of Stellenbosch, HOPE Project (no date), 'About the Hope Project'. Online. Available HTTP: <http://thehopeproject.co.za/hope/Pages/default.aspx> (11 December 2012).

University of Stellenbosch, Division for Institutional Research and Planning (2011) *Fact Book 2011*. Online. Available HTTP: <http://www.sun.ac.za/irp> (11 December 2012).

University of Stellenbosch (2000) *Strategic Framework for the Turn of the Century and Beyond*. Online. Available HTTP: <http://www.sun.ac.za/university/stratplan/index.htm> (accessed 11 December 2012).

Vale, P. (1997) 'Southern African universities: New times, old divides'. In: I. Krukkert, C. Sadee and G. van Westrienen (eds) *COHESA Directory: Co-operation in Higher Education Between the Netherlands and Southern Africa*. The Hague: Nuffic.

Van der Merwe, W.L. and Duvenage, P. (2008) *Tweede Refleksie: 'n Keur uit die Denke van Johan Degenaar*. Stellenbosch: Sun Press.

Van der Waal, C.S. (2002) 'Diverse approaches in a South African debate on language and diversity in higher education', *Anthropology Southern Africa*, 25(3&4): 86–95.

Van Louw, T. and Beets, P.A.D. (2011) 'Towards anchoring hope', *South African Journal of Higher Education*, 25(1): 168–82.

Van Niekerk A.A. (2012) 'Op soek na identiteit: Die taaldebat op Stellenbosch'. In: H. Ester, C. van der Merwe and E. Mulder (eds) *Woordeloos tot Verhaal: Trauma en Narratief in Nederlands en Afrikaans*. Stellenbosch: SunMedia.

Zanoni, P., Janssens, M., Benschop, Y. and Nkomo, S. (2010) 'Guest editorial: Unpacking diversity, grasping inequality: Rethinking difference through critical perspectives', *Organization*, 17(1): 9–29.

Part III
Critical Race Theory/Postcolonial perspectives on critical hope

7 Critical hope and struggles for justice
An antidote to despair for antiracism educators

Ronald David Glass

This chapter explores Paulo Freire's insight that "hope is an ontological need" (Freire 1994b: 8) and argues that critical hope grounded in struggles for justice provides the best antidote to despair about the persistence of oppression. It situates this analysis within elements of the author's personal history, and it deploys the argument to critique some false hopes that contribute to the despair that often limits the social and political commitments of white antiracism educators in the USA and related contexts. The chapter shows that an understanding of critical hope, a hope without a definite object, strengthens the resolve needed to keep antiracist social justice reformers moving toward their dreams.

Hope as ontological need and political force

The struggle for justice is a story of hope as a primordial human quality, as an ontological need, being shaped into a political force. Hope reveals possible futures in the present, but a particular future only comes into being through choices and commitments. As Freire (1994b: 97) argues, human beings cannot be understood as "simply *living*" but must be seen "as historically, culturally, and socially *existing*." That is, to be human is to make history and culture even as history and culture make us. This is historicity, and it is at the core of human reflective action, of the praxis that enables us to go beyond the limits of the present. Generally, our actions reproduce the common sense shaped by dominant ideologies deeply rooted in our past and pervasive in our present, and thus create a future that largely repeats the past and reinforces oppressive social conditions. But hope exists ontologically because alongside this future that is repetition is an always-available possibility of alternative futures that are opened up by our intentional commitments, conscious choices, goals, and dreams. These competing and contested futures get enacted step-by-step, and must traverse both exterior realities and interior psychological spaces; this journey constitutes the praxis of freedom that lies at the heart of the struggle for justice (Glass 2001; Horton and Freire 1990).

History and culture condition the opportunities as well as the limits within each situation; yet each situation is ineradicably open because human beings are the builders of the history, culture, and situations within which they exist. When we achieve the kind of distance from the situation that lets us see into its depths, we grasp that the given limits are not fated realities but are rather obstacles and boundaries created in the course of human events. We then can struggle to enact "a breach with the real, concrete economic, political, social, [and] ideological ... order" (Freire 1994b: 99) that intervenes into the historical causal forces of the situation. This intervention strives toward "untested feasibilities" embodied in specific committed actions aimed at remaking the world; these critically conscious "limit-acts" transform ontological hope into critical hope and a political force that emerges into history (Freire 1994a: 94, 1994b: 105).

Critical hope made manifest as political force "demands an anchoring in [a] practice" (Freire 1994b: 9) that is hard work and requires significant effort, not only by individuals, but also by movements. Actions that grasp the *raison d'être* of the present situation and reach beyond current limits, extend the horizon toward possible futures (toward our dreams of justice). This critical hope cannot be animated by a righteous perfectionism nor by wishful idealism; rather, it is grounded in actual situations with their particular limits and possibilities, and it clings to the truth of the human power to change what is within reach. Justice is not achieved in some once-and-for-all cataclysmic upheaval that gives birth to a *de novo* reality; instead, justice is achieved always incompletely, and only step-by-step, situation-by-situation, specific context by specific context. This is not to deny that in some unpredictable moments of history, localized changes expand rapidly into transformative leaps forward that reshape an era, and indeed this is when movements come fully into being. But such leaps and movements rely entirely on the innumerable small steps by many people that both precede them and underlie their continuing development. Critical hope identifies possible actions that embed strategic political force despite situational limits; it recognizes that justice lies beyond each new horizon and requires ongoing work and struggle. It is precisely the embodiment of this work and struggle in a way of life that avoids the trap of despair.

Some believe that the persistence of injustice and the disappointments of both individual actions and social justice movements show the futility of hope as well as of struggle; some claim that these struggles have proven to be failures. But these views miss the "fineness of the striving" and the value built into the ethic of the struggle itself; they don't understand that justice is "a job to do in history" and not an achievement that finds completion (Freire 1994b: 50). Those who lose hope over the limits of what can be done and despair over what remains unachieved despite the efforts and sacrifices of millions of people are caught in an illusion of the unqualified power of both individual agency and social movements in the face of pervasive oppressive ideologies. Ontological hope that becomes critical and exerts political force is not naïve about either the limits or the power of struggles for justice, and it persists in the determination to open up future possibilities through unending actions aimed toward visions of a better world.

When we understand ourselves as persons who make history even as it makes us, then we know that if we daily dedicate ourselves to the tasks immediately within our reach, the wheel of history would turn more quickly and enlarge the sphere of justice. But we cannot know with certainty when our individual efforts, each a raindrop on the parched earth of oppression, each making its own impression and change, might join others to form rivulets and streams that shape the countryside, and eventually the rivers and oceans that alter the face of the earth itself. Only when we are in the fight day-to-day are we prepared for the large battles, and only when many are prepared for large battles can we marshal the force needed to win substantive victories. The Nobel laureate poet Seamus Heaney (1991: 77; emphasis in original) put this truth into these telling lines:

> History says, *Don't hope*
> *On this side of the grave.*
> But then, once in a lifetime
> The longed-for tidal wave
> Of justice can rise up,
> And hope and history rhyme.

Hope in antiracism struggle

When hope is not critical, it can become lost in despair. This can often be seen among white educators desiring to follow an anti-racism road. Audrey Thompson (2004) argued that white engagement with racism in classrooms was necessarily marked by dynamic uncertainties deriving from its ongoing (re)construction of processes and pathways and its relational character. These "anti-racist work zones" elude detailed mapping to guide anti-racism efforts, and they cast doubt on any expectations of forward progress or of definite destinations. These conditions can unsettle the hopes of white anti-racism teachers, who want clear directions to follow and few delays, detours, or distractions along the way. They wish that theory could insure their arrival at an anti-racist future, that they could travel a "Freirean freeway," "Hybridity highway," "Race Traitor toll way," "Critical Race Theory thoroughfare," "White Stage Theory turnpike," or an "Exceptional Whites expressway" and soon be done with the difficult transformative work required of them (Thompson 2004: 389).

But movement toward justice is slow, with more stops than gos, and the anti-racism road requires constant fabrication; moreover, its builders do not always know what they are doing. "Half the time, the drivers themselves have to get out of their cars and work on the roads themselves, in addition to doing repairs on their own cars" (Thompson 2004: 389). Anti-racist whites generally travel alone, keeping their hopes up by imagining they will arrive somewhere, with their righteousness guaranteed, and with people of color waiting with open arms to greet them. Thompson argued that this "white solipsism" and desire to be a "good white" not only continued the marginalization of people of color but also failed to grasp the relational nature of anti-racism action and of race itself (Thompson 2004: 390–1).

Stephen Haymes, responding to Thompson at a conference of philosophers of education, puzzled over why whites seemed to be so distraught about this situation, and called for an "existential phenomenological exploration of the lived reality of whiteness" (Haymes 2004: 397). The interchange between Thompson and Haymes sparked an intense discussion among an almost entirely white audience of about twenty people. Tales of woe and despair similar to those that Thompson had analyzed and that perplexed Haymes poured forth. Several people shared their experience of a melancholy arising within them when they glimpsed the unreliable nature of the anti-racism road and the enormity of the tasks required to get anywhere at all given how deeply interwoven racism is throughout the US cultural and institutional fabric, even including the most intimate domains of everyday life. Some people shared a moral anxiety connected to the impossibility of extracting themselves from racial privilege, and to the difficulties of overcoming suspicions and being accepted as an ally within communities of color. Some wondered aloud if they should devote themselves to some more obtainable social justice goal.

Racial privilege positions whites to miss how race permeates each situation and interaction; thus when the weight of US racist history becomes manifest and felt by them, they can be shocked and subdued. When they do act in response, they usually are isolated and unattached to the actual anti-racism struggle that ceaselessly ebbs and flows around us, therefore it is easy for them not to understand that anti-racism struggle is not a particular act or part-time commitment, but rather is a way of life. Without a precise end or certain way forward, the struggle for racial justice is morally challenging and emotionally draining, but it is also morally grounding and deeply enlivening. The liberation road is "made by walking" (Horton and Freire 1990: 3), without shortcuts or other ways to travel; all who travel this road must walk their own way, but they still are never truly alone and are always sustained by the continuing force of historical liberation movements.

The audience comments in reaction to Thompson and Haymes reflected not only racial privilege, but also traces of our postmodern moment. As Frederick Jameson (2000) argued, we live in a time of depthless superficiality in which enthusiasm and transitory highs get mistaken for hope. The intensities and euphorias of late capitalist consumer culture masquerade as hope, and when not rapidly superseded by one another, despair readily overtakes them. Moreover, the postmodern fragmentation of the self and of time replaces the actual historical past with nostalgia, and replaces a possible future achieved through struggle with ephemeral passions easily dispelled by the resistance of the real. Thus liberal whites caught up in these ideological structures have no grounded basis for anti-racism work, and they pursue illusory destinations that are nowhere at all.

As the discussion unfolded, I recalled the stock greeting between my friend Marc and myself as we each battled cancer: "Down but not out!" Marc's ferocious malignancy had bested him only several weeks earlier, while my less virulent disease was vanquished. With death looming (as it always is), any life remaining offers hope enough for taking the fight forward. Critical hope is the most reliable antidote to despair in the struggle for justice because life means we still embody our enduring capacity to make history and culture at the same time as history and culture make us. Our continuing life in the struggle means that the evils and injustices of the day remain that much more precarious.

Of course false hopes and despair can tempt anyone; we cannot be immune to the times in which we live, nor to the racist, sexist, classist, and other ideologies that inhabit us. Moreover, anti-racism and liberation struggles exact a heavy toll. Even when movements achieve great victories, opening up social, economic, and political possibilities that were barely imaginable only a generation earlier, the distance separating us from a just society remains beyond measure as surely as the defining power of racism remains unrelenting. Such contradictions mark the most intimate paths as well as the most public roadways that we must travel; there is no escaping the multitude of ways that race matters in our society. Critical hope cannot take away the suffering, and it does not seek to do so; but it inoculates us from the despair that only undermines the efficacy of the struggle and comforts the enemies of justice. When one is engaged fully in the liberation struggle of antiracism work, then one might get down now and again, one feels the pain of the violence built into the situation of oppression, but that is far from being out, from being dead, and so hope and struggle live on together. As Paulo Freire (1994a: 73) declared, "As long as I fight, I am moved by hope; and if I fight with hope, then I can wait." This waiting is not passive or despairing; it is a readiness to take advantage of any strategic opening to carry the fight forward.

Every situation has possibilities for antiracist struggle, and as our experience in struggle grows we learn to discern those possibilities more clearly. When our personal agency is linked with collective action, then we see how critical hope becomes manifest as not just personal efficacy but political force. My own engagement with antiracist struggle over 50 years illustrates the evolution of the critical consciousness undergirding critical hope and the way individual actions achieve political force (Glass 2008, 2010, 2012). In my youth, small challenges to racist stereotypes or the tellers of racist 'jokes' still packed sufficient force to transform those immediate situations. With experience, my courage grew, and as my fears became less fearsome (without ever vanishing), I engaged a broader and riskier range of situations. I discovered that "[t]he more you recognize your fear as a consequence of your attempt to practice your dream, the more you learn how to put into practice your dream" (Freire and Shor 1986: 57).

My steps followed my parents' steps as they similarly overcame their fears; their steps followed countless others who had risked everything in movements for justice that could be traced back to the earliest memories of our people. My father admonished me to see our actions as fundamental life commitments and self-interested solidarity, not as charity. We were not seeking righteousness, nor proving our exceptionalism, but rather we acted from the moral and political obligations made evident in the historical shadow cast by the Nazi holocaust, which was halted only a few years before my birth. He made clear that, as Jews, we were safe only to the degree that the society was just for all. Each of us was responsible to history when we engaged the injustices we faced in daily life.

Yet however much transformative force we could enact in our particular situations, our actions did not move institutions or the community until they were part of the eruption of the Civil Rights movement in the early 1960s.

Becoming one among countless unnamed people across many generations who have fought racial domination and who have stood up for justice, I learned that antiracist struggle is not some particular action, or even a series of particular actions. Rather, it is a way of life that finds room for transformative action in every space, no matter how tight. My social and institutional resources expanded as I matured and collaborated with others in numerous organizations and committees, so the impact of my antiracism interventions extended into larger spaces. Yet even having adopted this antiracism way of life, I receive the benefits of 'white' skin privilege and I remain infected by racist ideologies that must be continually critiqued. The possibility of a non-racist purity is a myth for those who risk little and venture no further than their own feelings, clinging to a desire for righteousness and the comfort of their privilege. Yet it is only by becoming embodied in lifelong commitments that hope, as an ontological need, becomes critical, and becomes part of the ongoing assertion of political force on behalf of justice.

False hopes and induced despair in education

Global rightist forces seem intent on shaping a future for poor children and children of colour that will be defined by schooling without meaning, jobs without significance, consumption without satisfaction, and war without end. Related educational policies narrow schooling to instrumental and vocational ends whose achievement can be measured so that schools and teachers can be held accountable. In the USA, education bureaucrats articulate a hope for closing the 'achievement gap' among racial groups by promising that publicly measuring student standardized test performances will force schools to strengthen the teaching and learning for low-income, racially, culturally and linguistically diverse (LI/RCLD) students, thereby improving their life opportunities. But instead, this facilitates the coercive and punitive management of the teachers and students in LI/RCLD schools, and at the same time enables the government to evade responsibility for the negative consequences of its policies and the actual social conditions that impact test performances. Sadly, as pressures mount on schools to conform to test-driven mandates, creative teaching and critical learning quickly become casualties (McNeil 2000), and LI/RCLD students do not receive the learning opportunities needed for critical citizenship and for realizing the deepest possibilities for human flourishing.

The truth is that neoliberal schooling leaves unaddressed the test score gap's root causes in an "education debt" (Ladson-Billings 2006), in inequities in school funding, teacher quality, family income and employment, and access to health care and quality nutrition (Anyon 1997; Orfield and Kornhaber 2001). Even when educators strive toward "college for all" they generally fail to attend to the substantial class and race inequities hidden within that discourse and those policies (Glass and Nygreen 2011). That is, neoliberal schooling policies protect racial privilege even while purporting to challenge it, and the false hopes they raise provide cover for an agenda that actually hardens the inequities in the foundational systems of society. These false hopes and hardened inequities can readily engender despair in LI/RCLD communities, and this despair becomes easy to exploit by the dominant because it also undermines the very forms of resistance that the communities need to struggle for justice effectively. But critical hope challenges these deceptive policies and focuses on remedies that impact the underlying structures that shape everyday realities.

Critical hope "refuses both despair and naïve optimism" and "rests on an equally critical belief, the belief that human beings can make and remake things, that they can transform the world," overcome their "*state of non-being*, and go on to a *state of being*, in search of *becoming more* fully human" (Freire 1973: 144–145; emphases in original). This critical hope is grounded in our ontological need to be historical beings capable of going beyond the limits of our day, of collaborating with others to enact a future of our own choosing. "[I]t is impossible to humanly exist without assuming the right and the duty to opt, to decide, to struggle, to be political" (Freire 1998: 53). The radical nature of critical hope is its recognition of our ineliminable human capacity to improve the world, to strive toward justice; but with this capacity comes the risk of being wrong since no guarantees can assure the absolute rightness of particular choices.

Thus critical hope is infused with humility. Each response to the challenges of oppression is necessarily incomplete and temporary, still partially reinscribing dominant ideologies, and thus necessarily subject in its turn to ongoing critiques and further choices as the struggle continues. Critical hope, even when humble, boldly aims at the underlying structures of an unjust schooling system, and at empowering LI/RCLD communities and their allies. Indeed, there are liberatory forces at work in urban communities in the USA, Latin America, and elsewhere that link justice, democracy, and education, and that build on the voices and dreams of the least advantaged (Wong and Glass 2009). The Citizen School project in Porto Alegre, Brazil, not only transformed the municipal schools to integrate the experiences, needs, and interests of the poor, but pursued this effort within a broader political program to empower an impoverished and historically excluded population to participate in substantive decisions in city governance (Gandin and Apple 2002). Globally, myriad community-based organizations ceaselessly struggle against the odds to create self-determined futures (see Warmington in this volume); they draw sustenance from the margin, and use their personal and local knowledges to generate a "passion for the possible" (Cruz in this volume). These counterweights to the dominant classes and ideologies act through collaborative and democratic channels to demonstrate critical hope made manifest as political force.

The political force of radical education experiments would be far greater if they were multiplied. However, when education reform efforts, even progressive ones, focus narrowly on schools without strategic interventions in the other social, economic, and political structures with which they interact, little change occurs in the lives of the poor and people of colour who populate these schools (Anyon 1997).

Meaningful improvements can definitely be achieved when schools, districts, teachers' unions, and universities combine resources to focus on educational equity issues in classrooms, though even such politically engaged pedagogy lacks the force needed to realize its larger aims (Wong and Glass 2009). Despite their limits, these efforts ensure that the increasingly artificial and forced monoculture of school environments is enriched with local nutrients that draw on community funds of knowledge (González *et al.* 2005). While a broader movement to link education, democracy, and justice awaits coalescence there is much work to do to challenge the dominance of global economic logics that confine schooling to technical literacy and numeracy (Burbules and Torres 2000). Bulwarks must be built against the backlash that defines pluralist identities narrowly in opposition to national unity, and support must be given to diverse cultural spaces in schools (Feinberg 1998). With public education under a sustained assault by neoliberal policies, schools must revive their traditional aims and foster the dispositions and habits needed for democratic citizenship (Arnstine 1998). These struggles sustain the promise of public schooling and prepare the ground for more forceful movements to come.

Nonetheless, people can despair over injustice and the suffering it causes. The long odds of overcoming the challenges in public schooling and even longer odds of overcoming the systemic and institutionalized racism pervading the dominant culture can dishearten even seasoned activists. Given that the long road to justice is obscure and stretches far beyond the horizon in every direction, discouragement can set in. Much has been tried, to limited effect, and little relief is in sight, so many become broken and tired. People search for a path of truth and dignity that can navigate between the arrogant disregard of the dominant classes and the proud righteousness of many champions of justice. The temptations of despair are truly legion, and they beckon the hopeless to become resigned to a fate seemingly beyond human intervention.

Oppressed people can "have a diffuse, magical belief in the invulnerability and power" of the dominant; as long as they "remain unaware of the causes of their condition, they fatalistically 'accept' their exploitation" (Freire 1994a: 46). This resignation insinuates despair into everyday life, making the dominant ideologies and their violence seem inescapable, and making a desire for transformation appear vain or foolish. Such despair denies the precariousness of the present; however great the evil of the day, choices remain, some in favor of justice, truth, and life, others not. A fear of freedom leads one to hide from these choices and their difficult consequences. Magical thinking and feelings of fear are thus the dwelling place of despair, and keep those with the most to gain from the struggle for justice far removed from taking responsibility for their choices and possibilities.

The dominant rejoice in this induced despair of the oppressed since it allows the landscape to be shaped with false hopes and perpetual disappointment, causing the oppressed to abandon the terrain of struggle. Promoting a self-interested individualistic notion of the human condition, the dominant ideology suggests that suffering is either ubiquitous and simply to be endured, or caused by the suffering victims themselves. The only hope, it is suggested, is that one's children will have a better life tomorrow, so there is no need to demand justice today.

This dream deferred is a corollary to another hidden debilitating force in despair, which is the assumption that the only battle worth fighting is the one that brings the struggle against injustice to a close; patience, some believe, is the better part of valor if total victory cannot be assured. This patience is not the waiting in readiness for the fight that Paulo Freire talked about as a capacity of critical hope; it is the false hope of a complete revolution coupled with a stoic despair that prevents a struggle from being mounted.

Despair, whether among anti-racism activists and educators or within the LI/RCLD communities that most suffer from injustice, is related not only to impossible hopes for certainties about the world and its future, but also to impossible hopes for a kind of authenticity – one that yearns for a self without taint or contradiction. This latter form of despair sees evidence of the futility of every effort to make changes when the hollow righteousness of white exceptionalism is debunked or the shortcomings of any person who soldiers for justice and takes on the burdens of leadership is recognized and called out. Despair thus expects both too much and too little of the individual. It denies our connection to a legacy of resistance and struggle that has secured the ground on which we stand and that gives direction to our creation of a better tomorrow. Despair thus signifies a form of self-righteous privilege that rationalizes disengagement and undermines the collective agency needed for antiracism and liberation struggles.

A critical grasp of the human construction of reality, of historicity, engenders the critical hope that can crack open the seemingly closed situation that imprisons the victims of injustice to reveal paths to transformative political force. Critical hope acknowledges that we cannot accomplish all that must be done, and we cannot be faultless, but this relieves no one from the obligation to do whatever one can. "Hope is rooted in men's incompletion, from which they move out in constant search – a search which can be carried out only in communion with others" (Freire 1994a: 72). In solidarity, our steps carry the history of struggle forward, without maps, without roads, without guarantees, without moral perfection. We are never alone in the battle for justice, as despair and the dominant ideology lead us to believe, even if at times it can seem as if the world is against us and that we alone are fighting the world. The more deeply we grasp the relationships among oppressions, and the dynamics of the situational limits and obstacles that must be faced, the more clearly we can recognize our allies and envision the actions necessary to advance the cause for justice. Critical hope becomes realized as political force only when people become "involved in the organized struggle for their liberation that [enables them] to believe in themselves" (Freire 1994a: 47) and that enables them to avoid the trap of despair.

Living critical hope

In the midst of one of the most violent and genocidal moments of the bloody twentieth century, T.S. Eliot, a politically conservative man with a tangled moral outlook, meditated on the meaning of hope in these well-known lines (Eliot 1971: 28):

> I said to my soul, be still, and wait without hope
> For hope would be hope for the wrong thing; ...

Eliot fell short of a grasp of critical hope, just as he fell short in his considerations of the rights of those who suffered inequities and of the obligations of the privileged, but he still glimpsed certain truths about the nature of false hopes. He understood that when hope is attached to something specific – a person, an object, a situational outcome – then that concrete content will be the "wrong thing," a false hope. When the world and life itself seemed emptied of value and meaning, Eliot grasped that we must construct value and meaning in anticipation of the future, in a form of waiting that is nonetheless a kind of motion. What Eliot seems not to have fully appreciated is the ontological nature of hope; hope exists precisely in the realm of possibilities, in open futures yet to be realized. Our human need to transcend every present, to create history and culture, reveals hope in action. The future anticipated by our choices is never fully realized, and so hope carries us forward. Buoyed by a love and faith beyond thoughts and words, beyond anything specific, we make our way by walking it.

Hope is "a natural, possible, and necessary impetus in the context of our unfinishedness" and its absence is "not the 'normal' way to be human" but rather "a distortion" (Freire 1998: 69). The absence of hope and inducement of despair should provoke indignation focused at the structural causes of false hopes and persistent inequities. These feelings connect us with others who are similarly situated, just as hope and love without fixations on objects connect us to others who share our vision of a more just world coming into being. Critical hope is born in these connections, and in the resulting movements built upon organizing and actions that challenge inequities. Waiting for the right moment to fight is not standing still, but rather it is moving step-by-step to engage limit-acts whose strategic specificity cannot yet fill out the full picture of justice, the full picture of a future without racism.

Reality is not inexorable or fixed, but for it to be different in relation to injustice, we must struggle. Those who think there can be innocent spectators cannot face their choices in favor of the *status quo*. Adaptation to oppression denies one's capacity to make more radical choices toward a more just world. On the radical ground of critical hope there is neither the intensity of feeling in false hopes and manufactured euphorias, nor the loss of feeling in induced despairs, but rather there are resolute commitments, and feelings of solidarity, belonging, and love. Living critical hope means to experience the transcendence of an isolated monadic self and to become a conscious person in history, working with others to bring life to our dreams and dreams to our life together.

Living critical hope involves taking up the immediate task at hand in the struggle for justice and also letting go of the certainty that it is the right or only thing to be done. Living critical hope is acting to overcome situational limits, but in a way that is tempered by humility and critique, by a provisional commitment that nonetheless holds nothing back. Every transformative project that resists the dominant ideologies and renews the community's wellsprings of meaning contains its own fundamental limits; every revolution is incomplete and every radical action has conservative elements embedded within it. We are all to some degree implicated in the evil we deplore and seek to overcome. Because our knowledge of the world is always mistaken and limited in certain ways, because conclusions derived from any moral calculus can be ethically questioned, because the character of every warrior for justice is flawed and contradictory, living critical hope means to embrace the striving toward justice more tightly than the goal. It also means to accept the inward aim and difficult psychological struggle necessary alongside the outer battles. There is no final deep authentic self beyond ideological taint, so any celebration of exceptionalism is based on a false imagining of one's purity and on a divorce from the history of struggle against racism and other forms of oppression.

Living critical hope forges communities of purpose and meaning that provide an effective innoculation against the despair often induced by the dominant ideologies. It is a vital force, a tenacious historically informed way to struggle to make history and culture serve the aims of democracy and justice. The task of repairing and reinventing the world is neither a singular nor specific action to be completed; it is a form of sharing in a way of life with a particular people. Critical hope does not depend on some ultimate redemption or reconciliation, and instead it accepts the virtue of the striving for democracy and justice as the measure of our humanity. Love is foundational to critical hope as we seek to embody a commitment to a moral life (despite our shortcomings), a devotion to others (despite their flaws), and a dedication to the dream of justice (despite its obscurities and the obstacles to its realization). Only this kind of critical hope endures as communities move beyond the brutalities and suffering imposed by injustice to build an alternative future, step-by-step and hand-in-hand, through hard work and struggle. This is the critical hope of liberation struggles that is the most certain antidote to despair in the struggle against racism and unjust schooling.

References

Anyon, J. (1997) *Ghetto Schooling: A Political Economy of Urban Educational Reform*. New York: Teachers College Press.
Arnstine, D. (1995) *Democracy and the Arts of Schooling*. Albany, NY: State University of New York Press.
Burbules, N.C. and Torres, C.A. (2000) *Globalization and Education: Critical Perspectives*. New York: Routledge.
Eliot, T.S. (1943) *Four Quartets (Section II: East Coker)*. New York: Harcourt Brace & Co.
Feinberg, W. (1998) *Common Schools / Uncommon Identities: National Unity and Cultural Difference*. New Haven, CT: Yale University Press.
Freire, P. (1973) *Education for Critical Consciousness*. New York: Seabury Press.
Freire, P. (1994a) *Pedagogy of the Oppressed*. New York: Continuum.
Freire, P. (1994b) *Pedagogy of Hope*. New York: Continuum.
Freire, P. (1998) *Pedagogy of Freedom: Ethics, Democracy, and Civic Courage*. Lanham, MD: Rowman and Littlefield Publishers.

Freire, P. and Shor, I. (1986) *A Pedagogy for Liberation*. Westport, CT: Bergin & Garvey.
Gandin, L.A. and Apple, M. (2002) 'Can education challenge neoliberalism? The citizen school and the struggle for democracy in Porto Alegre, Brazil', *Social Justice*, 29: 26–40.
Glass, R.D. (2001) 'Paulo Freire's philosophy of praxis and the foundations of liberation education', *Educational Researcher*, 30: 15–25.
Glass, R.D. (2008) 'Staying hopeful'. In: M. Pollock (ed.) *Everyday Antiracism: Getting Real about Race in School*. New York: The New Press.
Glass, R.D. (2010) 'Memories of Paulo Freire'. In: T. Wilson, P. Park and A. Colon-Muniz (eds) *Memories of Paulo*. Rotterdam, The Netherlands: Sense Publishers.
Glass, R.D. (2011) 'Critical pedagogy and moral education'. In J.L. DeVitis and T. Yu (eds.) *Character and Moral Education: A Reader*. New York: Peter Lang Publishers.
Glass, R.D. (2012) 'Cultivating compassion: Lessons learned from community and family'. In: L.G. Denti and P.A. Whang (eds) *Rattling Chains: Exploring Social Justice in Education*. The Netherlands: Sense Publishers.
Glass, R.D. and Nygreen, K. (2011) 'Class, race, and the discourse of "college for all"', *Democracy and Education*, 19: 1. Online. Available: <http://democracyeducationjournal.org/home/vol19/iss1/7.html> (accessed "date"). http://democracyeducationjournal.org/home/vol19/iss1/7/ (accessed March 4, 2013).
Gonzáles, N., Moll, L.C. and Amanti, C. (2005) *Funds of Knowledge: Theorizing Practices in Households, Communities, and Classrooms*. Mahwah, NJ: Lawrence Erlbaum Associates.
Haymes, S. (2004) 'White students and the meaning of whiteness'. In: K. Alston (ed.) *Philosophy of Education 2003*. Urbana, IL: Philosophy of Education Society.
Heaney, S. (1991) *The Cure at Troy: A Version of Sophocles' Philoctetes*. New York: Farrar, Straus and Giroux.
Horton, M. and Freire, P. (1990) *We Make the Road by Walking*. Philadelphia, PA: Temple University Press.
Jameson, F. (2000) 'Postmodernism, or the cultural logic of late capitalism'. In: M. Hardt and K. Weeks (eds) *The Jameson Reader*. Oxford, UK, and Malden, MA: Blackwell.
Ladson-Billings, G. (2006) 'From the achievement gap to the education debt: Understanding achievement in U.S. schools', *Educational Researcher*, 35: 3–12.
McNeil, L.M. (2000) *Contradictions of School Reform: Educational Costs of Standardized Testing*. New York: Routledge.
Orfield, G. and Kornhaber, M.L. (2001) *Raising Standards or Raising Barriers? Inequality and High-Stakes Testing in Public Education*. New York: Century Foundation Press.
Thompson, A. (2004) 'Anti-racist work zones'. In: K. Alston (ed.) *Philosophy of Education 2003*. Urbana, IL: Philosophy of Education Society.
Wong, P.L. and Glass, R.D. (2009) *Prioritizing Urban Children, Teachers, and Schools through Professional Development Schools*. Albany, NY: State University of New York Press.

8 Agents of critical hope
Black British narratives[1]

Paul Warmington

Introduction

Critical hope offers a dynamic framework for theorizing aspirations towards the removal of social injustices, towards social flourishing and also concern with the process itself – *how* we strive for flourishing. The collective directions of critical hope are predicated upon an affirmation of the importance of praxis; a forging of alliances across social groups; democratic citizenship and participation; and a focus on relationality as central to how we think and learn. This chapter maps a particular, local history of praxis and alliances: a history of black British[2] social agency in struggles over education and social justice in the post-war period. In examining black British educational activism, this chapter suggests that while black education movements in the UK have been diverse, they have always been predicated upon *critical hope*, wherein critical understanding of the school system's maintenance of race–class inequalities and hope in education as potentially transformative, a site of liberation and solidarity, have existed in tandem and in tension.

Black British intellectuals and education

There are many possible maps that might be drawn of the history of black education movements, and this chapter makes no claim to be definitive in this respect. Its principal focus is upon the literature that has grown out of black intellectual activism. In Britain, black writing is too often marginalized in public debates; it is assumed that black communities are problems to be theorized by white intellectuals. Consequently, in accounts of race and education, writing on black social agency has often been obscured, with black communities drifting into civic debate only at moments of crisis – usually crises defined from outside – but remaining "objects rather than subjects, beings that feel yet lack the ability to think, and remain incapable of considered behavior in an active mode" (Gilroy 1987: 11). In contrast, by exploring the distinctive contributions that black intellectuals and education movements have made to education in Britain, this chapter offers a form of what Critical Race Theorists define as 'counter-storytelling.' Delgado and Stefancic (2001: 144) define counter-storytelling as "writing that aims to cast doubt on the validity of accepted premises or myths, especially ones held by the majority." Understanding the story of black education movements in terms of critical hope is one means of resisting historical accounts of education in which black people are 'other' and in which black children are other people's children. This chapter emphasizes black education movements as agents of critical hope, and black people as agents of social change – history in which black thinkers and communities have made demands and contributions, thereby shaping British social life on the grand scale.

The intellectual activism discussed here encompasses both the academic world and organic intellectuals in grassroots and informal settings. There can be no rigid distinction, particularly not in the 'early' post-war phase of the 1950s, 1960s and 1970s, between black British community activism and intellectual production. Post-war black social critiques were born out of community struggles around schooling, unemployment and policing but those community struggles also constituted social critiques in themselves, for they were not only local campaigns for immediate solutions to issues around busing, banding, IQ testing and curriculum; they were also emergent citizen movements, born out of the realization among black parents that they and their children had a stake in the future of British society. However, one of the effects of the marginalization of black British intellectual traditions has been the downplaying of links between diverse black British intellectual spaces. Thus, the black education movements that have focused on schooling are often thought of as protests but not intellectual movements. Conversely, the work of black scholars and academics – in particular, the remarkable generation of cultural theorists that transformed British scholarship from the late 1970s onwards – is not always thought of as part of an *educational* movement.

This chapter begins by explaining the distinctive British definition of political blackness that was produced, in significant part, by struggles against racism in education. It establishes that education has been central to black British identities since the mass migration and settlement of the 1950s and 1960s. Struggles over what it means to be black *and* British have been enacted repeatedly around sites of educational desire and despair, and, as this chapter shows, education is one of the significant fields in which black British intellectual positions have been defined and differentiated. It then considers the influence of Critical Race Theory (CRT) on my own 'counter-narrative' approach to reclaiming histories of black writing, intellectual activism and education. Finally, this chapter maps the development of black British education movements in the decades since what Dhondy *et al.* (1985) termed the 'black explosion' in British schools: the period during the 1960s and 1970s when the children of post-war migrants entered the British school system in large numbers. The black educational movements discussed in this chapter encompass a considerable range of philosophies, strategies and specific campaigns. What they have in common is that they have not merely sought superficial system adaptation; they have critiqued in fundamental ways the racialized nature of educational inequalities and acted on an understanding that African-Caribbean, South Asian and African communities were a permanent, settled presence in Britain.

Defining 'black British'

In Britain the term 'black' has a complex history and can, depending on context, denote *either* people of African/African-Caribbean descent *or*, via discourses of 'political blackness,' the assembly of African, African-Caribbean, Asian and Arabic peoples constructed in the post-war period of immigration – the collective sometimes referred to in the USA as 'people of color.' In the 1960s, 1970s and 1980s political blackness tended to dominate in the UK, with people of colour adopting 'black' as an inclusive, umbrella term (Alexander 2002). Since the late 1980s, Hall (1988, 1989), Modood (1992), Gilroy (2000) and Song (2003) have all interrogated the homogenizing tendencies of British political blackness. They have raised questions about the dominance within political blackness of certain forms of African-Caribbean maleness; the marginalization of women; the relegation of South Asian voices; the invisibility of queer sexualities; the complexities of articulation between religion and race; generational and class differences; the underplaying of the agentive potential of fluid negotiation of ethnic categories. Although Hall's (1988, 1989) proclaimed 'new ethnicities' have not entirely replaced political blackness, they have modified blackness' claims and necessitated critical self-reflection, hastening the emergence of unstable, decentered blackness. At the same time, it is still the case that many contemporary black British intellectual currents are derived from the moment (or idiom) of political blackness, even where they take issue with it.

In this chapter, the term 'black' is used in a contentious, even provocative, sense: with its umbrella, political meaning restored. In part, this is because it is concerned with *histories* of black intellectual production in Britain, covering periods when much work adhered to the uniquely British use of the term 'black.' I do not suggest the umbrella usage of the word exhausts all possible meanings of 'blackness.' Importantly, though, the term 'black British' signifies something far more radical than geographical location. As Procter (2003) argues, the emergence of the term signified a shift from being *black in Britain* to being *black and British*. Quoting Paul Gilroy, Procter (2003: 5) suggests that "it involves a radical deconstruction of the idea that 'blacks are an external problem, an alien presence visited in Britain from the outside.'" During the settlement phase of the 1960s and then in the 1980s and 1990s, as settled and 'second generation' black Britons began to write their own stories, black intellectuals began to appropriate Britain and Britishness as the legitimate objects of their work. This refocusing, this new self-representation constituted nothing less than a deconstruction of what it meant to be British. Note Hall's advocacy for:

> [T]he logic of coupling, rather than the logic of binary opposition [...] You can be black and British, not only because that is a necessary position to take [...] but also because those two terms [...] do not exhaust all of our identities. Only some of our identities are sometimes caught in that particular struggle. (Hall 1996: 472).

In relation to theorizing critical hope, this chapter traces the history of that uniquely British form of political blackness, its role in the formation of black British intellectual traditions and of wider black identities. As this implies, the term 'black' is understood here not principally as a reference to color or presumed cultural essence but as a strategic political tool. It is an idiom through which intellectuals of colour (and, it should be said, white anti-racist intellectuals – activists such as Chris Searle, Jenny Bourne, David Gillborn) have, at particular historical junctures, addressed racism and social injustice – a position from which they have entered into dialogue with the state, the schools and their white neighbours.

So this is not merely an effort to 'advocate' or 'honour' histories of black British intellectual activism but to do in practice the work of invoking their thought and their engagement in educational struggles as reference points in theorizing critical hope. I do not wish to claim them for some essentialist, ahistorical notion of blackness (this should be apparent from the fact that some of those I name in this chapter would not usually be considered 'black'). I do not attempt to characterize them all as crypto-Critical Race Theorists, though they are all 'critical.' Neither am I suggesting that there is a charmed, self-sufficient space of black intellectual activism. Black education movements in the UK have nurtured myriad alliances over decades. In addition, to black-led and organized groupings, such as the Black Parents Movement, New Beacon and the Asian Youth Movements of the 1970s and 1980s, there have been multiracial organizations, steered by teachers, unions and churches, such as the National Association for Multi-Racial Education (NAME) and All Faiths for One Race (AFFOR). In invoking black activists and the black education movements, I wish to signify something about particular intellectual concerns and approaches: the determination to *account for* the social construction of race as an organizing principle of (unequal and unjust) human relations, determination not to evade race, racialization and racism by treating them as unfortunate marginal, aberrant experiences or murky, transient policy issues (cf. Gilroy 1987; Gillborn 2008; Warmington, 2009).

Critical hope and education

'Critical hope' is almost too perfect a descriptor of the agency that has driven black British communities' encounters with the education system but it is no less apt for all that. For the story of Britain's black education movements is largely the story of how the hope that black parents initially invested in the British school system was very quickly refashioned by lived experiences into *critical* hope. From the early 1960s – a period that, for better and for worse, set the tone for ensuing decades of contests over 'race and education' – black parents and activists have asserted a commitment to their children's education. Yet that commitment has been asserted in the knowledge that too often the school system as it actually existed, deeply classed and racialized, operated not to counter racial inequalities but, to paraphrase the Critical Race Theorist David Gillborn (2008), to maintain them at manageable levels. In short, the praxis of the black British education movements emerged as an action-orientated challenge to the belief that working-class parents had no business encouraging 'unrealistic aspirations' among their children. From the 1960s and 1970s onwards, "black parents were challenging that supine 'realism'" (Farrar 1992: 9) and they have continued to do so, forging alliances, solidarity and connectedness.

Yet, while education is cited almost incidentally as being formative to black British experiences, particularly in the post-war period (Sivanandan 1982; Gilroy 1987), existing large-scale histories (Fryer 1984; Ramdin 1987) give surprisingly limited attention to education. Other very useful historical work, such as Grosvenor's (2007) *Assimilating Identities* and Tomlinson's (2008) *Race and Education* illuminate post-war struggles over race and education but their focus is primarily on policy ideology. One consequence of this has been the relegation of some of the seminal figures in black British intellectual history, such as the activist John La Rose and his New Beacon circle, Ambalavaner Sivanandan and the Institute of Race Relations, the Race Today Collective, educators Gus John and Maureen Stone, cultural theorist Hazel Carby and literary historian David Dabydeen. Exploring their work – and that of newer, sometimes unpredictable black voices – helps to explain why the story of race and education in Britain is larger than the hoary issues of underachievement or multicultural education.

Critical Race Theory

The chronicling of histories of black British education movements is one way of shifting beyond paradigms of black educational failure and underachievement. This approach to exploring histories of race and education in Britain might be read as a variant of what Critical Race Theory (CRT) refers to as *counter-storytelling*. Solórzano and Yosso (2009: 134) emphasize that CRT methodologies, such as counter-storytelling, are designed to challenge "ahistoricism and the undisciplinary focus of most analyses [...] analyzing race and racism by placing them in both historical and contemporary contexts." They define the counter-story as: "[...] a method of telling the stories of those people whose experiences are not often told [...] a tool for exposing, analyzing, and challenging the majoritarian stories of racial privilege" (Solórzano and Yosso 2009: 138). CRT emerged in the USA during the 1980s as a framework for understanding the endemic presence of race within the American social and political formation. Its key analytical principles are aimed at countering the ideological claims to neutrality and meritocracy customarily proffered in fields such as law, social policy, news media and education (Crenshaw *et al.* 1995). Through CRT analyses, the 'taken for granted' racialized processes embedded in those fields are made visible. CRT is now well established in the USA through the work of academics and activists such as Derrick Bell, Gloria Ladson-Billings, Kimberlé Crenshaw, Richard Delgado, Jean Stefancic and Zeus Leonardo, but it is a relatively new presence in Britain, where it has been utilized in the work of Gillborn (2005, 2006, 2008), Housee (2008), Hylton (2009), Preston (2010) and Warmington (2012).

One reason for scrutinizing CRT's transfer is that US CRT has uttered its key conceptual claims in both global and local registers. Thus, speaking 'globally,' Taylor (2009: 4) draws on Charles Mills' dictum that "Racism is global White supremacy and is itself a political system, a particular power structure of formal and informal rule, privilege, socio-economic advantages." However, CRT's 'local' origins lie specifically in the break with the US Critical Legal Studies movement made during the 1970s by legal scholars such as Bell and Crenshaw. In addition, one of the papers that signaled the transfer of CRT to the field of education, Ladson-Billings and Tate's (1995) 'Towards a Critical Race Theory of education,' speaks CRT at this local level. So, for instance, its propositions around race and property include assertions that "[r]ace continues to be a significant factor in determining inequity in the United States" and "US society is based on property rights" (Ladson-Billings and Tate 1995: 48). There is nothing peculiar about this; all social theory originates somewhere along the line in local observations. However, it does mean that we should pay due attention to the local materials out of which CRT might be crafted in the UK. Gillborn's analysis of education *policy*, for example, has redirected the focus on legislation that has historically driven the development of CRT in the USA. CRT's robustness in the UK will be dependent upon taking the same kind of historically grounded approach through which CRT has been taken forward in the States (Warmington 2012).

Black social agency

The reclaiming of 'hidden histories' of black educational activism is a contribution both to the development of Critical Race Theory in the UK, and to the building of a critical hope that is historically grounded in black British experiences. Educators and activists, such as Max Farrar (1992) and Jan McKenley (2001) have long called for what McKenley (2001) terms a 'cartography' of the impact of the black presence, black *agency*, on post-war education policy and practice, one that maps black intellectual work and educational activism. Black cartographers of education will, of course, produce multiple narratives; the current chapter offers just one of many possible tellings. Elsewhere, Farrar's (1992) recounting of the politics of race and education in Yorkshire, including the Leeds pupils' strike of 1973 (protesting against the alleged racism of a local head teacher) has done much to rectify the metropolitan gaze of black British writing. McKenley's (2005) *Seven Black Men* has, in its studies of fatherhood and schooling challenged representations of African-Caribbean hyper-masculinity. Anandi Ramamurthy (2005, 2006) and Zaiba Malik (2012) have each delved into the history of the Asian Youth Movements of the 1970s and 1980s, as a corrective to the erasure in the mainstream media, over the past twenty years, of secular Asian politics. And while Claire Alexander (2002) has cautioned against reducing black British history to the 'Windrush narrative' (that is, the idea that black Britain begins with the arrival of 500 Jamaicans at Tilbury Docks in 1948, and unfurls through a series of mostly African-Caribbean moments into a cool, culturally diverse Britannia), even that narrative is only a big fish in a small pond. Outside of specialist circles, the struggles in the 1960s and 1970s over the placement of African-Caribbean pupils in ESN schools (schools for the 'Educationally Subnormal') or the busing of Asian children in London and Bradford (aimed at limiting numbers of 'immigrant' children to no more than 30 percent in any school) are not well understood. Therefore, it is worth sketching of some of the landmarks that might populate a map perhaps titled 'black British intellectual activism and education.'

Mapping black education movements

The British school system did not require the presence of black children in order to reproduce social and educational inequalities. It was, as Basil Bernstein, Paul Willis and other social reproduction theorists argued across the 1960s and 1970s, more than capable of incorporating working-class children into their designated places in the labour process. The problem for black children in the 1960s, 1970s and 1980s was that the education system was not even sure that it could achieve that much. The shock, not so much of arrival as of permanent settlement, saw black parents and pupils *and* their teachers negotiating the unplanned, with minimal support from national government or local authorities (McKenley 2001; Tomlinson 2008). Amidst growing hostility, black parents campaigned locally against the seemingly arbitrary measures local authorities improvised out of a tangle of poor resourcing, prejudices about the educability of black children and panic over concentrations of black pupils. These kinds of experiences did not sit well, particularly with African-Caribbean parents, brought up to believe that a formal (colonial) education was *the* route to social mobility. They soon learned that in the British context, their aspirational view of education was, at best, misunderstood, at worst, derided by those in education, politics and news media, who were aghast at the expectations of black parents (Phillips and Phillips 1999).

The key early black educational campaigns (mid-1960s–mid-1970s) were over dispersal policies, low teacher expectations and the placing of Caribbean children, in particular, in schools for Educationally Subnormal (ESN) children (Sivanandan 1982; Dhondy *et al.* 1985). The relatively established black and anti-racist bodies, such as the Indian Workers Association (IWA), the Campaign Against Racial Discrimination (CARD) and the early incarnation of the Institute of Race Relations, were slow to turn their attention to the education of black children. Consequently, the key educational struggles of the 1960s and 1970s were waged most effectively by a wave of new activist groups, influenced by US civil rights and Black Power movements, as well as by their 'home' traditions and local British educational conditions (Warmington 2014). They initially included the North London West Indian Association (NLWIA); the Caribbean Educators and Community Workers Association (CECWA); those who organized around supplementary schools; the Black Parents Movements and Black Students Movements that emerged in London, Manchester and Bradford in the 1970s and '80s; and the Asian Youth Movements that formed in London, Leicester,

Bradford and Blackburn. Key to this period was the publication of Bernard Coard's (1971) pivotal *How the West Indian Child is Made Educationally Subnormal in the British School System*, which emerged directly out of the work of the London's black educational activists. Coard's book was the first by a black British intellectual to offer an extended structural analysis of racialized processes in British schooling. As such, it became the spectre haunting much subsequent work by black British academics and educators.

The struggles of the 1960s, 1970s and 1980s were, in the truest sense, organic intellectual activity. The new student and youth organizations increasingly located their analyses of schooling within the wider experiences of young Caribbean and Asian people, campaigning also around policing, unemployment and anti-fascism (Sivanandan 1982; Ramamurthy 2006). There were also the supplementary schools, which developed out of parental disillusionment with the lived experience of British schooling. Sometimes referred to as 'complementary schools' or 'Saturday schools,' these comprised classes that were set up, managed and staffed by black parents, teachers and activists, outside of the normal school day. While supplementary schools are often described as a movement (Reay and Mirza 2001), they, in fact, encompassed a complicated spread of aims and arrangements, in terms of the type of provision offered; their longevity and stability; the degree of formality and official recognition accorded by local authorities; and the balance of control between parents, teachers and other stakeholders. This is as much the case today as it was in the 1960s and 1970s.

In addition, many educators and activists were strongly linked with emergent black British publishing, the arts and other areas of cultural production (Alleyne 2002). It was during the 1960s, 1970s and 1980s that many black intellectual activists who would exert an enduring influence on black educational thinking became prominent through the grassroots community and educational campaigns, among them (and this is by no means an exhaustive list): Jeff Crawford, John La Rose, Jessica and Eric Huntley, Gus John, Len Garrison, Ambalavaner Sivanandan, Stella Dadzie, Farrukh Dhondy and Jan McKenley.

Hidden histories

There have been points when a momentum has been achieved in surfacing histories of black British politics (even if education did not always quite receive due attention). The mid-1980s, for instance, saw the republication of key works by C.L.R. James, and the publication of Peter Fryer's (1984) *Staying Power*, Buzz Johnson's (1985) biography of Claudia Jones, Beverley Bryan, Stella Dadzie and Suzanne Scafe's (1985) *Heart of the Race* and Ron Ramdin's (1987) *The Making of the Black Working Class in Britain*. The late 1990s saw a number of histories 'commemorating' the anniversary of the arrival of the Empire Windrush at Tilbury docks, a moment that has become synonymous with the initiation of post-war black migration to Britain. These included Kalbir Shukra's (1998) *The Changing Pattern of Black Politics in Britain*, and Mike and Trevor Phillips' (1999) *Windrush*.

However, the history of black British intellectual activism incorporates disparate strands, not always included in the conventional Windrush narrative: the work of bookshops and publishers (such as the Bogle L'Ouverture and New Beacon imprints), the Indian Workers Association, Southall Black Sisters, the *Race Today* Collective and the arts journal *Wasafiri*. It is certainly not confined to the academy; indeed, it might be argued that black British intellectual life and academia have intersected only fitfully. That said, from the 1970s onwards, powerful black academic voices that were also *public* intellectual voices began to stake out a presence in academia, beginning with the work of Chris Mullard and Dilip Hiro, achieving international standing through the work of Stuart Hall, Hazel Carby, Paul Gilroy, Kobena Mercer and others aligned to the Centre for Contemporary Cultural Studies, producing the literary histories of David Dabydeen and diversifying thereafter into myriad conceptual, pedagogic and policy-oriented fields. The work of Hall, Gilroy, Mercer and their contemporaries is too often considered separately from the 'grassroots' struggles of the 1970s, 1980s and 1990s. Yet many of the great, early strides in Hall's work came out of conditions and concerns akin to those being traversed by the likes of Sivanandan, Gus John and John La Rose. These conditions included the limitations of British models of race relations; the policing of black communities (both in the literal sense and in terms of the media and policy representations that pathologized black communities); the marginalization of black histories and cultural work; diaspora and the new identities that black settlement had produced. Hall's routes were different to those of Sivanandan (and they eventually drew Sivanandan's ire) but Hall's work too was created out of the black British hope and flux.

Diverse voices

The early stands taken by the black educational movements of the 1960s and early 1970s fed into radical structural analyses of British schooling. Bernard Coard (1971) and Farrukh Dhondy *et al.* (1985) both drew upon their experiences of teaching in London schools, Marxist analyses of schooling in capitalism and the radicalism emerging across the black Atlantic, as well as their belief in the emergence of 'second generation' black Britons as an oppositional force. Hazel Carby (1982), working alongside Stuart Hall at the University of Birmingham's Centre for Contemporary Cultural Studies, also saw black pupils and communities forming active opposition both to the authoritarian dimensions of schooling and the distractions offered by facile forms of multiculturalism.

These radical/left analyses contrast with the work of Maureen Stone (1981) and, later, Tony Sewell (1997, 2009) whose research was embedded in a rejection of radical 'deschooling' as utopian, combined with a rejection of liberal self-concept theories as being rooted in cultural deficit models. Both turned their emphasis towards school leadership as the key to improving the schooling of black pupils. Sewell's (1997) critical ethnographies have, in turn, been critiqued as being constrained by an adherence to subcultural analyses and a problematic conservatism (Warmington 2014). Alongside these shifts has been public intellectual work that has grown out of older traditions of black labor activism, pan-Africanism and feminism, such as Prescod and Waters (1999), Graham (2001), Alleyne (2002), and John (2006).

From the late 1980s onwards, the work of Mairtin Mac an Ghaill (1988), Hazel Carby and Heidi Safia Mirza (2009) on schooling and racialization began to draw upon notions of de-centred blackness that derived, in part, from Stuart Hall's work on 'new ethnicities' and his rethinking of articulations between race, class and gender. These were cultural analyses in the truest sense, showing the influence of both Gramscian and post-structural analyses. Attention to gendered modes of racialization countered the phallocentrism in which earlier accounts of resistance and opposition to the racialized processes of schooling were often embedded. Tariq Modood (2007), meanwhile, has persistently challenged dominant modes of political blackness and their reliance on both subcultural and Marxist analytical frameworks. There has also been research on exploring the creative ways in which young people have negotiated 'in practice' the fragmentation, dissembling and reconfiguration of racialized identities in the UK (see Reay and Mirza 2001; Song 2003).

That critical hope remains a principle of black educational activism in the UK is apparent in the determination of critical thinkers on race and education, to construct visions of hope that remain embedded in realistic appraisals of the current educational conditions. Mirza (2007) argues that decades of superficial discursive shifts (assimilationism, multiculturalism, diversity) only conceal "patterns of persistent discrimination, both blatant and subtle [...] the illusive chameleon nature of racism in education [...] changes its mantle over time [...] the more things change, the more they stay the same" (Mirza 2007: 114). Drawing on the emergent conceptual tools of Critical Race Theory, Gillborn (2008) goes further, naming the pervasive, 'conspiratorial' nature of white supremacy as a constant and arguing that, despite the contemporary rhetoric of social justice and cultural diversity, the function of schooling is not to counter racial inequalities but to maintain them at a manageable level. Gillborn's dictum carries the historical echoes of half a century of black educational struggles in Britain. What has characterized those struggles always is the commitment to seeing that initial analysis not as the cause for pessimism but as the basis of a critical, hopeful realism.

Conclusion

In her book *Teaching Community: A Pedagogy of Hope*, bell hooks recalls the publication in 1969 of June Jordan's seminal essay 'Black studies: bringing back the person.' In that essay Jordan declared that given the history of race and education in the USA, there was nothing optional about black studies for African-American students (hooks 2003). Given the post-war histories of black British communities, one might say that there is nothing optional about critical hope. In the early 1960s the culture of British schooling (that is, state schooling for working-class children) provided one of harshest lessons of arrival; black communities learned very quickly that the schools were not places to which they could, in an unproblematic sense, entrust their children or in which their children would necessarily acquire sound academic knowledge and skills or passports to social mobility. However, African-Caribbean and Asian parents and pupils would not accept the 'realistic' expectations: unquestioning horizontal integration into a stratified system. Today African-Caribbean, Pakistani, Bangladeshi and Somali communities, in particular, still experience the hard effects of a deeply unequal school system (Gillborn 2008; Tomlinson 2008). Those educational conditions have engendered critical realism among black educational activists; the transformations for which they continue to work necessitate hope, but of a critical kind. This chapter's account of black British educational struggles has underlined that understandings of critical hope must be historically grounded because the conditions from which critical hope emerge are local and particular, as well as being informed by 'universal' ideals of transformative education. This directs us, once again, to the paradoxical nature of critical hope but in a way that suggests that paradox is a social justice imperative.

Notes

1 Parts of this chapter appeared in the journal article, Warmington, P. (2012) 'A tradition in ceaseless motion': critical race theory and black British intellectual spaces, *Race Ethnicity and Education*, 15(1): 5–21. Thanks to Professor Dave Gillborn.
2 The term 'black British' may not be entirely accurate in all instances. For instance, it does not always overcome the old tendency to conflate 'England' with 'Britain'. For historical reasons most of the 'black British' intellectuals examined in this book have worked and written in England, not Wales or Scotland, and in a pre-devolution context. Importantly, though, the term 'black British' is used in this chapter because it has remained a preferred term among many black people because. In theory at least, it implies the possibility of a British identity comprising multiple ethnicities; it has allowed a creative fuzziness around the (still largely unpacked) limits of black 'Englishness', 'Welshness' and 'Scottishness'. As I have used the term 'black British', I have, for consistency's sake, also used the terms 'Britain'/'British' when describing country or nation.

References

Alexander, C. (2002) 'Beyond black: Re-thinking the colour/culture divide', *Ethnic and Racial Studies*, 25(4), 552–71.
Alleyne, B. (2002) *Radicals Against Race: Black Activism and Cultural Politics*. Oxford: Berg.
Bryan, B., Dadzie, S. and Scafe, S. (1985) *The Heart of the Race: Black Women's Lives in Britain*, London: Virago Press.
Carby, H. (1982) 'Schooling in Babylon'. In: Centre for Contemporary Cultural Studies (eds), *The Empire Strikes Back: Race and Racism in 70s Britain*. London: Hutchinson.
Coard, B. (1971) *How the West Indian Child is Made Educationally Subnormal in the British School System*. London: New Beacon.

Crenshaw, K., Gotanda, N., Peller, G. and Thomas, K. (eds) (1995) *Critical Race Theory: The Key Writings that Formed the Movement*. New York: New Press.
Delgado, R. and Stefancic, J. (2001) *Critical Race Theory: An Introduction*. New York: New York University Press.
Dhondy, F., Beese, B. and Hassan, L. (1985) *The Black Explosion in British Schools*. London: Race Today.
Farrar, M. (1992) 'Racism, education and black self-organization', *Critical Social Policy*, 35 (Autumn).
Fryer, P. (1984) *Staying Power: The History of Black People in Britain*. London: Pluto Press.
Gillborn, D. (2005) 'Education policy as an act of white supremacy: Whiteness, critical race theory and education reform', *Journal of Education Policy*, 20(4): 485–505.
Gillborn, D. (2006) 'Rethinking white supremacy: Who counts in "WhiteWorld"', *Ethnicities*, 6(3): 318–40.
Gillborn, D. (2008) *Racism and Education: Coincidence or Conspiracy?* Abingdon: Routledge.
Gilroy, P. (1987) *There Ain't No Black in the Union Jack: The Cultural Politics of Race and Nation*. London: Routledge.
Gilroy, P. (2000) *Against Race: Imagining Political Culture Beyond the Color Line*. Cambridge, MA: Harvard University Press.
Graham, M. (2001) 'The "miseducation" of black children in the British education system – towards an African-centred orientation to knowledge'. In: R. Majors (ed.) *Educating Our Black Children: New Directions and Radical Approaches*. London: Routledge-Falmer.
Grosvenor, I. (1997) *Assimilating Identities: Racism and Educational Policy in Post 1945 Britain*. London: Lawrence and Wishart.
Hall, S. (1988) 'New ethnicities'. In: K. Mercer (ed.) *Black Film/British Cinema: ICA document 7*. London: Institute of Contemporary Arts.
Hall, S. (1989) *Ethnicity: Identity and Difference*, Speech to Hampshire College, Amherst, Massachusetts, *Radical America*, 23(4), 9–20.
Hall, S. (1996) 'What is this "black" in black popular culture?' In: D. Morley and K. Chen (eds) *Stuart Hall: Critical Dialogues in Cultural Studies*. Abingdon: Routledge.
hooks, b. (2003) *Teaching Community: A Pedagogy of Hope*. New York: Routledge.
Housee, S. (2008) 'Should ethnicity *matter* when teaching about "race" and racism in the classroom?' *Race, Ethnicity and Education* 11(4): 415–28.
Hylton, K. (2009) *'Race' and Sport: Critical Race Theory*. Abingdon: Routledge.
John, G. (2006) *Taking a Stand: Gus John Speaks on Education, Race, Social Action and Civil Unrest 1980–2005*. Manchester: Gus John Partnership.
Johnson, B. (1985) *"I Think of My Mother": Notes on the Life and Times of Claudia Jones*. London: Karia Press.
Ladson-Billings, G. and Tate, W. (1995) 'Towards a Critical Race Theory of Education', *Teachers College Record*, 97(1): 47–68.
Mac an Ghaill, M. (1988) *Young, Gifted, and Black: Student-Teacher Relations in the Schooling of Black Youth*. Milton Keynes: Open University Press.
Malik, Z. (2012) *The Asian Youth Movements*, BBC Radio 4 Broadcast, 26 March 2012.
McKenley, J. (2001) 'The way we were: Conspiracies of silence in the wake of the Empire Windrush', *Race Ethnicity and Education*, 4(4): 309–28.
McKenley, J. (2005) *Seven Black Men: An Ecological Study of Education and Parenting*. Bristol: Aduma Books.

Mirza, H.S. (2007) 'The more things change, the more they stay the same'. In: B. Richardson (ed.) *Tell It Like It Is: How Our Schools Fail Black Children*. London: Bookmarks/Trentham.

Mirza, H.S. (2009) *Race, Gender and Educational Desire: Why Black Women Succeed and Fail*. London: Routledge.

Modood, T. (1992) *Not Easy Being British: Colour, Culture and Citizenship*. London: Runnymede Trust and Trentham Books.

Modood, T. (2007) *Multiculturalism: A Civic Idea*. Cambridge: Polity.

Phillips, M. and Phillips, T. (1999) *Windrush: The Irresistible Rise of Multi-Racial Britain*. London: HarperCollins.

Prescod, C. and Waters, H. (eds) (1999) *A World to Win: Essays in Honour of A. Sivanandan*. London: Institute of Race Relations.

Preston, J. (2010) 'Concrete and abstract racial domination', *Power and Education*, 2(2): 115–25.

Procter, J. (2003) *Dwelling Places: Postwar Black British Writing*. Manchester: Manchester University Press.

Ramamurthy, A. (2005) *Secular Identities and the Asian Youth Movements*, Paper presented to 10th International Conference on Alternative Futures and Popular Protest, Manchester Metropolitan University.

Ramamurthy, A. (2006) 'The politics of Britain's Asian youth movements', *Race and Class*, 48(2): 38–60.

Ramdin, R. (1987) *The Making of the Black Working Class in Britain*. London: Gower.

Reay, D. and Mirza, H. (2001). 'Black supplementary schools: Spaces of radical blackness'. In: R. Majors (ed.) *Educating Our Black Children: New Directions and Radical Approaches*. London: Routledge-Falmer.

Sewell, T. (1997) *Black Masculinities and Schooling: How Black Boys Survive Modern Schooling*. Stoke-on-Trent: Trentham Books.

Sewell, T. (2009) *Generating Genius: Black Boys in Search of Love, Ritual and Schooling*. Stoke-on-Trent: Trentham Books.

Shukra, K. (1998) *The Changing Pattern of Black Politics in Britain*. London: Pluto.

Sivanandan, A. (1982) *A Different Hunger: Writings on Black Resistance*. London: Pluto.

Solórzano, D. and Yosso, T. (2009) 'Counter-storytelling as an analytical framework for educational research'. In: E. Taylor, D. Gillborn and G. Ladson-Billings (eds) *Foundations of Critical Race Theory in Education*. Abingdon: Routledge.

Song, M. (2003) *Choosing Ethnic Identity*. Cambridge: Polity.

Stone, M. (1981) *The Education of the Black Child in Britain: The Myth of Multiracial Education*. London: Fontana.

Taylor, E. (2009) 'The foundations of critical race theory in education: An introduction'. In: E. Taylor, D. Gillborn and G. Ladson-Billings (eds) *Foundations of Critical Race Theory in Education*. Abingdon: Routledge.

Tomlinson, S. (2008) *Race and Education: Policy and Politics in Britain*. Maidenhead: Open University Press.

Warmington, P. (2009) 'Taking race out of scare quotes: Race conscious social analysis in an ostensibly post-racial world', *Race Ethnicity and Education*, 12(3): 281–96.

Warmington, P. (2012) 'A tradition in ceaseless motion': Critical race theory and black British intellectual spaces', *Race, Ethnicity & Education*, 15(1): 5–21.

Warmington, P. (2014) *Black British Intellectuals and Education*. Abingdon: Routledge (Forthcoming).

9 Decolonizing education
Discovering critical hope in marginal spaces

Merlyne Cruz

In this chapter, I recount varied ways in which colonial history has shaped Filipino ways of knowing, doing and being. My writing offers a re-theorizing of the 'anti-colonial' by offering context-specific narratives of local subjects, viewed as "agents of critical hope" (Warmington, this book). I discuss how various Filipino scholars and I have used diverse facets of critical hope to build decolonizing, transforming sites for personal and social emancipation.

Consistent with the anti-colonial framework used, I employ a combination of reflexive performance counter narrative (Richardson 2000) forms in this chapter, namely: personal narrative of the self; self-stories, fragmented, layered texts; cultural criticism and "accounts that disrupt discourse by exposing the complexities and contradictions that exist under official history" (Mutua and Swadener 2004: 16). The critical, counter narrative is a central genre of contemporary decolonizing writing (Denzin *et al.* 2008).

At the outset, I would like to state that, as a decolonizing person barely emerging from a "culture of silence" (Freire 1970), I find that my default approach in thinking and presenting ideas tends to lean on the "naming-reflection-action" approach espoused by Freire (1985). I realize that there are limitations to this method. One of these is the risk of the approach being interpreted as more of an introspective technique, a solitary self-dialogue in which I as the author, could be misunderstood as indulging in self-narration, probing personal meanings, and wallowing in subjectivity. The naming–reflection-action method that I have brought into this work is a consequence and part of the decolonizing process I am currently immersed in. Such ongoing process involves the silenced/marginalized/colonized in a) *naming* – naming internalized oppression; naming the oppressor and the oppressive structures; b) *reflection* – gaining the ability to question one's reality as constructed by colonial narratives; developing critical consciousness that can understand the consequences of invisibility and silence; asking: Where do I go from here? c) *action* – giving back to marginalized communities (in this case for me, in particular, the Filipino community); and telling and writing one's story – that in the telling and writing, others may be encouraged to tell their own (Strobel 2000). My sincere intention in taking on a naming–reflection-action mode in this chapter is to offer an invitation to the reader to engage in reflective conversation with me.

Colonial history, education, epistemic colonization

My birth country, The Philippines, was ravaged by a long history of colonization – first by Spain for four centuries and by the USA for half a century. Nothing was sacred in the colonization process. The long period of colonial rule resulted in the loss of traditions and recollections. Strobel (2000: ix) identifies this phenomenon as a colonial mentality, or "a state of marginal consciousness which lacks the critical awareness of the forces of domination and oppression that shape attitudes, values, and behaviour in the colonized." It is an intellectual captivity where people suffer from cultural amnesia and develop a warped sense of values and distorted picture of their own reality.

Pecson and Racelis (1959) tells how in the first decade (1898–1908) of US colonialism over the Philippines, the US government immediately sought to instill an educational system that would help train and enforce Filipinos of the duties of a colonial ideal. In 1901, under the Department of Public Instruction headed by the USA, the Philippine Commission developed a centralized public school system. The following year, there were 1,074 US teachers in the Philippines whose mandate was to train Filipino teachers (Pecson and Racelis 1959). Filipino historian Renato Constantino (1966) has argued that educational institutions became an instrument for instilling the idea that colonial ideas, culture, and educational system were superior to the cultural and educational legacies of the indigenous Filipino culture. He further claims that, rather than encouraging the advancement of Philippines' literature and language, colonizers imposed Western practices, ideals and values and created schools that closely resembled the US public school system arguing that Filipino self-rule would be possible only through their guidance and direction. Constantino (1966) has aptly described this as an aftermath of the masterstroke to use education as an instrument of colonial policy and to serve as a powerful weapon in instituting colonial conquest. Kane reinforces these conclusions:

> To co-opt the language of the colonizer is to co-opt racism and to "betray" one's own self and culture, and to internalize one's own inferiority. Through this historical process, the gradual loss of language and hence, culture, the history of the colonized is buried in the past: its great accomplishments and thinkers lost.
>
> (Kane 2007: 357)

Kane (2007) argues that one of the tasks of the colonist was/is to replace indigenous histories and cultures and replace them with the newly constructed ideologies. By gaining control over education, our colonizers were able to reshape history and alter the memory of the Filipino people. Constantino (1966: 8) described this as the beginning of our 'mis-education,' for the people learned no longer as Filipinos but as 'colonials.' Shaped by the overriding factor of expanding the colonizers' control, the pattern of education fostered certain attitudes on the part of the governed.

The moulding of human minds, notes Constantino (1966), is the best means of conquest. Centuries after our first colonizers came to our shores, epistemic colonization continues to manifest in different ways in the lives of many Filipinos (Nadal 2009). The everydayness and systemic effect of colonization remains in people's episteme: imbibing 'White love' (Rafael 2000) syndrome ('White is beautiful,' 'White is intelligent,' 'White is powerful') while devaluing one's own indigenous culture; tolerating (neo)colonial mentality; embracing a Western-dependent identity resulting in an inability to articulate one's ethnic identity (David and Okazaki 2006).

Filipino studies critic Maria Root (1997) points out that trauma stemming from colonialism fragments and fractures the essence of the colonized person's being and self-knowledge. Lily Mendoza explains:

> In a national life where the doxa is that of a racialized colonial ideology, assimilation becomes the only logical mode of survival [...] Whether in the case of Filipinos living in the Philippines growing up dreaming of snow, white Christmas and ambitioning someday to [...] live forever in the land flowing with milk and honey, or of Filipino Americans frantically erasing traces of their otherness by unlearning their native accents, erasing their past, denying their ethnic background, or simply acting white, internalized racism for many centuries served as the naturalized defining condition of the Filipino.
>
> (Mendoza 2002: 10)

As a child, I have heard relatives and friends make fun of our 'brown, native' physical features. Skin whitening has always been a perennial preoccupation, a daily obsession for many Filipinos (Pierce 2005). Imported, Western goods are preferred over locally made products; the latter perceived as always of lesser value (Quezon 1966). English continues to be esteemed as the language of the educated, of the higher class, of the cultured, of the successful, while local dialects are viewed as means of communication used by the poor, the lowly, and those considered ignorant and uneducated members of the community (Nadal 2009).

As individuals, and as a people, many of us continue to live our 'raced identities' (MacNaughton 2001) in and through the power relations that constitute our daily lives. Notions of hope in my country have always been strongly attached to education. The key to an individual's success in life has always been taught to us as being access to colonial education regardless of the fact that it silences and oppresses indigenous knowledge and values, glorifies everything Western and thwarts critical thinking.

Throughout all my academic pursuits, I have been immersed in Eurocentric knowledge and, consequently, developed a 'natural' inclination to learn mainly from White scholars. The idea of researching a group of early childhood educators' commitment to cultural diversity in my Doctoral study emerged from my consuming interest in episteme and epistemology. I was unaware then that deeper reasons for my preoccupation with worldviews were embedded in the larger contexts of my socio-cultural history.

Through my reading, I learned that an end to oppression would require the ability to critically perceive one's existence in the world (Freire 1970). This marked the start of an active journey in unmasking the discourses of colonialism that pervaded my world. Although often, my desire for my White master's approval would drive me back to mimic his ways and thinking, this time, a simultaneous, nagging voice that prods to resist, begs to subvert and betray the mimicry. The Filipino-American scholar Linda Pierce explains this struggle:

> You come to understand that your life, your day-to-day interactions that were once so personal are actually part and parcel of particular constructions of race, gender, class, and nation. You inherit these struggles by virtue of being born. And then, only after processing painful emotions, uncovering relevant historical context, and recognising your relationship to others in the trajectory of the past and present – you begin to comprehend your life. You are exhausted. But now you are ready to begin.
> (Pierce 2005: 34)

Critical hope

I consider hope as located, first and foremost, in highly situated practices of people struggling to live within desperate conditions. In a country where individual hopes can easily be thwarted, the temptation to despair and to be passive in life, it seems, could have easily engulfed a nation's existence. And yet, there are elements that help go beyond nourishing individual hopes and continue to overcome the numerous obstacles brought about by our socio-cultural, historical and political contexts.

Hope most centrally involves the practice of building lives even in the midst of suffering and oppression, uncertainties, risks and difficulties. Hope opens up spaces for individuals to mediate between what is and what might be (Freire 1994). It draws upon the confidence engendered by the very act of survival in order to fuel further acts of transformation. Webb speaks about a hope: "full of risk that takes as its objective a liberating utopia; an adventurous hope grounded in the capacity of human beings to construct new ways of organising life, a precarious hope which moves beyond open critique and emphasizes the necessity of transforming society" (Webb 2010: 337). As a colonized/decolonizing being, I am convinced that a major component of critical hope is a critical consciousness of the ways power operates to legitimate oppressive social divisions. Such consciousness empowers individuals to name inequities and to discern the ways that individuals are discursively, ideologically, and culturally constructed as human beings (Ladson-Billings and Donnor 2008). It provides the strength to draw upon discursive traditions to explain social and political phenomena for multiple knowing (Dei and Kempf 2006).

I contend that critical consciousness is about knowing one's authentic story (the socio-political construction of self) and the ability to synchronize interpretations of one's story to form a meaningful position. Having critical hope is being actively conscious about one's self and one's place in a diverse society. This kind of hope, Glass (this book) argues, can be transformative; it reaches beyond the specificities of today and the material horizons of the moment, not in an empty way, but in actions that connect us with others. For Glass (this book), the story of the struggle for justice is the story of hope as an ontological need finding expression as a political force. Gutierrez (1990) describes such hope as that which spurs us to action; it frees us to commit ourselves to social praxis. Critical hope, when anchored in practice, could serve as a powerful impetus to sustainable social change (Freire 1994).

Warmington (this book) argues that there is nothing optional about critical hope. Critical hope openly proclaims its affiliation with efforts to produce an egalitarian and democratic world that refuses to stand for the perpetuation of human suffering (Kincheloe and Steinberg 1997). Critical hope, embodied as political force, Glass (this book) argues, infuses purpose into suffering so that it fuels empowerment; the hope that animates liberation struggles emerges from deep engagement with the historicity of human life itself, with our enduring capacity to make history and culture at the same time as history and culture make us.

How might those immersed in the negative impact of colonial violence – those against whom education has been utilized as a tool of dispossession – use critical hope? How can critical hope serve as counter narrative for both personal and social liberation? Together with Zournazi (2002), I ask: How can we build new sites for contemporary struggles? What revolutions in hope can make a difference? How could we establish discontinuities in which something new gets born?

The academic project of anti-colonial thinking and practice is to challenge and resist Eurocentric theorizing of the colonial encounter. Dei and Kempf (2006) have argued that in many ways, the 'anti-colonial thought' is the emergence of a new political, cultural, and intellectual movement reflecting the values and aspirations of colonized and resisting peoples/subjects. Both stress that colonized peoples require an anti-colonial prism that is useful in helping to disabuse our minds of the falsehoods told about our peoples, our pasts and our histories. The approach to anti-colonial discursive thought and practice is informed by the academic and political project calling for knowledge that colonized groups can use to find viable solutions to our own problems (Dei and Kempf 2006). Glass (this book) refers to hope made manifest as revolutionary futurity; political force demands practice that requires significant effort and avoids the trap of despair.

Decolonizing praxis

Rabaka (2003: 7) has argued that one of the most important tasks of a critical anti-colonial theory is "to capture and critique the continuities and discontinuities of the colonial and neo-colonial" in order to make sense of one's colonized life and worlds. In this struggle, we can point to some positive developments. In this section, I discuss multiple ways that people of colour, particularly Filipino scholars and activists, have used facets of critical hope to build decolonizing, transforming sites for enacting one's responsibility to others and for personal and social emancipation. The power of the anti-colonial prism lies in its offering of new imaginings and philosophical insights to challenge Eurocentric discourses to pave the way for indigenous intellectual and political liberation (Dei and Kempf 2006). Here, I present a re-theorizing of the 'anti-colonial' by offering context-specific praxis of local subjects, viewed as 'agents of critical hope' (Warmington, this book). The examples below, namely: thinking from the margins, drinking from one's own wells, *barangay* (community) building pedagogy, and *pinayist* (Filipina feminist) praxis illustrate how critical hope – as a political force – can evolve.

Thinking from the margins

In her essay *Choosing the Margin as a Space for Radical Openness*, the Black feminist theorist bell hooks suggests that we reclaim the word 'margin' from its traditional use as a marker of exclusion and see it as an act of positive appropriation for people of colour:

> Marginality is a central location for the production of counter hegemonic discourse. It is found in the words, habits, and the ways one lives [...] It is a site one clings to even when moving to the centre [...] It nourishes our capacity to resist [...] It is an exclusive space where we recover ourselves, where we move in solidarity to erase the category coloniser/colonised.
> (hooks 1990: 149–50)

Thinking from the margins is a form of critical hope that enables the oppressed to circulate counter discourses to formulate oppositional interpretations of their identities, interests and needs (Brettschneider 2002). It involves asking how particular ideas come to dominate our understandings of and actions in the social world and contribute to inequities in it. Enacting a 'thinking from the margins' praxis seeks to foster an 'oppositional consciousness' (Collins 2000) and nourishes the understanding that knowledges, subjectivities, and social practices take shape within "asymmetrical and incommensurate cultural spheres" (Mohanty 1991: 181). Beginning from the lives and interests of marginalized communities, one is able to access the politics of knowledge and the power investments that go with them to engage in transformative work (Mohanty 2003).

Thinking from the margins provides vantage points to understand and deconstruct mystifications of dominance and oppression within one's immediate realms. One's marginality could operate as a location of possibilities, a source of strength, and a site to engage in critical hope as one pays special attention to 'Other' ways of reading and re-reading the world (Dillard *et al.* 2000).

Drinking from one's own wells

Gutierrez (1984: xix) expands our notion of critical hope to include drinking "from our own wells, from our own experience not only as individuals but also as members of a people." Drinking from my own wells means honouring my Indigenous Filipino ways of thinking and being and making these ways visible in my teaching and research work. It involves reclaiming my Filipino Indigenous 'self' – a self underpinned, among other things, by elements of spirituality and holism. From here on, my scholarly pursuits evolved into a political, symbolic act of welcoming back a part of me that centuries of colonization have stolen before I was even born. I chose to drink from the wells of wisdom of past and present Filipino activists and scholars who introduced me to counter-narratives I never knew existed. Their input provided concrete examples of how critical hope and Filipino praxis serve as decolonizing tools in education.

Re-meeting history, learning critical pedagogy from Filipino mentors

On the surface, many Filipinos habitually analyze Philippines in the light of colonial myths and foreign concepts. We seem to act on the basis of premises that reveal a lack of understanding of the rich experiences contained in our history of struggles for freedom. History appears as a segmented documentation of events that occurred in the past, without any unifying thread, without continuity, save that of chronology, with the present.

Constantino's writings (see for example *Identity and Consciousness, Miseducation of the Filipino, Neocolonial Identity and Counterconsciousness*, and *Westernizing Factors in the Philippines*) reveal how resignation and passivity, respect for the master and depreciation of indigenous ways – imposed by the colonizers to make us good colonial citizens – had been passed on by our ancestors as virtues. Constantino (1975) instructs us to value the need for a real people's history. Such a history, according to him, must rediscover the past in order to make it reusable. Our understandings of *kasaysayan* (history) must take a critical turn of drawing out the *saysay* (meaning, sense, or relevance) of events for a constituent people. Reclaiming Filipino history is a process of reclaiming memories that have been submerged, taught to be unimportant, inconsequential, and must be negated (Strobel 2000). From Constantino, I learned to face history in a proactive way, believing that history, as an analytical guide in perceiving present reality, is a liberating factor.

The Filipino cultural theorist Epifanio San Juan, Jr. (2004) taught me that there are models to draw from for social change and justice on the Philippine legacy of liberatory praxis. I re-learned history through the lens of critical scholars who taught that the leaders of our first revolutionary movements (1896–8) possessed courage and brilliance to fight our colonizers. The works of our national hero José Rizal (1912), whose core writings on individual rights and freedom are found in his works *Noli Me Tangere* (published in Berlin in 1887) and *El Filibusterismo* (published in Ghent in 1891), expanded my understandings of the dynamics of submission and resistance under colonialism.

Vicente Rafael's (1993) innovative interpretation of the early Spanish period, his focus on translation and conversion makes his works of great value to someone like me interested in the role of language in history. Virgilio Enriquez (1986, 1992), founder and pioneer in the field of indigenous Filipino mindset, expresses the importance of looking to the indigenous past as a reference to break the chains of colonialism. This form of epistemology, identified as *Sikolohiyang Pilipino*, is both a narrative and a call for action. It questions the imposition of Western theoretical models in explaining why the Filipino is the way s/he is and seeks to explain realities from the Filipino perspective, taking into account the distinct values and characteristics of the Filipino (Enriquez 2004). Enriquez sought to undermine his students' excessive awe and unquestioning acceptance of Western norms of scholarship. He encouraged Filipino students to trust their own instincts and believe in their own ability to create new knowledge (Mendoza 2002). In lieu of outside (mostly Western) authorities, he motivated them to use their own voices, think their own thoughts, and look to each other, and to local scholars for intellectual challenge.

Sikolohiyang Pilipino becomes more than just a 'school of thought;' it demands a fundamental transformation in worldview and personal valuing. Personal alignment in this regard entails bringing one's life into alignment with a new set of values, priorities, goals and actions. These include the centering of Filipino worldview(s) in one's teaching and research studies. Employing the principle of 'indigenization from within,' one sees the need to reject the colonial framework and to replace it with an entirely new paradigm that, once adopted, generates a set of associated social values. For example, Indigenous Filipino epistemology refers to *malay* or consciousness such as *paninindigan* (courage of one's critical convictions) and *pakikibaka* (level of fusion in a common struggle). *Pakikibaka* awakens the consciousness of present day realities and motivates individuals and collective groups of people to be as one in their struggle to break away from clutches of oppression and domination existing in the world (Enriquez 1986). The Filipino value of *kapwa* (the other in one's self) connotes the shared being of all humanity. *Ang kapwa ay sarili din* (the 'Other' is oneself also) is a common Filipino saying. Thus, *pakikipagkapwa* (the act of sharing one's being) is always for the good, always for a positive purpose.

Such vision of the world includes a critical realization that people are agents and creators of change. Linked to this is the understanding that we are utterly reliant upon each other. Critical hope, when linked to *kapwa* and other core Filipino Indigenous values, underlies inter-subjective communion. Hope, in this sense is located on the spiritual plane, where communion and hope stem from a love that drives one to care for, respect, honour and value others.

Barangay (community) building pedagogy

Daus-Magbaual (2010) identifies a model of *barangay* (community) building pedagogy that emphasizes communal spirit based on community teaching. *Barangay* pedagogy supports a leadership pathway that provides learners to engage in social justice education. It inspires communities to form political, social, historical, and dialogical spaces to engage youth to understand their history and identity to become teachers for future generations. The activities of Filipino scholars in a global diaspora who are learning about the world, not simply by reflecting on it but by changing it, is an invaluable resource to augment critical pedagogy (San Juan, Jr. 2007).

What are some concrete examples of teaching and learning projects that engage in this type of critical pedagogy? The Filipino youth leader Efren Peñaflorida developed an out-of-the-box delivery of education services called *Kariton Klasrum* (Quismundo 2012). The programme uses pushcart (*kariton*) as classroom (*klasrum*) to seek out its intended target: out-of-school, homeless children. With a group of committed teenagers, Peñaflorida pushes a makeshift pushcart which he calls *kariton ng karungan* (pushcart of knowledge), packed with school supplies and books to teach homeless street children in several cities in the Philippines. Taking his pushcart to slum areas of massive dumps, Peñaflorida enthralls children for love of learning. The youth volunteers in his project, who serve as teachers and role models to the young urban learners involved in their programme, illustrate the importance of youth helping communities engage in social justice endeavors. The *Kariton Klasrum* project is now being replicated in other communities locally and abroad to bring a holistic learning experience for children who cannot go to school through providing an alternative learning environment and healthcare.

A number of Filipino educators currently based in North America have begun to look at developing curricula and pedagogy with decolonization curriculum frameworks. Patricia Halagao (2004, 2010) examined the impact of *Pinoy Teach*, a curriculum framework that focuses on Philippine and Filipino American history and culture using a problem-posing pedagogy that encourages students to think critically through multiple perspectives on history. As part of the learning process, college students mentor and teach what they are learning to younger students. *Pinoy Teach* provides a venue "to create a curriculum conceived by Filipinos, about Filipinos, and for Filipinos to liberate them from shackles of colonial ignorance" (Halagao 2010: 499) and is integral in moving participants through stages of decolonization.

Halagao (2010) theorized from her decolonization experiences of pain, passion and background. Harnessing the pain from colonialism, capitalizing on the passion of a renewed commitment to oneself, and inspiring hope for change became the bases of this decolonizing curriculum. A decolonizing curriculum must have, among other things, a social–action component that develops leadership, models activism, produces empowerment, self-efficacy, and inspires carving one's own niche in giving back to the community to effect social change (Halagao 2010).

Pinayist (Filipina feminist) praxis

Tintiangco-Cubales and Sacramento (2009: 179–81) define *Pinayist* praxis as:

> a process, place and production that aims to connect the global and local to the personal issues and stories of *Pinay* [Filipina women] struggle, survival,

sisterhood, and strength. It is an individual and communal process of decolonization, humanization, self-determination, and relationship building, ultimately moving toward liberation. Through this process *Pinays* [Filipinas] create spaces where their epistemologies are at the center of the discourse/dialogue/conversation and organizing [...] *Pinayist* pedagogy aims to uncover challenges that *Pinays* face, while creating plans of action that pursue social change for the betterment of their lives [...] Similarly, spaces of *Pinayist* pedagogy become places of healing for both *Pinayist* teacher and student.

The *Pin@y Educational Program* (PEP) is one example of a *Pinayist* service-learning programme that creates critical spaces where teachers and students study the struggles and survival stories of Filipinos in the USA and throughout the world (Tintiangco-Cubales 2007). It provides opportunities for students in various levels to teach and learn from each other and offers training for students interested in teaching and research. The program addresses the larger needs of the lack of Filipino-American educators and the underrepresentation of a critical Filipino-American studies curriculum.

What difference do these decolonizing frameworks and educational resources make to students, teachers, families, communities, and the larger public? Studies (Halagao 2010; Daus-Magbaual 2010) point to similar results:

a   Identity transformation as impact at the level of personal awareness, identity and pride – this includes love and appreciation of ethnic history, culture, and identity; feelings of lasting empowerment and self-efficacy; life-long embodiment and commitment to principles of diversity; and continued activism in the teaching profession and/or involvement in social and civic issues in the community.
b   New ways of learning and teaching – *Pinayist* pedagogy has impacted the ways in which *Pinays*, particularly young people, are viewed and how they view and treat themselves.
c   Reproduction of impact – the critical impact of these curricula resources continues to grow in terms of increased collaboration among community organizations and more Filipinos opening their minds to decolonizing, anti-colonial perspectives. Some have developed ongoing activism in their work as teachers, in other professions, and/or through civic engagement where they lived.

The preceding examples illustrate the kind of hope Zournazi (2002) speaks about: to hope that things can be born in your life; hope can be a dialogue about gifts and exchange in another – about acts of giving that open a gateway to possibilities in the midst of difficulties and uncertainties. It is the hope that Filipino activists and critical scholars mentioned in this essay enact – one founded on community vision and collective activism. It is this kind of critical hope that is imperative for us to articulate and express through our shared responsibility to each other.

Looking forward

This chapter demonstrates the broad context which understandings of critical hope and anti-colonial framework bring. The lessons for educators and students are numerous. For educators, critical hope is a hope that calls us to action. Hope calls us to look to the rich and varied knowledges of the different learners in our settings to facilitate transformative inclusive education (Dei and Kempf 2006). This means addressing the histories, strengths, aspirations and desires of our students. Critical hope prods me to "drink from my own wells" (Gutierrez 1984) and to continue to refer to critical pedagogy – the humble, evolving kind that learns from diverse peoples in differing historical and socio-historical, cultural and political locations and asks questions of itself, and induces us to ask questions of ourselves (Kincheloe 2008).

As teachers full of hope, we need to learn to ask critical questions, to be willing to ask questions of our own thinking and practice, to be ready to ask challenging questions, and engage in the consequences of the answers. Hope gives us the courage to ask questions that open up spaces for deepening and enlarging our work for social justice, equity and diversity. Questions such as: How could educators engage with – not the 'feel good,' 'sanitized,' stories of life – personal narratives of oppression, of racism, of difficulties and of suffering of marginalized individuals and groups? How do you build a critical awareness of suffering caused by colonizing/normalizing discourses among educators? How do you use narratives with co-educators, children and families that talk about hope, inspiration, agency and transformation? What hopes and visions guide the actions of educators? What theories/other thinking help educators to enact their hopes and visions? What policies support educators to enact their hopes and visions? What challenges confront educators in enacting their hopes and visions?

In deconstructing and decolonizing those structures within educational institutions that privilege Western knowledge systems, we could ask: How could educational settings turn pedagogies of oppression into pedagogies of liberation? How could educators be supported in their decolonizing tasks, particularly those that involve the return of dignity and self-determination among marginalized groups? In what ways could we support educators' strategies to build decolonizing epistemology and open up new knowledge? How can these new understandings move within and beyond the realms of current thinking and pedagogical practices?

Critical hope and anti-colonialism present opportunities to address the questions raised in this final section. These questions have been constructed to assist action-oriented solutions to real issues. These questions challenge us to engage in strengthening local research capacities, to find ways to better comprehend sources and sites of agency, and search for new perspectives that would destabilize oppressive paradigms that control our ongoing colonized worlds.

The development of critical consciousness should be a major objective in all educational endeavours. Critical hope therefore stirs us to be part of 'critically knowing communities' (MacNaughton 2005) engaging in bringing about change in education. Our critically knowing communities must extend to White allies and anti-colonial people of colour, scholars and theorists in marginal spaces whose works honor Indigenous/'Other' marginalized epistemologies and, in so doing, heal the wounds of colonization. We learn that, education generally, and resistance specifically, must be community-building exercises (Dei and Kempf 2006).

For those against whom education has been an instrument for dispossession, critical hope and decolonizing education calls for summoning one's past – our re-usable past – and place within the present and future. Critical hope has the possibility to create and sustain educators' practices of exposing what it has meant for particular groups of people to survive; of ensuring that transgressions are remembered and that the resistance acts are reinterpreted and re-applied to further emancipatory projects.

All these lessons beckon us to build critical hope, the kind that will stir us to imagine what is possible so we do not only transcend the challenges in which we find ourselves but dismantle the structures and spheres that fortify colonial domination. It is this kind of hope that prods us to engage in ongoing conversation, critical reflection and collaborative, transformative action.

References

Brettschneider, M. (2002) *Democratic Theorizing From the Margin*. Philadelphia, PA: Temple University Press.

Collins, P.H. (2000) *Black Feminist Thought: Knowledge, Consciousness, and the Politics of Empowerment*. New York: Routledge.

Constantino, R. (1966) *The Making of a Filipino: A Story of Philippine Colonial Politics*. Quezon City: Malaya Books.

Constantino, R. (1975) *The Philippines a Past Revisited*. Metro Manila: Tala Publishing Corporation.

David, E.J. and Okazaki, S. (2006) 'Colonial mentality: A review and recommendation for Filipino American psychology', *Cultural Diversity and Ethnic Minority Psychology*, 12: 1–16.

Dei, G.S. and Kempf, A. (eds) (2006) *Anti-Colonialism and Education: The Politics of Resistance*. Rotterdam: Sense Publishers.

Denzin, N.K., Lincoln, Y. and Smith, L.T. (2008) 'Introduction: Critical methodologies and indigenous inquiry'. In: N.K. Denzin, Y. Lincoln and L.T. Smith (eds) *Handbook of Critical and Indigenous Methodologies*. London: Sage.

Dillard, C.B., Abdur-Rashid, D. and Tyson, C.A. (2000) 'My soul is a witness: Affirming pedagogies of the spirit', *International Journal of Qualitative Studies in Education*, 13: 447–62.

Enriquez, V.G. (1986) 'Kapwa: A core concept in Filipino social psychology'. In: V.G. Enriquez (ed.) *Philippine World-View*. Singapore: Institute of Southeast Asian Studies.

Enriquez, V.G. (1992) *From Colonial to Liberation Psychology*. Quezon City: University of the Philippines Press.

Enriquez, V.G. (2004) *From Colonial to Liberation Psychology: The Philippine Experience*. Dasmariñas, Cavite: De La Salle University Books.

Freire, P. (1970) *Pedagogy of the Oppressed*, trans. M. Bergman Ramos. New York: Seabury Press.

Freire, P. (1985) *The Politics of Education*. South Hadley, MA: Bergin and Garvey.

Freire, P. (1994) *Pedagogy of Hope: Reliving Pedagogy of the Oppressed*. New York: Continuum.

Gutiérrez, G. (1984) *We Drink from Our Own Wells: The Spiritual Journey of a People*. Maryknoll, NY: Orbis Books.

Gutiérrez, G. (1990) 'Toward a theology of liberation'. In: A.T. Hennelly (ed.) *Liberation Theology: A Documentary History*. Maryknoll, NY: Orbis Books.

Halagao, P.E. (2004) 'Holding up the mirror: The complexity of seeing your ethnic self in history', *Theory and Research in Social Education*, 32: 459–83.

Halagao P.E. (2010) 'Liberating Filipino Americans through decolonizing curriculum', *Race, Ethnicity and Education*, 13: 495–512.

hooks, b. (1990) 'Choosing the margin as a space of radical openness'. In: *Yearning: Race, Gender, and Cultural Politics*. Boston, MA: South End Press.

Kane, N. (2007) 'Frantz Fanon's theory of racialization: Implications for globalization', *Human Architecture: Journal of the Sociology of Self-Knowledge*, 5: 353–62.

Kincheloe, J. (2008) 'Foreword'. In: A. Churchill (ed.) *Rocking Your World: The Emotional Journey Into Critical Discourses*. Rotterdam: Sense Publishers.

Kincheloe, J. and Steinberg, S. (1997) *Changing Multiculturalism*. Buckingham: Open University Press.

Ladson-Billings, G. and Donnor, J. (2008) 'Writing for the call: The moral activist role of critical race theory scholarship'. In: N.K. Denzin and Y.S. Lincoln (eds) *Handbook of Critical and Indigenous Methodologies*. London: Sage.

MacNaughton, G. (2001) 'Voices of Anglo-Australian children: Colonialism and change', *Every Child*, 7: 8–9.

MacNaughton, G. (2005) *Doing Foucault in Early Childhood Studies: Applying Poststructural Ideas*. London: Routledge.

Mendoza, S.L. (2002) *Between the Homeland and the Diaspora: The Politics of Theorizing Filipino and Filipino American Identities*. New York: Routledge.

Mohanty, C. (1991) 'Under Western eyes: Feminist scholarship and colonial discourses'. In: P. Mongia (ed.) *Contemporary Postcolonial Theory*. London: Arnold.

Mohanty C. (2003) *Feminism without Borders: Decolonizing Theory, Practicing Solidarity*. Durham, NC: Duke University Press.

Mutua, K. and Swadener, B.B. (2004) 'Introduction' In: K. Mutua and B.B. Swadener (eds) *Decolonizing Research in Cross-Cultural Contexts: Critical Personal Narratives*. Albany, NY: State University of New York Press.

Nadal, K.L. (2009) *Filipino American Psychology: A Handbook of Theory, Research, and Clinical Practice*. Bloomington, IN: Author House Publishing.

Pecson, G.T. and Racelis, M. (1959) *Tales of the American Teachers in the Philippines*. Quezon City: Carmelo and Bauerman.

Pierce, L.M. (2005) 'Not just my closet: Exposing familial, cultural, and imperial skeletons'. In: M.L. de Jesús (ed.) *Pinay Power: Feminist Critical Theory: Theorizing the Filipina/American Experience*. New York: Routledge.

Quezon, M. (1966) 'Philippine racism', *Philippine Graphic*, 2 November.

Quismundo, T. (2012, 14 January) *Kariton Klasrum on Streets Soon*. Philippine Daily Inquirer.

Rabaka, R. (2003) '"Deliberately using the word colonial in a much broader sense", W.E.B. Du Bois's Concept of "Semi-colonialism" as Critique of and Contribution to

Postcolonialism', Online. Available HTTP: <http://english.chass.ncsu.edu/jouvert/v7i2/rabaka.htm> (Accessed 14 October 2012).

Rafael, V. (1993) *Contracting Colonialism: Translation and Christian Conversion in Tagalog Society under Early Spanish Rule*. Ithaca, NY: Cornell University Press.

Rafael, V. (2000) *White Love and Other Events in Filipino History*. Durham, NC: Duke University Press.

Richardson, L. (2000) 'Writing: A method of inquiry'. In: N.K. Denzin and Y.S. Lincoln (eds) *The SAGE Handbook of Qualitative Research*. Thousand Oaks, CA: Sage.

Rizal, J. (1912) *The Philippines: A Century Hence*. Manila: Philippine Education Company.

Root, M. (ed.) (1997) *Filipino Americans: Transformation and Identity*. Thousand Oaks, CA: Sage.

San Juan Jr., E. (2004) *Working through the Contradictions: From Cultural Theory to Critical Practice*. Lewisburg, PA: Bucknell University Press.

San Juan Jr., E. (2007) *In the Wake of Terror: Class, Race, Nation, Ethnicity in the Postmodern World*. Lanham, MD: Lexington Books.

Strobel, L.M. (2000) *Coming Full Circle: The Process of Decolonization Among Post-1965 Filipino Americans*. Quezon City: Giraffe Books.

Tintiangco-Cubales, A. (2007) *Pin@y Educational Partnerships: A Filipino American Studies Sourcebook*, vol. 1: *Philippine and Filipina American History*, Menlo Park, CA: Phoenix Publishing House International.

Tintiangco-Cubales, A. and Sacramento, J. (2009) 'Practising Pinayist pedagogy', *Amerasia Journal*, 35: 179–87.

Webb, D. (2010) 'Paulo Freire and "the need for a kind of education in hope"', *Cambridge Journal of Education*, 40: 327–39.

Zournazi, M. (2002) *Hope: New Philosophies for Change*. Wollongong: University of Wollongong.

Part IV
Philosophical overviews of critical hope

10 Hope

An emancipatory resource across the ages

John Horton

Hope's origin

Just what is *hope*? How is *hope* emancipatory? Why a resource? From where did *hope* come? How does 'ordinary' hope transition to critical hope, the distinctive perspective of this book?

Hope is a somewhat slippery term, used very casually in everyday fashion, 'I hope your day is going well.' But hope can also be deep and serious. Hope can have gravitas. *Serious* hope is a clustering concept that seemingly melds with a family of related notions, words like emancipate, imagine, transform, flourish, all verbs that connote action and imply agency. Serious hope is more than a state – like, say, optimism. We hope *for* something, with a future happening in mind, but hope seems also to convey the notion of bringing something to fruition, a goal to be somehow realized. Likewise there are some nouns, as we shall explore, that have close kinship to serious hope: dignity, humanity, freedom, altruism and, perhaps controversially, the very idea of knowledge, and its potential link to openness, to access and to critical empowerment.

The cluster of concepts associated with hope provides the basis for discerning the criticality of hope. Critical hope, then, provides a synoptic understanding of the dynamic fusion of critique and possibility. It is in the domain of opening up of human knowledge that our hope story begins.

The classical story of hope is popularly attributed to Greek mythology, with an account by the historian Hesiod that describes a trick played on the supreme god Zeus, by a lesser god, Prometheus.[1] It had been the task of Prometheus, a Titan god, to populate the world with men and animals. Believing that the human race which he had created was in need of fire, he stole a flaming torch from Zeus, passing it to mortals, a deed for which he suffered an eternally gruesome fate. The audacity of this theft and its inordinate benefit to mortals has taken on special resonance through history in poetry, art, music, drama and philosophy. The Promethean act of magnanimity has been seized on by artists and philosophers ever since, largely because it represented three symbolic breakthroughs for humanity: a more hopeful future for the human race, an open portal to new and liberating knowledge, and a template of audacious agency in the service of humankind.[2]

How to interpret hope has been the subject of much debate for more than 2000 years. In considering the origin of hope in the mists of time, the myth of Prometheus reminds us of hope's presence as part of a creation story that involves originary explanations of the genesis of the world; with Prometheus, the notion of hope takes on an early identification with human curiosity, knowledge and power. The eponymous Promethean came to signify new hope for western humanity, with the light and heat of fire representing the liberatory struggle to transcend the 'given' through the acquisition of new, enlightening knowledge.

Fire devolving onto the human race became synonymous with 'progress' in mythology, with stories and poems offering different variations on the Hesiod myth within that leitmotif. In philosophic thought, Plato offered his own translation of the Promethean myth in which he declared fire to be the means of life and the source of reason and mind. The new hope for humankind, delivered by Prometheus, was picked up famously centuries later by Francis Bacon, and equally famously in Hegel and Marx.

For the main part, then, hope as symbolized by Prometheus – historicized hope – is a positive word, replete, as I will attempt to show, with cognitive and conative power. But Promethean hope's downside also has had its innings, most notably by Frederic Nietzsche (1878): '[H]ope is the worst of evils, for it prolongs the torment of man.' Nietzsche is not alone in this view, since Promethean acts have become to some a cautionary symbol of transgression, dangerous consequences, and reckless risk as well as a cause of Nietzchean tormentedness.

Along with risk and its consequences, hope becomes importantly identified in the Promethean myth with self-sacrificing philanthropy, agency with an altruistic mission, promulgated and enacted within a hostile environment. Prometheus overcomes benightedness through daring, foresight and determination. Emboldened to improve the creative possibilities of humankind, he defies the social order as ordained by the gods, thereby issuing a first challenge to the sovereignty of convention. With the translation and revival of Greek myths in the Renaissance, that startling tale of subversion of authority for a deeply humanitarian cause did not go unnoticed by Francis Bacon.

Francis Bacon: Promethean fire and the early enlightenment

Our story of early modern hope picks up in the early-seventeenth century, a time known as the Early Enlightenment. If ever there was a 'renaissance man,' it would surely apply to Francis Bacon, novelist and essayist, scientist, jurist and all-around scholar. Bacon modeled the awakening that was taking place in that era, a time of unprecedented expansion in a great many areas: geography, exploration, law, culture and science being examples of Bacon's personal contribution to the knowledge explosion.

An important contributant to knowledge growth during the early renaissance was the translation and publishing of the classical language, bringing an infusion of ideas and culture from those flourishing cultures back into social circulation within Europe. Versed in Latin and Greek, Bacon seized on the myth of Prometheus as a symbol of hope for enlightenment, an intellectual expansiveness in all fields of learning that Bacon felt was badly needed by his rapidly developing society, with its aspirations for mercantile ascendancy and New World colonization. Some say Bacon modeled himself on Prometheus, and indeed as a creator, enabler, and dispenser of new knowledge his giftedness did seem larger than life.

Francis Bacon translated the myth about Prometheus from the Greek, wrote about its significance and used the myth allusively as a symbol in his voluminous writings. Promethean-like, he became a philosopher of expanding scientific knowledge, describing and theorizing about it; his encyclopedic learning included a fascination with the dramatic advances in astronomy and the unrolling of the new map toward the Americas, with its burgeoning discoveries, colonies and prospects. To portray his expansive vision of what one might hope for in a society of the future, he composed the *New Atlantis*, a utopian tale about an imaginary Pacific island onto which he projected his vision of social progress through more sophisticated governance and culture that would be enriched through the more systematic and creative use of science.

Bacon (1605) had already achieved fame for inventing the inductive method of empirical research for scientific experimentation, an innovative theory so powerful that such legendary scientists as Newton and Darwin were to credit it with inspiring their respective research projects. Hope for humankind, Bacon believed, would be predicated on acquiring useful new knowledge. In the *Magna Instauratio* (1620) he called for nothing less than 'a spring of progeny of inventions, which will overcome, to some extent, and subdue our needs and miseries.' Hope and learning, hope and invention, hope and scientific imagination – these were the watchwords that drove the vision and boundless ambition of Francis Bacon.

The society that Bacon idealized was a more open society, collaborative in problem solving, convivial and communal in organization. Bacon emphasized both ends and means. Social planning involved clear goal setting: '[I]t is not possible to run the course aright when the goal has not been rightly placed,' he says in the *Novum Organum*.

Harking back to Prometheus in his book, *The Wisdom of the Ancients*, Bacon lauds Prometheus for his philanthropy in gifting fire, 'the help of helps, the mean of means.' The ends of knowledge were of paramount concern. Knowledge was for the benefit and use of life, the gift of knowledge becoming for Bacon an adumbration of a better life. Baconian social hope was thus future-focused, a combination of visioning and systematic practitioning, a creative blend of theory and practice, with altruism as its moral centre.

Immanuel Kant and hope: 'We feel our freedom' (Kant 1987: 182)

As it had been for Francis Bacon a century earlier, knowledge was an emancipatory idea for the great German philosopher, Immanuel Kant. His famous

Critiques have been philosophical landmarks with respect to understanding the organization of the mind and how we come to acquire knowledge.

Kant's interest in exploring the ways of establishing truth was framed by a hope-incited vision of intellectual freedom. Hope for humankind was bound up in the exercise of God-given reason and the social responsibility that went with the power to reason. 'Dare to be wise' was the challenging motto that expressed Kant's strongly worded mandate for persons or society growing to intellectual maturity, by which he meant using one's own understanding without the guidance of another. Famously, he defined the epoch of the Enlightenment in a 1784 essay as 'man's emergence from his self-incurred immaturity'.

For Kant, freedom had political as well as moral and epistemological dimensions. He studied and supported the human rights manifestos of the American and French revolutions. Kant had deep sympathy for the revolutionary cause in France and the USA, the Kantian scholar Hannah Arendt notes; it inspired hope by 'opening up new horizons for the future' (Arendt 1982: 56). From cognitive and moral standpoints, Kant felt compelled to distance himself from revolution. But as he himself points out in the *Critique of Judgement*, in a matter like human freedom, the human imagination expands the very concept. The imagination at work in the presentation of aesthetic ideas, says Kant, 'expands the concept itself in an unlimited way' (Kant 1790: 142–7). The idea of freedom at work in the human imagination lends extraordinary emotive power to the concept. In this way, 'hope' enters into what Kant calls the free play of the imagination.

Kant is an important figure to be seen through the lens of hope, in part because of his leadership in the Enlightenment movement as reflected in his faith in human progress, guided by reason. As well, Kant brought a new perspective to this-worldly hope the way he positioned the rational human subject at the centre of the cognitive and moral worlds. Kant's contribution was not limited to the rational, however, as noted above. He saw beyond the purely cognitive by bringing illumination to the notion of affect, and its relation to imagination, human potential, and benevolent change.[3]

Hegel: Critical hope, history and the spirit of progress in history

"For what may I hope?" Immanuel Kant had asked, as he ruminated on the meaning and purpose of life. A bold answer to that question was attempted a few years after his death by fellow German philosopher Georg Hegel, who was to offer a novel perspective on the meaning of human history, a view so persuasive that it would ultimately impact on much of the western world.

Imagine writing a philosophic tract while a battle was raging around you. Hegel did just that, writing the famous *Phenomenology of Spirit* in his home city of Jena. In 1806, ears resounding with the pounding of cannons, Hegel confronted old ways of thinking about philosophy with brilliance comparable to Napoleon's tactical success on the nearby battlefield.

Hegel's purpose was to show that history, rather than being a giant jumble of random events, actually represented an enormously hopeful story of human progress, a tale that had traversed human history from its beginning. History, he claimed, was imbued with a *Geist* (spirit) of reconciling hope. By delving into the depths of factual detail about cultures, the way societies were organized and governed, their wars, social mores and the like, Hegel argued that a pattern or schemata was clearly discernible. What was revealed by studying the trajectory of events through time was a persistent search: the human odyssey questing for freedom. The very meaning of history, he claimed, was to be found in the grand liberatory theme of the evolving freedom of humankind.

History in the raw was rife with contradiction, division and conflict; in short, history was a dialectical narrative. Within history's story-line, the presence of master-slave relationships was endemic to all societies. But over the centuries, according to Hegel, flagrant inequities and oppressions can be seen to be lessened and displaced by the notion of a social order where mutual respect between persons supersedes antagonism and mistrust. This was the positive trajectory of history that Hegel believed had brought western civilization to a higher moral plane, one which officially endorsed human freedom. Hegel pointed to the powerfully hopeful examples of the American Constitution and the dramatic freedoms achieved by the French Revolution to substantiate his argument for human progress.

Hegel was acutely aware that his society, indeed the entire world, was wracked with suffering. Despite its dark side, when Hegel surveyed the sweep of history he discerned the evolutionary emergence of a healthy pattern of 'hope', powered by a combination of human reason and the desire for freedom. Humankind was edging closer and closer to fuller consciousness and self-understanding of what was needed for individual fulfillment and a profounder recognition of the value of mutually beneficial relations with one another.

Hegel's ambitious new philosophy had, as he intended, provided a new platform of philosophic hope. It brought reassurance. His theology was attuned to secular ambitions, but secularity within a providential purview, an interpretation that accommodated reason and science, the burgeoning arts. Most importantly, it blended harmoniously with an economic-centered new order. But Hegel also recognized that he was living in a precarious moment in time, one in which the human condition was vastly afflicted by unmet basic needs and burdened by moral shortcomings. The tension between dire need and progress, both material and spiritual, was perfectly captured in the fate of Prometheus chained to the rock for stealing fire for humankind. Hegel was stirred by the Promethean fate of captivity and torture.[4] To Hegel, the fettered Prometheus represented the extent to which a suffering humankind must struggle to redeem its historic destiny.

Marx and Engels model revolutionary hope, and set the stage for critical hope

Marx spent a lifetime working on a revolutionary project to bring hope to humankind. An ardent fan of the Promethean myth, his life ambition became to release the working class from the imprisoning grip of what he regarded as the inexorable law of capitalism. In *Das Kapital*, his famous critique of capitalism, Prometheus turns up representing the proletariat chained to capital. So inspirational was the Greek myth to him, Marx was said by a biographer Edmund Wilson to have reread the Aeschylus poem, *Prometheus Bound*, every year!

Analyzing Marx's 'hope' is to first recognize his humanist impulses, beginning with his passion to restore dignity to all human beings, a condition which, to him, could only occur in a truly free society. His critique of the human condition led him to accept the Hegelian dialectic, but utterly repudiate Hegel's teleology of historical hopefulness. His rejection of Hegel galvanized Marx to search for a liberating schema centered on radical economic restructuring, in general, and revolutionizing the process of production, in particular. His conclusion: to produce was the means of life. By assuming control over production, workers could reorganize and control the way they lived in the world, so he claimed, and thus achieve personal fulfillment in their lives.

The proletariat was the victim of false consciousness, said Marx's colleague Engels, a coinage whose variants were to reverberate through the years in worldwide struggles to restore the integrity of the oppressed self, an expanded need for emancipation not only from class and caste, but from racial and gender inequity and exploitation. Half a century later in the New World, for example, the same concern for an alienated consciousness preoccupied W.E.B. Du Bois. Sometimes called the black Prometheus of America, for Du Bois, the struggle was to erase the double consciousness that demeaned the integrity of the black spirit, the 'twoness' that 'one ever feels' (Du Bois 1969: 45). In a spirit of revolutionary hopefulness, 1897 finds Du Bois issuing a turn-of-the-century challenge: with destiny firmly in mind: "the oppressed are girding themselves in the van of progress, not simply for their own rights as men but for the ideals of the greater world [...] the emancipation of women, universal peace, democratic government, the socialization of wealth, and human brotherhood" (Du Bois 1897: 182). The revolutionary hope of Marx and Du Bois was born of critical elements, fired first by the desire to supplant injustice with equity, but also in recognition of the need for practical measures to effect radical change. For Marx, praxis dictated that only a society led by the proletariat would produce the radical change that would correct the global injustice that afflicted the world. Du Bois was also advocating the practical need for solidarity, seeing a Pan-African movement as needing world-wide coalescence of black peoples, a common resolve to bring an empowering new consciousness.

Alliance and solidarity of the oppressed became critical elements of revolutionary hope, those aspirations becoming central in the mid-twentieth-century struggles of Frantz Fanon, the Algeria-based social activist and Steve Biko, the emerging leader of the black consciousness movement in South Africa in the late 1960s.[5] For both, the envisioned self was a free self, who believed that the psychological and cultural liberation of the black mind was precursor to political freedom. One could substitute the peasantry for the working class, and read much in the early Marx's passionate impulse for freedom in Fanon and Biko.

Fanon and Biko, like Du Bois and Marx before them, represent an expanded conception of humanity, and a firing of the moral imagination in the direction of radical social change.

A thumbnail sketch of Marx cannot begin to do justice to the complexity of his economic doctrine. What is important with respect to the hope theme, however, is his belief that only through social revolution can the fettering of capitalism, and the class system it entrains be shattered and society rebuilt in accordance with the authentic interests of humanity.

The implementation of Marxist theories in Russia took on a direction that was ultimately to distort and destroy the project that he had envisioned. Marx did not live to see the perversions of his theory under Stalin, whose regime remains infamous for its horrific criminality. One would assume that Stalinism, with its abject denial of human rights, would have been total anathema to him. What Marx did supply to the world was a grid of new possibility, an alternative form of social hope.[6]

As we have seen, the revolutionary hope became a template for cultural change in many parts of the world where colonization, slavery and other forms of bondage were endemic. Similarly, in education the Marxian model would continue to influence in varying degrees emancipatory frameworks wherein the goals of personal and social flourishing lie in the direction of human development, new possibilities for transformation, responses to twenty-first-century geo-social pressures, attention to progressive approaches, and engagement with pedagogies of possibility.

Critical-utopic hope in the twenty-first century

For Ernst Bloch, studying and writing about hope was the passion of a lifetime. Hope, he believed, was central to human thought. Bloch's homeland was Germany, where he attracted attention to his unique vision of the relationship of human hope to the human spirit with the publication in 1918 of *Spirit of Utopia*. While he was inspired by the revolutionary socialism of Karl Marx, his philosophy was shaped by many other influences – for example his studies of Jewish Messianic philosophers, the idealism of Georg Hegel and a passion for the spellbinding novels of Karl May. What emerged, however, was a career-encompassing philosophical inquiry into hope that is renowned for its breadth, originality and, for many, its profundity.

Bloch fervently believed in the revolutionary social mission of Karl Marx, having studied his work in university and participated in intensive Marxian discussion as a member of the Frankfurt Institute of Social Research. It was principally Marx's humanistic goals that attracted Bloch; Marxism had provided him with praxis, an actual grid or schemata of what revolutionary change could accomplish if realized. Animated by an ardent belief in the possibility of change, Bloch probed the phenomenon of hope, investing it with singular power: our world is kept 'by the presence of futuristic properties within it, a world full of propensity towards something' (Bloch 1986: 18). The world of Bloch is not a settled entity, not a determinate world. Bloch postulates human hope as an engagement with the world that is, above all, open to the future.

In his master work, the *Principle of Hope*, Bloch (1986) attempts to bring philosophy to hope by reconstituting philosophy along the lines of a principle. The principle of hope rejects philosophy as contemplation. He wishes to reorient philosophy to the future, and to the 'not yet' condition of 'becoming.' The philosophy of hope looks to the future, and entails a commitment to change the world. Hope is thus transformative in its very nature, a future-oriented faith in the human capacity to create a better human future.

Bloch was an unabashed utopian, not in the sense of a fixed state utopia, but utopia in the sense of moving towards something, a processive utopia that Angelika Bammer calls a 'movement beyond set limits into the realm of the not-yet-set' (Bammer 1991: 7). Hope knows itself as the utopian function, claims Bloch. Its contents are first represented in the ideas of the imagination, 'extending material into future possibilities of being different and better' (op. cit: 144). Again, Prometheus makes an appearance, this time with a focus on the envisioning nature of hope. In his magnum opus on hope, Bloch called attention to the myth of Prometheus, highlighting that his name in Greek meant 'forethought'.

Bammer writes glowingly of Bloch's characterization of hope as 'the driving force of our creative and political energies [...] a potentially transformative force in the dialectics of history' (Bammer 1991: 17). Bloch's principle of hope is not dead at all, she claims, but 'very much alive in people's longing for a more just and human world, their belief that such change is possible, and their willingness to act on the basis of that belief' (p. 3).

Like Marx, Bloch was interested in the practical, and that meant grounding the utopic project, giving it some hold on the present as opposed to a dream world with no prospect for realization. As with all great utopic thinkers of the past, Bloch's goal was not crassly material in the sense of a blueprint for better bourgeois comfort, but a liberatory utopia, that would alleviate or end human suffering and misery.

His was a critical hope examining history and culture for its worthwhile elements with a view to incorporating them into future visioning. Similarly, he believed in rigorous interrogation of the present, critiquing the politics of the day and again, discerning what was worthy of salvaging as utopian content for envisioning a better world. Little wonder that major theorists of critical education theory today, viz. Michael Apple, Henri Giroux, Douglas Kellner, pay homage to Ernst Bloch's seminal and inspirational ideas on critical hope.

Bloch presents a hugely imaginative role for hope. Hope becomes the discourse of critique and social transformation. Hope has inbuilt capacity for change agency simply by virtue of its ontology, that anticipatory, envisioning nature of hope that mobilizes, intervenes and effects change. Critical-creative hope, as uniquely delineated by Ernst Bloch, is a pedagogy of possibility with powerful resonance for the purposes of this book. With Bloch's coupling of social justice with openness to change and to the future generally, critical-creative hope seems especially suited to counteract the vicissitudes, angst and despondencies of our time.

Paulo Freire: Critical hope and pedagogical liberation

Near the end of his career, Paulo Freire wrote a book with a title that sums up his great passion, the *Pedagogy of Hope* (1994), the story of his life-long struggle to understand and communicate what genuine education is really about, and the role that hope played in that quest. 'I do not understand existence,' he says, 'apart from hope and dream' (Freire 1994: 2). Hope is a human need, explains Freire, an ontological need, a concrete imperative. But hope, by itself, is not enough. Hope has to be embedded in the larger struggle, or praxis, which cycles through theory, application, assessment, reflection and returns to theory. Hope is a crucial starting point, says Freire, but hope needs anchoring in practice in order to become historical concreteness. The progressive educator unveils opportunities for hope whatever the obstacles may be. Hope evokes passion. Without 'rage and love,' 'there is no hope' (Freire 1994: 4).

Freire is deservedly the most universally celebrated of critical educators. Beginning with his attack on the banking model of education, one which conceives of the student as an empty account to be filled by a teacher, Freire sees the teacher's role to 'instill awakening of critical consciousness,' (1994: 19) the independent self-consciousness called for by Hegel. As Freire points out, attaining conscientization was essential to becoming an authentic person, a responsible subject with an awareness of the world that impinges on one's consciousness. In *Pedagogy of the Oppressed*, Freire's landmark work (1970), his message is a *cri de coeur* on behalf of the oppressed. The methodology, he warns the readers, is radicalization, a form of pedagogy 'committed to human liberation'[7] (Freire 1970: 23).

To understand the revolutionary tenor of Freire's work, it is important to recognize the personal and geographical context in which *Pedagogy of the Oppressed* was written. Freire had spent 25 years in the midst of dehumanizing living and working conditions forced upon illiterate Brazilian peasants. Only by immersing himself in their culture, he believed, could he problematize and then empower people to alter their relations with society.

Embedded in the oppressive conditions of northeast Brazil for years, and later in the economic marginalization of rural Chile, it is little wonder that Freire compares these people to the *Wretched of the Earth*, vividly described by Franz Fanon some twenty years earlier. Little wonder also, that Freire identifies with the arch-revolutionist of his time, Che Guevara, seeing his 'humility and capacity to love,' as making possible 'his communion with the people' (p. 170). Freire himself had experienced poverty and hunger as a child. His zeal to help the socially afflicted had led him to reject the practice of law, for which he had qualified, and immerse himself, with the peasantry, in the fields of Brazil, striving to unlock a methodology that would give hope to their lives. His efforts, plus giving a published voice to his beliefs in 'education as the praxis of liberation', were to lead to his exile from his country.

Freire's challenge to the establishment articulated in *Pedagogy of the Oppressed* was an attack on what he called the culture of silence, the many forms of domination by race, class and education that would shut down paths of thought that lead to a language of critique. The revolutionary pedagogy that has become universally associated with his name is the dialogical encounter. Dialogue for Freire meant first recognizing the 'true word,' by which he means the educand being encouraged to name the world 'as it really is.' Maxine Greene connects the Freirean notion of 'reading the world' with Michel Foucault's notion of breaking with the habitual, the human capacity to 'step back' (Greene 1995: 190) from the enmeshments of society, with its blockages and manipulations. As Foucault puts it: 'Thought is freedom in relation to what one does, the motion by which one detaches oneself from it, establishes it as an object, and reflects upon it as an object' (Foucault 1984: 388).

For Freire, uttering the authentic happens as an encounter with the world, in dialogue with 'the Other.' True dialogue is an act of creation, an act of love, an act of freedom. Thus we see that the language of liberation and the language of development become symbiotic. It is in this silence-shattering verbal communion that learners come to an understanding of the new possibilities, what Freire calls the possibility of a 'lovelier world,' to which they aspired.

The lovelier world, to Freire, is the product of pedagogy of hope, a liberating hope. Enabling the development of one's own language, the language of conjecture, design, anticipation of a new world – this is the pedagogy of hope.

In Freire's *Pedagogy of Hope*, we note his dramatic testimonial to the emotive side of hope, its capacity to evoke rage and love, and the concomitant fortitude for struggle that hope induces. Freirean hope comingles the passion inherent in hope with our leitmotif of this chapter, freedom. Freire is a Promethean figure, a struggling, transgressive and combative activist in the service of justice for humanity.

The originality and force of Freire's praxis has brought widespread acknowledgements of his inspiration and influence. *Pedagogy of the Oppressed* opened a floodgate of contributions on critical pedagogy in many domains. Eminent educators such as Michael Apple, bell hooks, Megan Boler, Maxine Green, Henri Giroux, Peter McLaren and Cornel West, Joe Kinchelo, among many others, pay explicit homage to Freire's inspiring and empowering vision. Freire's recognition of the importance of humility in dialogue, says Megan Boler, reminds us that 'our perspectives and vision are partial and striving and must remain open to change' (Boler 2004: 131). To Cornel West the publication of *Pedagogy of the Oppressed* was a 'world-historical event' (West 1993: 1). Nel Noddings credits Freire's explication of dialogue as the most fundamental component of moral education, the care model (Noddings 1995: 140). Their writings, in turn, reflect Freire's valorization of hope, the creative-critical spirit and the 'life-necessity' importance of self-liberation.

In summary

My attempt in this chapter has been to call attention to the character of hope by exploring one of many possible tracings of its protean journey through time.

An analysis of hope within a variety of historical contexts reveals a syncretic blend of characteristics from its mythic roots, most importantly from the earliest accounts of creation, and the interrelated myth of Prometheus as a symbol of hope. The very name Prometheus, meaning foresight, brings the dimension of hope's futurity into play, the expanding vision and utopic impulse associated with hope.

An interpretative framework of hope foregrounds reason and emotion at work in the act of hoping. The legendary passion of Prometheus for advancing knowledge links, in turn, to another element of hope, its altruistic desire to improve the human condition. Also embodied in the Promethean myth, as exemplified in the philosophical thought-leaders in this chapter, is the struggle for freedom, a historic theme that resonates within hope's genealogy.

In this chapter, I have explored the phenomenon of hope as a transhistorical and cosmopolitan force, a word, especially when prefaced with 'critical,' that becomes thickly connotative with transformative ideas of freedom, expanding knowledge, fullness of feeling and audacity of purpose and action. Does that claim for hope clash with the Foucauldian dictum of the contingency of history, the lack of continuity of historical ideas? The famous Chomsky-Foucault debate[8] focuses the contending approaches to history. Historical hope, to Chomsky is 'a kind of groping towards the true humanly valuable concepts of justice and decency and love and kindness and sympathy, which I think are real' (Chomsky and Foucault 2006: 55). For Foucault, a concept such as justice is an idea 'put to work [...] as an instrument of a certain economic or political power, a contingency of momentary need' (p. 54). Justice is in no way reflective of 'the essence of human beings' as Chomsky (2006: 57) asserts, but is simply the use of an idea as a means to achieve immanent power. But the individual is not totally held hostage by the hegemony of power, however pervasive. Foucault champions the individual's obligation to confront the carceral power that would control our lives. Hope lies in the agency of individual will to resist normalizing power, to find potentially open spaces. In the face of governmentality, 'the will of individuals must make a place for itself, to speak out against every abuse of power, whoever its author, whoever its victims' (p. 212).

Thus, while the particular contexts of liberatory hope, as I have shown, vary in intent and emphasis, and certainly in ideology, the bold Promethean fusion that engages both the emancipatory and the philanthropic re-emerges in time and place throughout history.

Given early description by the historian Hesiod, the Promethean story emerged in a famous play by Aeschylus, *Prometheus Bound*, about 430 B.C. His story resurfaced after two millennia, when Francis Bacon took up the cause of expanding human knowledge by trying to systemize scientific investigation introducing the inductive method. Immanuel Kant recognized the transcendent power of the revolutionary spirit when he vicariously experienced the American and French enthusiasm to implement radically new governance. A 'founding father' of critique, Kant spent his life formulating critiques to illuminate the workings of the mind's capacity to unite reason with experience and make enlightened judgments. Georg Hegel was similarly an emancipationist, discerning new paradigms evolving through history, their contradictory nature, he claimed, becoming reconciled in progressive ways. The hope-incited liberatory theme took a radical turn in the philosophy of Karl Marx. Marx famously turned Hegelianism 'on its head' by eschewing the idealistic dialectic for the materialistic dialectic, in an argument that it is political consciousness that inscribes a person's sense of self; political economy became, for Marx, the engine of the mind, and, as such, defined authentic consciousness.

The polemical force of Marx's challenge to false consciousness had widespread international implications for global emancipation, with the Afro-American movement in the United States, liberation struggles in Latin America and diverse anti-colonial and anti-apartheid uprisings in North and South Africa and South-East Asia. W.E.B. Du Bois brought fervid eloquence to negating the black 'double consciousness' in America, a cause to be picked up by Frantz Fanon in Algeria, and Steve Biko and co-revolutionaries in their emancipatory struggles in Africa in the last half of the twentieth century. Powerful voices in search of liberatory post-colonial hope emanated from India, exemplified by Gayatri Spivak's aspirations for subaltern consciousness and expunging the epistemic violence of imperialism. In complementary fashion, contemporary hope for a reborn consciousness is heard in Homi Bhabha's crusade to bring new possibilities for enunciating culture within pan-global situations of hybridity.

A believer in Marx's emancipatory efforts, Bloch spent a lifetime trying to reveal the inner nature of hope, and its 'capability to imagine the totality as something completely different,' (Bloch 1988: 3–4) and to prepare the ground for something new, the not-yet of social possibility. Paulo Freire famously challenged the culture of enforced silence, seeing in dialogical encounter the hope for change in the oppressive structures of society.

Conclusion

My selective investigations of the signal meaning of hope, past and present, yield a picture of hope as a resource. They reveal an axial quality to hope, linking freedom, knowledge and critical confrontation and, with education in mind, a link to pedagogic possibility. My analysis argues for critical hope's capacity to open up society, to incite a creative-critical spirit of social reform and human empowerment. Dashed hopes and catastrophic failure darken the story of hope from age to age. But there is a dynamic and resilient quality, a survivability about hope that transcends defeat and cynicism, engenders moral imagination and renews the transformative impulse. Critical hope, thought of as a resource, is an active presence, weaving its way between vision and critique, transformation and suffering.

Critical hope is far from naïve. Our protagonists of hope from Prometheus onwards, were engaged in struggle. The contributors to *Discerning Critical Hope*, moreover, would surely concur with the trials of hope, the Promethean contestation and agony of bringing hope to realization. In the words of

Raymond Williams, 'once the inevitabilities are challenged, we begin gathering our resources for a *journey of hope*' (Williams 2003: 127) [*emphasis mine*]. There are rarely easy answers, Williams reminds us, but that must not disrupt hope's journey. '[T]here are still available and discoverable hard answers, and it is these that we can learn to make and share' (p. 127).

Notes

1 A useful reference: Jasper Griffin, 'Greek myth and Hesiod,' in *Oxford History of the Classical World*.
2 Marty Sulek, <http: hdl.handler.net/1805/2763>, *Gifts of Fire: An Historical Analysis of the Promethean Myth*.
3 For the interpretation of Kant's view on imagination, and Arendt's explanation of same, see Linda Zerilli, '"We feel our freedom": Imagination and judgment in the thought of Hannah Arendt'.
4 A useful reference is Ian Fraser, *Hegel and the Concept of Need*, University of British Columbia Press.
5 Frantz Fanon, *The Wretched of the Earth* and Steve Biko, *I Write What I Like. Selected Writings*.
6 See, for example, Marxist historian Eric Hobsbaum, *On History*.
7 Paolo Freire (1994) *Pedagogy of the Oppressed* (p. 23).
8 In 1971, Noam Chomsky and Michel Foucault were famously brought together at the height of the Vietnam War to debate the age-old philosophical question: Is there such a thing as innate human nature independent of our experiences and external influences?

Bibliography

Arendt, H. (1982) *Lectures on Kant's Political Philosophy*, Ronald Beiner (ed.) Chicago, IL: University of Chicago Press.
Bacon, F. (1857) 'Of the Wisdom of the Ancients'. In: *The Works of Francis Bacon*, J. Spedding, R. Ellis and D.D. Heath (eds) London: Longman.
Bacon, F. (1937) *Essays, Advancement of Learning, New Atlantis, and Other Pieces*. New York: Odyssey Press.
Bammer, A. (1991) *Partial Visions*. New York: Routledge.
Bhabha, H. (2008) 'Notes on globalization and ambivalence'. In: D. Held and H. Moore (eds) *Cultural Politics in a Global Age*. Oxford: Oneworld Publications.
Biko, S. (2002) *I Write What I Like. Selected Writings*. Chicago, IL: University of Chicago Press.
Bloch, E. (1988) 'Something's Missing: A discussion between Ernst Bloch and Theodor W. Adorno on the Contradictions of Utopian Language (1964),' *The Utopian Function of Art and Literature: Selected Essays*. Trans. by Jack Zipes and Frank Mecklenburg. Boston: MIT Press.
Bloch, E. (1986) *The Principle of Hope*, trans. N. Plaice, S. Plaice and P. Knight. Cambridge, MA: MIT Press.
Bloch, E. (2000) *The Spirit of Utopia*, trans. A. Nassar. Stanford, CA: Stanford University Press.
Boler, M. (2004) 'Teaching for hope'. In: D. Liston and J. Garrison (eds) *Teaching Loving, Learning: Reclaiming Passion in Educational Practice*. New York: Routledge-Falmer.

Chomsky, N. and Foucault, M. (2006) *The Chomsky–Foucault Debate on Human Nature*. New York: The New Press.

Du Bois, W.E.B. (1969) *The Souls of Black Folk*. New York: New American Library.

Du Bois, W.E.B. (2007) *The Conservation of Races and the Negro*, Penn State Electronic Series. Online. Available HTTP: <http://www2.hn.psu.edu/faculty/jmanis/webdubois.htm> (Accessed March 27, 2013).

Fanon, F. (2004) *The Wretched of the Earth*, trans. R. Philcox. New York: Presence Africaine.

Foucault, M. (1984) *The Foucault Reader*. New York: Pantheon Books.

Fraser, I. and Burns, T. (2000) *The Hegel–Marx Connection*. New York: St. Martin's Press.

Freire, P. (1970) *Pedagogy of the Oppressed*. New York: Seabury Press.

Freire, P. (1994) *Pedagogy of Hope*. New York: Continuum.

Greene, M. (1995) *Releasing the Imagination: Essays on Education, the Arts, and Social Change*. San Francisco, CA: Jossey-Bass Publishers.

Griffin, J. (1985) 'Greek myth and Hesiod'. In: J. Boardman, J. Griffin and O. Murray (eds) *Oxford History of the Classical World*. Oxford: Oxford University Press.

Hobsbawm, E.J. (1997) *On History,*. London: Orion Publishing Group.

Kant, I. (1774) 'What is the enlightenment?' Online. Available HTTP: <www.columbia.edu/acis/ets/ccread/etscc/kant.html> (Accessed 27 March 2013)

Kant, I. (1987) *Critique of Judgment*, trans. W.S. Pluhar. Indianapolis, IN: Hackett.

Nietzsche, F. (1878) 'On the History of Moral Failings' #72. in *Human, All Too Human*, The Online Books Page, HTML at holtof.com.

Noddings, N. (1995) 'Care and moral education'. In: W. Kohli (ed.) *Critical Conversations in Philosophy of Education*. New York: Routledge.

Spivak, G. (1996) *The Spivak Reader*. New York: Routledge.

Sulek, M.S. (2011) *Gifts of Fire*, Indiana University. Online. Available HTTP: <http//hdl.handle.net/1805/2763> (Accessed 27 March 2013).

West, C. (1993) 'Preface'. In: P. McLaren and P. Leonard (eds) *Paulo Freire, A Critical Encounter*. London: Routledge.

Williams, R (1983) 'Towards 2000'. In: D. Halpin (2003) *Hope and Education*, London: Routledge-Falmer.

Wilson, E. (1940) *To the Finland Station: A Study in the Writing and Acting of History*. New York: Harcourt Brace.

Zerilli, L. (2005) 'We Feel Our Freedom': Imagination and Judgment in the Thought of Hannah Arendt', *Political Theory*, 33(2): 158–88.

Afterword
Critical hopes – gratitude and the magic of encounter

Mary Zournazi

> Gratitude, as it were, is the moral memory of mankind.
>
> Georg Simmel

> 'You do not interest me.' No man can say these words to another without committing a cruelty and offending against justice.
>
> Simone Weil

Encounters

The chapters in this book look at critical hope in education practices as well as social and political action. In this afterword, I want to reflect on how critical hope emerges out of the contingency of action and everyday experience, as well how this action can shape emotional and political thought. For me, discerning critical hope is about engaging in a world of reflection and social change, and thinking about how social change requires new hopes and responsibilities; a social imagination built on encounters with each other and the world.

Let me begin with a story

In 2003, I was invited to attend a festival for early childhood education. The festival was organized around the themes of hope and dialogue that I had established in my book of the same name. I was thrilled to be invited to such an event, given that the relationship between hope and education seemed to beg fundamental questions such as: what are the genuine conditions needed for learning and how do we cultivate such learning for others and ourselves? In other words, what is the human potential for hope in our most formative relationship: childhood.

Just before the festival, I got a serious bout of writer's block. Even though I was inspired by the questions of education and hope, I felt I did not have the tools to address the issues at hand. I knew this was not strictly the case, but I became stumped on how to address hope and its relation to education and learning.

During this time, I took daily walks to help release some of the tension and consternation that was surrounding me. One day, quite by accident, I came across a rather enchanting scene: at a local cake shop two young girls aged around four years or so were standing on either side of the shop's glass door entrance – one girl was inside and the other girl was outside, the door was slightly ajar – each child had their face and arms pressed against the door, peering at each other through the glass panels.

The girl on the inside said with much anticipation and excitement: 'I'll let you in when you come to the other side'. I was struck by the strange logic of this young child. She'd let her friend inside when she reached the other side?

Something magical was happening here; I was witnessing some mysterious exchange between the two children. I can only explain it as a shared moment of happenstance, and in this shared moment the girl on the inside saw her friend as already *with* her, and in this spontaneous encounter with the other girl, their *being together* made complete sense. This togetherness was spontaneous just as it was unique. Neither child knew each other before that moment, but in the presence of each other's company they shared a mutual joy, a certain trust and pleasure that comes out of the threshold of experience.

For me, the children's encounter echoed Franz Kafka's description of the 'magical'. Kafka writes:

> It's entirely conceivable that life's splendor surrounds us all, and always in its complete fullness, accessible but veiled, beneath the surface, invisible, far away. But there it lies – not hostile, not reluctant, not deaf. If we call it by the right word, by the right name, then it comes. This is the essence of magic, which doesn't create but calls.
>
> (Kafka 2006: 133–134)

After this encounter, I had a different sense of hope and how it could manifest in the educational setting and creative potential; this 'critical hope' had something to do with shared experience and commonality as well as gratitude. At the time, I wrote about hope as a spirit of dialogue; I described this dialogue as a kind of generosity and spontaneity as well as the joyful engagements possible with other people. This joy was clearly demonstrated by the children; it was a moment of genuine encounter with another person, it was as much relational as it was magical.

I would say these two children had no sense of obstacle, even though the physical obstacle was there – they had a door separating them, but their hope was manifest simply in their meeting, and being *with* each other. In each other's presence, the children were calling each other by the right name. This relationship of presence and encounter is what the philosopher Martin Buber suggests is the requirement of living. He states very precisely: 'all real living is meeting' (1975: 48).

In many ways, this story of the young children might sound utopian; however, it seems to me that hope emerges through joy: the wonder and mystery that is built in the recognition of others and their difference. Human existence, as Buber and philosopher Emmanuel Levinas have put it, is the response to another's call to us; this 'call' is the ethical relation that exists in human encounters. It is what comes before any sense of duty or obligation, but it is what creates our social bonds and relationships to justice. This ethical space manifests through dialogical encounters – it is what occurs between people – the historical and material relationships that exist between us. As both thinkers remind us, this dialogue may be silent, and it is not limited to humans alone.

For Buber, this dialogical relationship emerges out of what he calls the *I/Thou* (I/You) relation as the primary relation of human experience. Buber makes the philosophical distinction between what he calls 'I/It' and 'I/You';[1] the former is the objectification of self and others, the latter is the dialogic relation between others and ourselves. He writes: 'the primary word I-Thou can only be spoken with the whole being. Concentration and fusion into the being can never take place through my agency, nor can it ever take place without me. I become through my relation to Thou; as I become I, I say Thou' (1975: 48). Levinas would suggest that the fundamental word spoken 'you' must always recognize the unequal distribution of sociality and social hope; otherwise put, this ethical relationship involves the recognition of suffering and vulnerability of others and ourselves. For Levinas, this is a justice that moves beyond the limits of law and social constraint. Levinas often cites after Dostoevsky, 'We are all responsible for all for all men before all, and I more than all others'. And furthermore, he states:

> One must yield to the other the first place in everything. From the 'après vous' before the open door right up to the disposition – hardly possible, but holiness demands it – to die for the other. In this attitude of holiness, there is a reversal of the normal order of things, the natural order of things, the persistence of being (2001: 1).

Today, I would say 'critical hope' is based on this kind of responsibility and gratitude in living encounters – whether in the classroom, in political action and engagement, or in everyday life. Hope resides in ethical relations that are the co-extension of action, that is, in the recognition of our common and shared experiences as well as our differences. It is a simultaneous longing and belonging together, a different sense of wish fulfillment – a different sense of community and communion. For me, the essays that comprise this book demonstrate how hope exists in the realm of gratitude as the fundamental ethical relation that exists between people; it is part of a genuine attempt to address oppressive situations and their social and political affects.

In the rest of this afterword, I will reflect on how I see critical hope as the rebirth of everyday action, that is, a sense of gratitude and shared communion, the hope that arises out of the space between *I* and *you*. This is an ethical realm that is about daily action, the choices we make to help improve life *as it is* lived in gratitude and freedom; as the sociologist Georg Simmel (1964: 395) states of gratitude: 'every human relationship of any duration produces a thousand occasions for it'.

Gratitude

Returning to my opening vignette, the element of intrigue and beauty in the children's encounter with each other was their sense of gratitude; they demonstrated a spontaneous as well as joyful response to each other. It was a direct experience of 'gift' giving that arises out of being *with* others. Said differently, hope and gratitude are the recognition of others in the subtlest of forms and the energy that cultivates the potential for harmonious social relations. As Simmel (2012: 395) notes, gratitude is the 'memory of mankind'. Gratitude is the place of genuine exchange between people.

For Simmel, gratitude is often viewed as the exchange of gifts and reciprocity of gifts; however, this understanding of gratitude promotes an objectification of social relations and coerciveness; that is, gratitude becomes a duty and obligation that is forced rather than given (and indeed, this was Simmel's analysis of the philosophy of money and exchange at the threshold of modernity). He writes:

> Exchange is the objectification of human interaction. If an individual gives a thing, and another returns one of the same value, the purely spontaneous character of their relation has become projected into objects. This objectification, this growth of the relationship into self-contained, movable things, becomes so complete that, in the fully developed economy, personal interaction recedes altogether into the background, while goods gain a life of their own. Relations and value balances between them occur automatically, by mere computation: men act only as the executors of the tendencies toward shifts and equilibriums that are inherent in the goods themselves. The objectively equal is given for the objectively equal, and man himself is really irrelevant, although it goes without saying that he engages in the process for his own interest. The relation among men has become a relation among objects.
>
> (Simmel 2012: 388)

Yet real gratitude exists on another plane. We might say that for Simmel that gratitude is the hope that resides in: 'The first gift [that] is given in full spontaneity; it has a freedom without any duty, even without the duty of gratitude' (2012: 392). Such gratitude is what transpired between the children, and it is what Buber, and Levinas after him, would situate as the primary ethical relation. That is, our response to others is a gift given without expectation but with genuine *connection* to others; this connection has the propensity toward joy and movement, rather than stasis, foreclosure and constraint. As Simmel writes:

In fact, we do not thank somebody only for what he *does*: the feeling with which we often react to the mere existence of a person, must itself be designated as gratitude. We are grateful to him only because he exists, because we experience him. Often the subtlest as well as firmest bonds among men develop from this feeling. It is independent of any particular act of receiving; it offers our whole personality to the other, as if from a duty of gratitude to *his* whole personality.

(2012: 389–90)

For Simmel, it is only when we give first that freedom arises. The first gift does not expect reciprocity or equivalent action, it is simply the response to the care of others, to the sociality of experience. Simmel writes that the 'first gift is the spontaneous devotion to the other,' it exists without coercion or constraint as well as without the sense of duty. This gratitude may engender new actions: 'it is an ideal bridge which the soul comes across again and again, so to speak, and which, upon provocations too slight to throw a new bridge to the other person, it uses to come closer to him' (2012: 388).

How do we create this potential 'new bridge'?

For the political philosopher Hannah Arendt, this action would be an exercise in political thought. For Arendt, this exercise is the commonality and shared experience that arises out of what she terms common sense. She writes:

Common sense – which the French so suggestively call the 'good sense,' *le bons sens* – discloses to us the nature of the world insofar as it is a common world; we owe it to the fact that our strictly private and 'subjective' five senses and their sensory data can adjust themselves to a nonsubjective and 'objective' world which we have in common and share with others.

(Arendt 1961: 221)

If we consider Arendt's notion of common sense, and Buber's idea of meeting, we might say that gratitude is the space between us; it is the 'gap' in time – Arendt might call this 'interval'; Buber might call it the 'eternal' – regardless, this gap is the infinite possibility that exists between 'I and you'. It is the space between us that can engender new action. This action comes out of the energy of love and care for the other. Concretely speaking, it is through our everyday experiences and choices that gratitude manifests in its subtle as well as substantive forms. Infinitely tough, this energy and force is what can provide more relational and creative potential for people in all settings and circumstance.

For Buber, the only hope for this hour is through this kind of gratitude and common reality, what calls the 'rebirth of dialogue'. He writes: 'what is called for is not "neutrality" but solidarity, a living answering for one another – and mutuality, living reciprocity; not effacing the boundaries between the groups, circles, and parties, but communal recognition of the common reality and communal testing of the common responsibility' (1957: 102).

Rebirth of dialogue

The world becomes communion and commonality insofar as it is a world that we share with others. This critical hope is a means to consider the affective bonds we share in relation to others as well as the responsibility toward diverse and collective needs. In a fundamental sense, this dialogical approach is necessary when we consider our responsibility toward each other; if we translate this experience the educational setting we might say it is the openness of dialogue that provides the curiosity and recognition of human potential. Dialogue – in this regard – opens out the space of difference; it is about potential that emerges in the presence of each other, in our meeting. It has a magical quality.

bell hooks (2003) describes this type of hope and community as a dialogue that recognizes the need for openness on both sides; each person in dialogue must be willing to change. In the classroom context, the teacher and the student actively share a space of learning and therefore share responsibility toward each other. This responsibility involves the space in which difference can arise, even if it is tainted by discontent or discomfort. In this light, gratitude is this gift between people; it is the realization of hope in difficult contexts, or what Megan Boler earlier in this volume calls a 'shattering of world views'.

This dialogical relation also enters the realm of the author and the text as a shared communion of this world. Perhaps this point is demonstrated most fruitfully in Russian theorist Mikhail Bakhtin's analysis of Dostoevsky's poetics (see Bakhtin 1973). Bakhtin writes that Dostoevsky writes *with* his characters; he does not judge them. It is this dialogical model that purports to working with a community of people. It is a framing of human consciousness that partakes of spirit and historical circumstance; this consciousness evolves through listening as well as imagination. This is the potential for hope.

In this sense, the 'dialogical method' is inherently ethical; it is based on relations between people. And it is through dialogue and its 'surprise' that Dostoevsky reminds us: 'Reality is not limited to the familiar, the common place, for it consists in part of a latent, as yet unspoken future Word' (cited in Bakhtin 1973: 73).

In my mind, hope might be seen as a spontaneous act without reserve. It is a communion. It might be considered 'common sense' – a shared experience as well as the ethical realm in which we can cultivate gratitude and compassion in our social relationships, in our chance encounters with others.

The chapters in this book come together as a kind of 'dialogic' community to address hope as an 'ontological as well as material necessity' (c.f. Freire). The collection is an invitation to consider new paradigms of hope just as the chapters demonstrate the potential for change that is closely aligned to historical circumstance and 'exercises in political thought' as Hannah Arendt might put it.

This book attests to the need for affective and critical emotional praxis as well as approaches to pedagogy that address skills to work against false hopes and power that are so easily translated into neo-liberal thinking on choice and diversity.

Collectively, then, this book is the exercise in political thought. Critical hope is emergent and contingent on experience and the potential for change; new hopes arise out of the choices made in daily encounters and experiences. (c.f. Zournazi *et al.* 2003).

In the final instance, critical hope is about the potential to work effectively within the constraints and possibilities of power. It involves creating new social imaginaries based on the contingency of experience just as the need for common action. In many respects, critical hope is a movement toward the future that arises from the material conditions of the present; our everyday practices, our calling to responsibility and justice, our common sense.

Note

1 In this chapter, I use the *I-You* translation of *Ich-Du* rather than *I-Thou* as most often used as it relates closer to the informality of the original German usage. However, I use Ronald Gregor Smith's translation of Buber's I-Thou as the basis of my analysis and understanding of Buber.

References

Arendt, Hannah (1961) *Between Past and Future – Six Exercises in Political Thought.* London: Faber and Faber.
Bakhtin, Mikhail (1973) *Problems of Dostoevsky's Poetics*, trans. R. W. Rotsel. US: Ardis.
Buber, Martin (1957) *Pointing the Way*, trans. Maurice Friedman. London: Routledge and Kegan Paul.
Buber, Martin (1975) *The Way of Response*, N.N. Glatzer (ed.) New York: Schocken Books.
Buber, Martin (2004) *I and Thou*, trans. Ronald Gregor Smith. New York and London: Routledge.
Freire, Paulo (2004) *Pedagogy of Hope*, trans. Robert R. Barr. London and New York: Continuum.
hooks, bell (2003) *Teaching Community – A Pedagogy of Hope*. New York and London: Routledge.
Kafka, Franz (2006) *The Zürau Aphorisms*, trans. Roberto Calasso. London: Harvill Seckor.
Laclau, Ernesto and Mouffe, Chantal (1985). *Hegemony and Socialist Strategy: Towards a Radical Democratic Politics*. Verso: London.
Levinas, Emmanuel (2001) *Is it Righteous to Be?* J. Roberts (ed.) California: Stanford University Press.
Simmel, Georg (1964) 'Faithfulness and Gratitude'. In: *The Sociology of Georg Simmel*. Illinois: The Free Press.
Weil, Simone (2005) *Simone Weil – An Anthology*. London: Penguin Classics.
Zournazi, Mary (2003) *Hope – New Philosophies for Change*. New York: Routledge.

Index

alternatives to educational systems 64–6
annihilation of self 31
anti-racism 103–6
apartheid segregation 41
Australia 43
awareness 28, 37, 60, 127, 135–6

Bacon, Francis 144–5
Black British: critical hope and education 116–17; defining 115–16; education movements mapping 119–20; hidden histories 120–1; history 115–16; inequalities 122–3; intellectuals 113–14; movement 114; options 122; second generations 121; voices, diverse 121–2
Bloch, Ernst 149–50
brief genealogy of critical hope 12–14

challenging education systems 60–1
co-existence 159
colonialization 127–9; anti-framework 126, 136; violence 130
commitment 63
common vulnerability 15
compassion 26–9, 31, 34–5, 37–9
concept of critical hope 1–2
conscientization 62–3
context 3
corporate social responsibility 90–2
critical emotional praxis: contribution of in pedagogies 16–21; creating spaces for hope 22–3; despair and hopelessness, feelings of 18–19; engaging 23–4; implications 21–4; meaning 12; solidarity and connectedness, nurturing feelings 19–21; vignette 17–21
critical theory 1, 5, 82, 91

critical-utopic hope 149–50
culture of silence 126

decolonization: community building 133–4; critical consciousness 136–7; differences to education 135; 'drinking from own wells' 132; history, re-meeting 132–3; legitimization 129–30; margins, thinking from 131; praxis 130–3
deferred hope 14
despair 51–2; induced 106–9
dialogical relationships 159
dialogue, rebirth of 162–3
discomfort 42; beyond 36–7; clarity of reality 30; comfort zones 29; diversity work 44; loss, making up for 37–8; pedagogy of 27

early Enlightenment 144–5
educated hope 78
education debt 106–7
emotions: ambivalence 21; engaging 11; role 21; selectivity 30–1; willingness 13
encounters 157
engagement 51
Engels, Friedrich 148–9

false hopes 106–9
fatalism 11–13
Filipino: critical pedagogy, learning from 132–3; education 127–8; feminist praxis 134–6
Freire, Paulo 151–2

gratitude 159–63
Greek mythology 143–4

Hegel, Georg 146–7
history: hope, of 152–4; progress in 146–7

Index

hokey hope 13–14
HOPE project: ambiguity 88–9; barriers to transformation 92; critical social responsibility 92; deconstruction 88–9; diversity 89–90; fundraising 88; institutional transformation 87; metaphorical discourse, as 94; rebranding Stellenbosch 86–8; Rector Chris Brink 85–6; Stellenbosch University genealogy 83–4; strategic framework 84–5; success 94; support 93
human condition 108, 147–8, 153
human rights education: declarationization 72; deconstruction 73–5; definition 71–2; dominance 69; form 74–5; hopelessness 70; left-over 69–77; plasticity 76–7; questioning 70, 73; regeneration of 77–8
humanism 77
humility 38, 107, 110, 152

inequality 26–7; systems of 36
intellectuals 62

journey of hope 155
justice: culture 101–3; history 101–3; living critical hope 109–11; movement 103; oppression 108; struggle 102, 104–5

Kant, Immanuel 145–6

legal rights 76–7
literature 3–4

Marx, Karl 147–9
mobilization of affects 15
mythical hope 14
myths 26

naïve hope 2, 4–5, 13, 16, 35–6, 40, 72

obstacles and hope 158
ontological need, hope as 101–3

ontology of hope 12
origin of hope 143–4

pedagogies 14–16; challenges 16; liberation 151–2; potential 11
plasticity 71–7
political forces, hope as 101–3, 107–8
process 2, 14, 52
progressive pedagogies 59–64

race: Black social agency 118–19; Critical Race Theory 117–18; literature 113; privilege 104
reality, construction of 109–10
redemption: beyond narrative 59–64; discourses 57–9; narratives 61–2
resistance 28; suffering, and 31–4; unexpected shift 34–5
results 62
revolutionary hope 147–9

school reform 13, 72
social justice: emotional fallout 31; struggling 18–19, 39; studying 27
social praxis 11, 14–16, 23, 130
solidarity 161
South Africa 40; community, self and identity project 41, 43–49; final thoughts about course 51–2, HOPE project 82–94, racial segregation 84, student responses 49–51; techniques 44–7
space, hope as 129

third space dialogue 52
twenty-first century 149–50

unified concept 14
USA 44

vulnerability 22

willingness to change 31